Great
adventures
in
Florida

Great
adventures
in
Florida

M. TIMOTHY O'KEEFE

MENASHA RIDGE PRESS
BIRMINGHAM, AL

O'Keefe , M. Timothy.
Great adventures in Florida / by M. Timothy O'Keefe.–1st ed.
p.   cm.

ISBN 0-89732-183-9
1. Florida–Guidebooks. 2. Adventure and adventurers–Florida.
I. Title.
F309.3.034   1996
917.5904'63–dc20   95-43094
                                    CIP

Cover photography & additional photographs: M. Timothy O'Keefe
Cover & text design: Grant Tatum

Menasha Ridge Press
700 South 28th Street
Birmingham, AL 35233
800/247-9437

Warning: Many of these adventures are assumed risk activities. The ultimate responsibility for safety lies with the reader. Use of this book is acknowledgment of this responsibility. This guide cannot be expected to replace appropriate courses or precautions in whichever activity you decide to participate.

Dedication

To my parents, who never said "Don't try."

Table
of Contents

APPENDICIES

ABOUT THE AUTHOR 266

Introduction

Seeking out adventure is the most exciting and challenging way to meet life. What you find may startle you . . . or thrill you . . . or astound you. It will rarely bore you. Adventure travel offers what we all need, a little more excitement and mystery in our lives.

Most of us can forecast with amazing accuracy what we'll be doing next week, next month and possibly even next year at this same hour. We're victims of the same old routine . . . day in and day out . . . our lives are so predictable they've become blueprints for boredom.

Vacations are supposed to break up this monotony, to recharge and refresh us, but they rarely do. Getting sunbaked and stuffed with food at a resort provides little meaningful diversion. Even the most die-hard shoppers usually find that the thrill of bargain hunting diminishes after a few days.

No wonder more and more people are abandoning traditional resort vacations for adventure travel. I like to define adventure travel in the broadest sense possible: something that challenges us physically, mentally, or emotionally. The best experiences include all three, absorbing us so completely that we forget everyday life. That's the most refreshing kind of vacation anyone can enjoy.

A family or couple which shares an adventure together is going to become more strongly bonded together. It's fun to explore the unknown with people you care about. Furthermore, the feelings of satisfaction and accomplishment after an adventurous outing are almost euphoric. The adrenaline rush can be addictive.

It's also possible to collect more than meaningful memories. Adventurous experiences may impart lifetime benefits if you allow yourself to attempt challenging situations on vacation. Later, back home, you'll probably start handling unpleasant predicaments with a lot more confidence. Deadlines and squabbles somehow will become less important and be easier to deal with. After all, if you've been sleeping with alligators, or just come from your first face-to-face meeting with a mermaid, you're not as likely to get worked up over minor aggravations, either at work or at home. Your whole perspective changes.

And since Florida's ecosystem is unique compared to any other part of the country, Florida is obviously the place to go for some truly unique adventures. As a peninsula with more than 6,000 miles of coastline (second only to Alaska), Florida offers many activities that are water-related, taking place both above and below the surface.

But not all the excitement occurs along the coast. Consider the Everglades, a huge sea of grass that covers more than a million acres at mainland Florida's southern-most tip. It's an area still so remote and desolate that a week-long canoe trip through the Glades' Wilderness Waterway is a true expeditionary experience.

The Everglades is also the home of the Seminoles, the only Indians who never surrendered to the United States. Now, for the first time ever, the Seminoles are willing to share a little more of their life with visitors. You can even sleep on a reservation in a traditional chickee, a South Seas-styled thatched hut built on stilts with all sides open.

Yes, Florida may be the fourth-most populated state in the United States, but it still has considerable tracts of wild habitat for black bears, the elusive Florida panther, and countless bird species. And there are more than 3,000 miles of hiking and nature trails on which to look for these and many other animals.

This book has two purposes. One is entertainment. But the primary goal is to motivate you to experience a wilder, more adventurous side of Florida.

Unfortunately, as technology becomes more sophisticated, fewer people are exercising their option to go out and directly experience the world around them. Ever larger numbers of people seem to see little sense in canoeing a river or getting chewed on by mosquitoes when they can sit at home in a media padded room, safe and sound, and watch an exciting movie or read a thrilling book. But any temporary elevation of blood pressure these man-made diversions provide is a sham. It's not the same as being in the middle of something authentic and real.

In most instances, people come down from an exciting book or movie in few hours or, at most, a few days. But when you've undergone an exciting experience in real life, the impact may last for a lifetime. Adventure travel can alter substantially how you view yourself, your work and your world.

And it's amazing how often you come away with a new appreciation for life. I've found nothing fosters a better sweetness for living than coming face to face with your own mortality, something an adventure traveler routinely does when elements of risk and danger are involved.

Furthermore, away from our normal environment, most of us seem to be more open to investigation and appreciation. We tend to view the world through a different, less rigid set of glasses. We're more open to new things.

Every experience in this book can be easily duplicated by you and your family. Furthermore, nothing in these pages–except perhaps gritting your teeth and holding on for dear life aboard Central Florida's best thrill rides–requires a great deal of courage or stamina.

As a few chapters illustrate, some of the best adventurous situations are ones you create for yourself. Your own initiative and spontaneity will often transcend any arranged program.

After all, if you ignore the possibilities of adventure, are you really living?

FLORIDA GLOSSARY

We have a few words and terms that are peculiar to Florida, as most states do. These are some of the most popular ones that appear regularly throughout the chapters.

Bug Goop: A shorter name for insect repellent, an important survival aid that must accompany you anytime you are out of doors in Florida, particularly around twilight. Visitors usually forget to carry it only once. (See "Mosquitoes")

Cold Front: This word is peculiar to Florida because we see so few of them. You will observe these tend to occur whenever you are camping or canoeing in the Everglades, where the temperature is always somewhere in the 30-degree range. Means just the opposite of "happy camper."

Conch: Pronounced "konk," not "konsh." A mollusk found in the Keys, but also how the residents of the Keys refer to themselves. The Keys is also known as the Conch Republic because residents often get fed up with bureaucrats and threaten to secede. This is never likely to occur since they know that if they ever establish their own republic, most of the people in other parts of Florida will want to join them.

Gators: Short for alligator, which litter the Florida landscape like pet rocks. Never get between a gator and the water or between a gator and its nest. And never take your pet dog into their territory, since gators regard them as snack food. Seriously. They are normally harmless to humans unless they are harassing me at night when I am in the Everglades (see "Cold Front").

Hammock: Not a misprint for "hummock." Hammock is an Indian term meaning "shady place." It's normally used today to refer to any grouping of trees, such as live oaks and cabbage palms, which are often found growing together. The trees remain green year-round.

Florida Cracker: The name for early Florida pioneers of the 1800s, many of whom were cowboys and used whips to herd cattle. The sound made by the cracking of the whip is where the term originated.

Mosquitoes: You may have some back home, but we have lots, lots more and in sizes you can't imagine. Florida has sixty-seven different mosquito species, and they come in both fresh and salt water varieties. They are present year-round, though least troublesome in winter. Frequent references are made to mosquitoes in the text since, at times, the creatures can dominate your thoughts and your life. Also referred to as "skeeters" and occasionally "damn bugs."

Real Frog Strangler: Any heavy downpour that results in standing water. It does not affect the welfare of frogs, which are quite accustomed to water.

Seminole Indians: Florida's only remaining tribe. The chairman of the Seminole tribe views himself as an Indian. He calls himself an Indian. The term Native American is not a normal part of his vocabulary (see Chapter 19, Seminole Swamp Safari). Since this is the term the Indians themselves currently favor, this is how they are referred to throughout the book.

Sportfisherman: A large boat used for offshore fishing, such as trolling for billfish or dolphin, especially in the Keys. Another politically incorrect term.

1

Sleeping Underwater
at Jules' Undersea Lodge

Many times my luggage has seemed filled with lead, but this is the first time forty pounds of lead weight have been added to my T-shirts and underwear in order to have them delivered to my room. The bellman standing on the dock advises me, "It's the only way to keep the suitcase from floating away." Then he lowers the waterproof container into the water, and it rapidly sinks to the lagoon floor twenty-three feet below.

The bellman and I, both dressed in swimsuits, are about to follow the same glide path as my suitcase. My room is several fathoms down, completely immersed underwater. Once my suitcase disappears into the depths, I gear up and prepare to follow it. I slip on my fins, don my mask, and accept the special regulator that will supply the air I need to enter this unusual resort. The regulator, known as a hookah, is connected by a long hose to a compressor on the surface. The hookah is supplied a constant stream of fresh air from the compressor, so it breathes on demand, just like a normal scuba regulator. With this arrangement, no cumbersome tanks are required for our swim below.

I'd been warned that recent heavy rains and the accompanying runoff had drastically reduced visibility. Under water, it turns out to be real pea-soup stuff, and I can see only a few inches ahead. On good days, you should be able to see between twenty to forty feet.

Near the bottom, a bright light coming through one of the bedroom portholes acts as our beacon in this undersea fog. We swim to the underbelly of the long metal cylinder and enter it through a large "moon pool." The moon pool is actually a rectangular hole cut in the floor. The continually circulating compressed air inside the cylinder is the only thing that keeps the water from surging inside. I soon think of it as an underwater swimming pool, since a swimming pool is exactly what it looks like.

I climb out of the moon pool and, like every other guest, stand dripping water on the floor of one of the most unusual and exclusive resorts in the world. This is Jules' Undersea Lodge in Key Largo, Florida. Named for science fiction writer Jules Verne, Jules' Lodge is the world's first undersea hotel.

A night here may be the ultimate getaway. Surrounded by millions of gallons of water, I will have no live TV or radio. My only connection to the outside world is by telephone. Obviously, this is a place to visit only with a very close friend.

Jules' Lodge is more select than most hotels about whom it accepts. Admittance is based not on credit rating or dress code (swimsuits and T-shirts are the norm) but on swimming ability. Because of the need for an underwater entry and exit, all lodge guests either must be certified divers or take a four-hour resort scuba course on site.

Although Jules' Lodge is advertised as a luxury hotel, I find the experience more like exotic camping with lots of frills. It definitely is not a place for claustrophobes. The entire complex is only fifty feet long and twenty feet wide, with the ten-by-twenty-foot entry room with the moon pool the largest area by far. My bedroom is an intimate eight-by-ten oval with bunk beds and a private fourty-two-inch porthole for watching marine life. My bed is opposite an elaborate VCR/TV/tape deck (which plays only prerecorded tapes) and a small but well-stocked refrigerator.

I inspect the video tapes, finding many water-oriented themes such as *20,000 Leagues Under the Sea* and *Beneath the Twelve Mile Reef* but no *Jaws, Creature from the Black Lagoon,* or *Killer Mermaids from Brooklyn.* Only the positive side of undersea life will entertain us here.

The term *fully carpeted* takes on new dimensions in our bedroom—beige carpeting covers the floor, the walls, and even the ceiling. Ian Koblick, who along with Dr. Neil Monney codeveloped Jules' Lodge, told me there was a special reason for this: to hide all the graffiti.

He explained that the lodge is the second incarnation for the underwater habitat. Originally known as "La Chalupa," it was one of the largest, most sophisticated undersea laboratories of the early 1970's. The twenty-foot long, cylindrically shaped chamber was formerly a decompression chamber where five aquanauts would spend as long as forty-eight hours readjusting to surface pressure after long stints deep on the ocean floor. Every team left its own comments on the decompression chamber walls. Those messages are still there, under the carpet. I wanted to peek to see what thoughts the aquanauts might have expressed, but the carpet is too securely attached to the chamber walls.

Before exploring further, I decide to unpack. The suitcase had been provided by the lodge. Waterproofed by an O-ring seal, it is large enough only for a few items, yet it's still sufficient. There won't be any formal dinners here.

Once my things are put away, I try a soft drink from the refrigerator. However, the cola is flat due to the pressure at even this shallow depth. Honeymoon couples here who often bring a small split of champagne must find their bubbly a mild disappointment. For insurance reasons, honeymooners are the only ones allowed to bring alcohol to the lodge. None is provided with meals. Well, some hardship must be expected when living on the ocean floor, although I seem to recall Captain Nemo had a better stocked bar aboard the *Nautilus*.

I soon become intrigued by the bathroom facilities. Although each bedroom has its own sink, the complex has a single shower and toilet that have been specially engineered to avoid polluting the lagoon. Shower water is pumped back onshore and disposed of, while a regular Port-a-Potty that can be emptied on land handles the other waste. A nifty arrangement that works quite well.

Regardless of the number of guests, I suspect most people will want to spend their time in the spacious eight-by-twenty-foot dining/entertainment chamber opposite the chamber's two bedrooms. It has two tables and a set of long benches that double as single beds when the lodge is at capacity; a microwave oven; another VCR/TV arrangement; and another porthole. A depth gauge above the kitchen sink permanently reads a level of twenty-three feet.

So there are no mix-ups, guests' meals are stocked in the bedroom refrigerators and later heated in the communal dining room's microwave. For dinner, I choose Florida lobster with fresh broccoli, a long grain–wild rice mixture, dinner rolls, and real Key lime pie (the yellow kind) for dessert. Other entree options are a fillet, chicken, or vegetarian menu. Breakfast is also in my refrigerator: Belgian waffles with strawberries and whipped cream, orange juice, coffee, and rolls.

I prefer to cook the meals myself rather than hire a "mer-chef." The meals are precooked in an above-water kitchen, then transported down in sealed plastic containers. The microwave has very explicit instructions for warming up each item, so everything tastes as if fresh from the kitchen.

Following dinner I want to take a swim outside to investigate the lagoon, but visibility is still disappointingly poor. I see several fish that swim right up to the portholes, but I can't spot the forty-foot sunken boat nearby because of the murk. Several friends who dived here a few months earlier when the water was clearer were very enthusiastic. They reported loads of fish in the lagoon, including parrot fish, gray angelfish, Bermuda chub, mangrove snapper, and even a harmless four-foot nurse shark. Lobsters, too, live in the rocks, some almost tame enough to stroke. Using the tethered hookah units, divers can stay out as long as they like. Since the lagoon floor is only thirty feet at its deepest point, no one need fear the bends for staying too deep too long.

Instead, I stay inside and feed the fish that congregate at the moon pool. My favorite is a triggerfish that is so bold it demands to be fed. When it's hungry, it comes to the moon pool and spits water to catch my attention. This fish is yet unnamed, so I decide to title him after me: Tim the Triggerfish.

Sleeping underwater proves no problem whatsoever, possibly because I review the security measures just before retiring. A telephone in my bedroom will instantly put me in touch with the command room which is manned around the clock when the lodge has guests. The moon pool is monitored with both a video camera and two-way microphone. If a power failure caused the compressor to stop working, the lodge still would have enough air trapped inside to last for several hours. Not that I'd expect to stay that long in case of trouble: I have an emergency air tank and regulator standby at the moonpool. Of course, one of the staff would be down to take me out in minutes in case of trouble. Otherwise, I am on my own. I like it this way, since it makes it seem more of an adventure. I cap off the night watching a favorite videotape I've brought with me: *Das Boot*.

In the morning, I notice something strange. The lodge does not feel so cramped, but has somehow expanded overnight. This perception reflects how I have adapted. I now feel truly comfortable with my surroundings. I even make the impatient triggerfish wait as I eat breakfast. I am quick to claim my mastery here, even if it's only my second day living under water.

Who

For complete information, contact Jules' Undersea Lodge, P.O. Box 3330, Key Largo, FL 33037; 305/451-2353. The telephone is manned from 9 AM to 3 PM daily. An answering machine records messages the rest of the time. The Internet address is http://www.jul.com.

What

Jules' Lodge offers several package programs, all based on double occupancy. The Aquanaut package costs $295 per night per person, with a check-in time of 1 PM and a check-out time of 11 AM. Meals, prepared by the mer-chef, include a dinner choice of lobster or steak. The European package is $195 per person per night, with a check-in time of 5 PM and a check-out of 9 AM. You prepare your own dinner (chicken and broccoli and rice) and breakfast in the microwave. Vegetarian dishes are an option for both packages. People who stay here for multiple days but want to explore the Keys during daytime may prefer the European package. The resort course for nondivers is $125. Special discount rates apply after the first day, especially for those who decide to take meals outside the lodge. How do you do that? Simply swim back to the surface, dry off, and drive to an interesting restaurant. I never realized before how much I like the tingle of carbonation in my soft drinks.

When

To make sure you get a room with the best view, avoid anytime it's been raining in the Keys for a prolonged period. It's impossible to predict conditions precisely, since even during the summer, when showers are common almost every day, the lagoon can be crystal clear. The key to making the most of this experience is to be able to take a relaxing swim outside, in the lagoon, when it is clear. My visit was during August after a heavy downpour, and I really missed out on the full experience. To be certain of the conditions, call ahead before leaving home.

Where

Jules' Undersea Lodge is located at Mile Marker 103.2, also Transylvania Avenue (how can any movie buff forget that?), on the ocean side of Key Largo.

2

Orlando Canoeing:
The Wekiva River

The Wekiva, located a few miles northeast of Orlando, is a waterway of many faces. Near its headwaters, the spring-fed stream is narrow and crystal clear with small, sunlit pools where white sand bottoms dazzle with brightness. As the river meanders along and is fed by its many tributaries, it broadens for hundreds of yards across to truly become a river. The richness of the foliage and wildlife along its banks is often breathtaking.

A lot of Central Floridians like myself think the Wekiva is special: so many of us let our appreciation be known that the state investigated, agreed, and designated the Wekiva River an Outstanding Florida Waterway. This title has more than just a pretty sound to it: it also the strongest environmental protection offered by Florida.

This means no treated sewage can be dumped into the river system, nor can there be any development along the banks of the protected zones. For outdoor enthusiasts, it also means permanent preservation of what is still one of the most unspoiled rivers in the entire state. No matter how large Orlando's population grows, even if it doubles, the length of the Wekiva should remain just as clean as the forty-eight million gallons of spring water that pour into it daily from Rock Springs and Wekiva Springs.

More importantly, the twenty-two species of rare, endangered, or threatened plants and animals that live along the Wekiva have a far better opportunity to live out their natural life. These animals include numerous black bear, possibly Florida panther, and three snail species found only in the springs feeding the river.

But despite all the formal designations and militant protection, the Wekiva is still very much a people's river. Unlike some scenic spots, the Wekiva receives fairly heavy use, especially on weekends, when flotillas of canoeists paddle the river for a relaxing day well away from the comforts of civilization. In some stretches, buildings are so scattered and so far apart it's easy to imagine you've taken a wrong turn and ended up lost in the wilderness.

Not to worry. All the streams head in the same direction, eventually ending in the St. Johns River near Sanford. Not only is there no danger of getting lost, but also the Wekiva is quite helpful in making your journey enjoyable, supplying just enough current to make paddling unnecessary in many sections. All you need to do is keep the bow off the bank, settle back, relax, and rubber-neck the scenery.

This friendly quality undoubtedly is what makes the river so popular among canoeists, even those who've never lifted a paddle before. There's nothing that can go wrong—unless, of course, you tip the canoe over, but you can hardly blame the river for that. An unanticipated plunge is always the result of "human error." The first extended canoe trip I ever took happened to be on the Wekiva a good many years ago. "Extended" is probably a bit of an exaggeration since the entire river is only sixteen miles long, and I sampled only a small bite of it. Still, the trip was long enough that it took a couple of hours coming and going (I returned to the launching point instead of going downstream only, a bad mistake since the return meant going against the current), and it left me feeling as if I'd just completed a tryout for the local college crew team.

I was fortunate on that trip. My companion was a long-time canoeist who happily shared all his knowledge before we set out. The first thing he told me was that I was going to sit in the bow, out of the way and out of trouble.

"You guide a canoe from the stern," he explained. "You don't do it by paddling frantically, trying to turn the bow around. Leave all the steering to me."

Gladly.

"We're also going to load all our gear only after the canoe is afloat," he advised next. "Otherwise you can put too much stress on the backbone and damage the craft. A canoe looks fragile, but it's not if you use it properly. It can carry a heck of a heavy load if loaded properly—up to ten times its own weight."

Our canoe weighed somewhere between 60 to 70 pounds. I was relieved to realize the ice chest full of soft drinks, food, cameras, etc., wouldn't (if you'll pardon the expression) put the slightest dent in our craft. On this very warm day, I was certain I would require all the nourishment aboard.

Not trusting the fate of my camera gear to the river gods, I packed it in a small Playmate ice chest where it would be protected against the sun and splash, yet still easily accessible. Just to be safe, I tied a life preserver to the handle in case we did tip. I don't know what good that would've done, but it made me feel better.

Extra clothes were packed in a large garbage bag. I left enough air in the bag that it looked like an inflated balloon, which meant the clothes could fend for themselves and float if we went over.

It may seem I did a lot of worrying about taking the plunge, but as I said, this was my first real canoe trip.

The next advice I was given pertained to boarding the canoe. The easiest time to tip a canoe is when you're first getting in it, before you realize just how "tippy" it is. If you step aboard as you would a regular boat, you may find yourself catapulting through the air so quickly you don't have time to shout a complaint.

"When you get in, grab both of the sides, which are called gunnels," my friend advised. "Crawl forward one foot at a time and stay low toward the center of the canoe. Whatever you do, avoid any sudden shifts to the side. A canoe moves faster than you ever can. That's why they pitch clumsy people so easily.

"If we encounter any boat wakes, get off the seat and move down onto your knees. The lower you are, the more stable the canoe is."

It seemed kneeling had another unmentioned benefit if we got mired in a wall of wake. It would be an easier position from which to pray.

With a few final words about how to paddle properly, we were finally off: "Cup the top of the paddle with one hand and place the other just above the narrow part of the blade. Use long, steady strokes instead of short, choppy ones. Short strokes don't move you as far and they wear you out more quickly."

It may seem like I got a lot of know-it-all instruction from this fellow and that he spent the entire day lecturing me. However, I was grateful for the advice—I've used it every time since—and it was also the last time he spoke for thirty minutes. Once out on the water, he simply paddled and looked.

The Wekiva can do that to you, take away all your desire for conversation. You can be so far away from city sounds and surrounded by such natural silence that something as common as the click of a fishing reel can seem terribly out of place.

Mechanical things intrude on the sounds of the natural "silence," which sometimes gets quite noisy: the cry of a bird or the crackling of underbrush by some unseen creature can be as startlingly loud as an unexpected gunshot. Yet you grow accustomed to the pattern quickly, this stillness punctuated by sudden, piercing animal sounds.

These days I can maneuver a canoe well enough that it no longer performs like a corkscrew ride at a theme park. I enjoy introducing people to the Wekiva, showing them this almost-wilderness in the heart of burgeoning Central Florida.

Because the Wekiva is so popular with canoeists, it's possible to rent a canoe at one of several spots, float downriver for several miles, then disembark and leave the canoe where the outfitter will pick it up at the end of the day. That is such a convenient arrangement that many canoe owners, including myself, prefer to rent rather than use their own craft. That way you avoid paddling the canoe back upstream or hassling with two cars—one to drop the canoe off at the launch point and another to wait at the finish to pick up the canoe.

My last outing couldn't have been on a more perfect day. The temperature was in the mid-70s, the sky a crisp clear blue. Our only concern was where to start. One place we could have started from was Rock Springs Run, located just off State Road 435 near Apopka. This canoe trail starts off a little turbid at first, then clears slowly to a sparkling aquamarine. Once you pass the homes at the beginning, it's mostly wilderness the rest of the way. The finish is at Wekiwa Marina on Wekiva Springs Road, about eight miles south and four hours away.

Or we could have started from the Wekiwa Marina itself for an extended journey that goes from the Wekiva into the St. Johns River and concludes at High Springs Road three miles west of US 17-92 in DeBary. That's an eight-hour run.

That was just a bit more paddling than we felt like doing. We ended up selecting Katie's Landing on Wekiva Park Drive near Sanford. Although this is farther from Orlando than either of the other two starting points, you are transported by van back towards Orlando and placed on the Little Wekiva. This is about a twelve-mile, seven-hour journey that takes you from the Little Wekiva to the Wekiva River itself and right past Katie's.

I'm very partial to the Little Wekiva; I think it may be the prettiest stretch of the entire waterway. As the water in the Little Wekiva flows fairly fast, very little paddling is required. Instead, it's more a matter of steering, simply by trailing a paddle from the stern to allow it to act as a rudder.

However, there is one drawback in starting from Katie's. You have to plan your departure according to the van schedule on weekends (although during the week when things are slower you can pretty much set your own timetable).

I was amazed at the amount we had to stow in our canoe: two ice chests, a plastic bag of clothing, a small cooler, a small tackle box, and a fishing outfit. What was worse, most of it was mine. Camera equipment occupied one entire ice chest, with spare lenses and extra film in the small cooler. When I'd gone on a two-week photo safari to Africa, I'd carried just as much camera gear, leaving behind only the ice chests. Well, once on the Little Wekiva, I wouldn't be able to run back to the car for anything I might need, so I took it all with us. Still, it was an embarrassing load, more befitting a weekend outing than a simple day trip.

Our launching point on the Little Wekiva had scattered development along its banks. Several large homes overlooked the water and, not unexpectedly, a few had canoes placed conspicuously in their yards. I was glad we were only leaving from here and not returning since the flow was much too fast for a leisurely paddle back.

I told my companion how at one time a development company had planned to build a 50,000-resident subdivision along the west bank of the Wekiva in Lake County. That would have turned the river into little more than a large drainage canal.

Fortunately, the state Cabinet revoked the building permit. The Wekiva's natural beauty had already come to the attention of state officials who were considering how to preserve it. Through a series of steps, the protection quandary ultimately ended with the Outstanding Waterway designation.

It was frightening to imagine the Wekiva with a city of 50,000 along one shore. It was also enough to make you wonder about the sanity of humans, who are continually lured to beautiful unspoiled areas and then foolishly pay large sums of money to destroy them. The reason for becoming part of the community would have been obliterated with the first lot clearing.

The Little Wekiva was shady and cool most of the way, a canopy of trees forming a green-colored tunnel. White egrets and blue herons perched on the limbs in many places, moving so little they reminded us of those grotesque plastic birds some people stick in their yards. We stopped to watch a heron stalk the shoreline. It raised its long, ungainly legs high above the water like it was trying to keep its feet dry. Its head never wavered but stayed pointed forward, almost as if attempting to hypnotize the small fish it sought. Its head struck suddenly downward, almost as a snake would. Then the dripping beak reappeared above water, a flapping fish securely in place. The heron raised its head backward and, like someone downing a raw oyster, swallowed the fish whole. It resumed its stalk.

Just a little farther along, we spotted a gator. It wasn't very big, only three to four feet long, but it had positioned itself at a turn in the river bank where most canoeists would never notice it unless they looked behind them. This must have been its way of enjoying the sun while remaining sheltered from the almost non-stop stream of weekend canoeists.

As we neared the gator, I wondered what it thought about having several hundred noisy canoes caroming down the narrow waterway, filled with overly boisterous people who frequently littered beer and soft drink cans all over his front yard. Orlando residents may become irritated at all the tourist traffic and garish attraction signs, but that's nothing compared to what this poor gator must go through.

I suddenly realized I was guilty of the obnoxious tourist role by seeing how close to the gator we could get. Too much more and it would need to seek sanctuary under the water. Rather than disturb it further, we quietly drifted/paddled several hundred more yards, then heard a terrific crashing in the underbrush behind us. Was it a wild hog? Or a black bear? Believe it or not bear sightings are not uncommon in the Rock Springs area. Whatever it was, it stayed hidden in the dense undercover, tantalizing our imaginations. So off we went again, wondering what we literally would find around the next bend.

A short time later we passed a canoe from the Wekiwa Springs State Park, located not far from the Wekiwa Marina. I've always found the spelling of place names here maddeningly inconsistent. While the Wekiva River ends in "va," the nearby park and marina end in "wa." So, it is the Wekiwa State Park and Wekiwa Marina on the Wekiva River. I've never heard a good explanation why the two are spelled differently.

Our trip down the last leg of the river required considerably more muscle power since the current is not as swift. For a brief period my companion took over the piloting while I shot a few photos. We paddled about another mile, then pulled in close to a tree near the edge of the water. Five turtles were sunning themselves on a floating log next to the tree, but they departed as our canoe came near. About midway up the tree a box turtle was sunning itself; several branches below it was a large, basking water snake. Across the river another blue heron was looking for a snack.

We joined him by unpacking for a late lunch. At the moment, we were the only people around. Except for a small shack hidden in the trees on a small island, there was no indication man had tried to leave his mark here.

Who

Rental canoes are easily available for both Rock Springs Run, the Wekiva River, and the Little Wekiva:

Katie's Wekiva River Landing
(On the Wekiva River, off SR 46
just west of Sanford);
407/628-1482.

Rock Springs Run
5714 Baptist Camp Rd.,
Apopka, FL;
407/886-0859.

Daily eight-mile guided canoe trips leave at 9AM from King's Landing,

Wekiwa Springs State Park
1800 Wekiwa Circle,
Apopka, FL;
407/889-3140.

Wekiwa Marina
1000 Miami Springs Dr.,
Longwood, FL;
407/862-9640.

There's an excellent restaurant here where you can watch other canoeists flail and almost tip as they careen by. The turtle and jalapeno cornbread are memorable.

Carry drinks and snacks in a small cooler; sunblock and a hat may be useful. Wear old tennis shoes so you can at least walk in the cool spring runs. Ditto for a bathing suit. If you want to carry a camera, seal it in a plastic bag and place it in its own ice chest to protect it from rain and splashing. Plan for a wet trip; it's more fun.

Those trained in the Tom Sawyer tradition may camp on the islands in the river. As you would expect, it requires careful planning and packing since the few designated campsites are quite remote.

You may also want to visit Wekiwa Springs State Park either as part of your canoe trip or as a separate outing. The spring there is the river's main springhead, but the bottom is relatively shallow, making it ideal for family swimming. A popular snorkeling site, it's also possible to rent canoes there as well. (See under Who.)

When

Weekends can be very crowded; a weekday is preferable. Summer afternoons can be very warm unless you cool yourself in the water occasionally.

3

Ten Great Places
to Photograph Wildlife

A photographer's idea of what constitutes good wildlife viewing is totally different from that of a serious seer, such as a birder. Photographers need to get right up to their subjects for good pictures, while a birder will be ecstatic at identifying a new species even when it's at flyspeck distance. Getting close to wild animals is not always easy.

Despite such a difficulty, wildlife photography is one of the most popular hobbies in North America. More people take pictures of wildlife, flowers, and plants than collectively hunt and fish.

Florida has some of the most diverse photographic opportunities of anywhere in the country, from the coral reefs of the Keys to the cypress swamps of the Panhandle. Nowhere else do you have the opportunity to lens aggressive alligators, shy manatees, and beautifully plumed snowy egrets all in a single day.

Wildlife photography also poses considerable challenges because you are dealing with creatures with a mind and will of their own. Photographing animals is one of the best ways to become closely acquainted with their habits and their habitats. And sometimes there is a real element of risk involved—standing only yards away from an unpenned alligator who can move faster on land than you can.

Fortunately, alligators run fast only for short bursts, and you can foil them even then by running zig-zag, a maneuver they apparently cannot do. I say "apparently" because I have never been chased by an alligator, and I don't know anyone who has. Like many accepted truisms, this one is still unproven as far as I'm concerned. So, whenever a gator seems agitated, I move away quickly before I get to test the theory.

After photographing wildlife professionally for more than two decades, I have come to recognize that animals photographed in natural preserves look no different from those roaming freely through a forest. Even in a preserve, there's no absolute assurance the animals will appear when and where you expect them to. Furthermore, most Florida preserves are not fenced, so the animals may come and go as they wish.

There's certainly nothing wrong with being a purist and sitting in the woods, hoping something interesting will wander by. I just find it a lot more satisfying to pick a place where I know I have the best chance to see animals.

The following places come close to guaranteeing good photo subjects that you can approach very closely.

ST. MARKS NATIONAL WILDLIFE REFUGE

Located on the Gulf of Mexico just south of Tallahassee, St. Marks offers a tremendous variety of wildlife throughout the year. Perhaps its most unusual feature is the annual monarch butterfly migration in October, when thousands of monarchs gather at the refuge while in transit to their wintering grounds in Mexico.

Monarchs won't fly directly across the Gulf to Mexico. Instead, they follow a coastal route. Thousands of monarchs flying down the East Coast of the United States end up, at least temporarily, at St. Marks because of its unique location in the Big Bend area.

The best time for viewing the normally huge butterfly population is on quiet, still days when they fill the skies like miniature Chinese kites. Yet it's difficult to get good portrait shots of constantly moving butterflies.

The best time for picture-taking is on windy days when the butterflies cling to the vegetation while waiting for better flying conditions. You can approach within two or three feet of a bush covered with the orange and black beauties when the wind is blowing.

The best place to photograph butterflies is also one of the easiest to reach: the St. Marks lighthouse. Follow Lighthouse Road past the visitor's center to the lighthouse. Park there and start looking. You will probably be amazed at the number of butterflies present.

At other times of the year, look for shorebirds, brown pelicans, gulls, and terns near the lighthouse, particularly around the pilings and the narrow strip of beach. Wading birds are common in the pools by the roads, as are hoards of waterfowl during the winter months.

If you want to test your luck, hike the dikes to Stony Bayou and the Mounds Pools where you may spot nesting bald eagles in winter. Early or late in the day, anytime of year, you might also spot bobcats and white-tailed deer.

For complete information on photographing at St. Marks, call the refuge office at 904/925-6121 (closed Mondays). St. Marks is located off US 98 near the town of Newport, just south of Tallahassee.

WAKULLA SPRINGS STATE PARK

No, you don't need to go to the Everglades to shoot lots of alligators. The crystal clear stream flowing from Wakulla Springs is so loaded with them that swimming (by humans, at least) is unsafe and not permitted except in a very small area.

You'll find the best variety of shots by taking a half-hour guided cruise on one of the park's boats. Hiking the nature paths will keep you confined to the woods and well away from the wildlife.

The cruise boats are covered for protection from sun or light rain and have open sides ideal for photography. It's always tough to decide where to sit. The front seat is good, but I prefer to stand at the back of the boat. That way I can shoot from both sides without getting in anyone's way, and there's the added opportunity to keep shooting as the boat moves away from an animal.

Besides basking gators, you'll get close to sunning turtles, a herd of white-tailed deer (which is always in the same spot, on the right, shortly after starting out), and iridescent gallinules (or mud hens) that walk atop floating plants at the edge of the run. Two birds common to Florida and uncommon elsewhere, the limpkin and anhinga, are also easy year-round photo subjects. Regardless of the animal, you'll need to be alert and shoot quickly since the ranger rarely slows or stops his boat for very long.

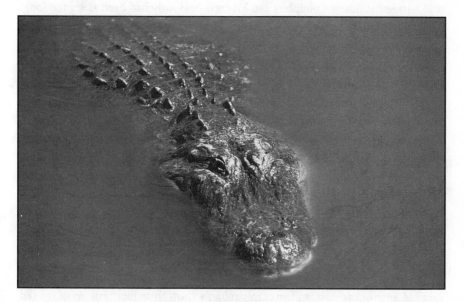

Wakulla Springs is so loaded with alligators that swimming is unsafe.

Wakulla Springs is one of the world's largest springs, and the park has glass-bottom boats that are supposed to show you the world below. In the past five years, I have yet to see one running. This is not a good place for fish photos.

For complete information, call the park at 904/922-3632. From Tallahassee, go south on US 319 or SR 61. Take SR 61 to SR 267.

HOMOSASSA SPRINGS STATE WILDLIFE PARK

Now here is where you'll find plenty of fish as well as one of the rarest and most endangered of animals, the West Indian manatee. My book, *Manatees, Our Vanishing Mermaids*, which is sold here, will fill you in on the life history of this remarkable animal. The manatees at Homosassa are being rehabilitated for possible release back into the wild. That means there is a good manatee population here year-round, not seasonally as elsewhere.

This is the only spot where you can view the animals under water as well as from the top. The manatees congregate near the glass-walled underwater observatory at the main spring during and after scheduled shows/feeding periods.

If you miss the scheduled shows, look for the manatees gorging on romaine lettuce at the bridge that spans the spring run. Sometimes all you can see are a few raised nostrils among the floating salad. Eventually, more of the body floats amid the lettuce. It's a peculiar shape: like a stuffed sausage with a beaver tail.

Christopher Columbus sighted a manatee on his first trip to the New World and mistook it for a mermaid. Considering a manatee's facial features (jowls, whiskers, and a large flat nose), Columbus and his crew obviously had been at sea too long. There ain't nothin' sexy about a manatee . . . except possibly to another manatee.

Photographic opportunities are not limited to manatees. In winter, big schools of jack crevalle, snapper, snook, and other saltwater species swim in from the Gulf of Mexico to take advantage of the warmer, 72-degree spring water. Many kinds of birds, including owls and hawks, reside at the Homosassa Wildlife Park throughout the year. Alligators are also present year-round.

For complete information, call the park at 904/628-2311. The park is located off US 19 in the town of Homosassa Springs, about two hours north of Tampa.

ORLANDO WETLANDS PARK

Although Canaveral National Seashore and the Merritt Island National Wildlife Refuge are located nearby, I prefer this much smaller, 1,200-acre wetland where you can become a lot more intimate with the animals, particularly the varied birdlife. Furthermore, the conditions are always ideal for birds year-round and not just seasonally.

Orlando Wetlands Park attracts so much wildlife because of its ponds and lakes. A man-made habitat, it receives roughly thirteen million gallons of treated wastewater daily. Aquatic plants remove the nutrients from the wastewater, a process that takes about fourty days. More than 140 bird species, plus deer, fox, and otter have chosen to make this place home.

You'll have no difficulty moving through and to different parts of the wetlands, thanks to a series of walking trails. Real snipe—not the kind you may have hunted for at night with a bag when you were a kid—reside here during the cooler winter months. Other migratory species include white pelicans, blue-winged and green-winged teal, and northern shovelers. Year-round you'll normally find great blue herons, snowy egrets, limpkins, and both black and turkey vultures.

Gators, raccoons, and turtles round out the many photo opportunities. For complete information, call the Orange County parks department at 407/246-2800. The park is located off US 50 between Orlando and Titusville near the town of Christmas.

MARINELIFE CENTER OF JUNO BEACH

The Atlantic shore of Florida between Brevard and Broward County contains some of the most important nesting beaches for the loggerhead turtle in the entire world. Loggerheads, which are classified as a threatened species, come ashore to nest after dark primarily in the months of June and July.

You'll need to make reservations at Marinelife Center to go on a turtle walk; these are extremely popular. Photographing the loggerhead is challenging, to say the least, since flash is not permitted during the nesting process. The guides illuminate the event by flashlight, so a tripod and fast film are mandatory to capture the actual egg-laying, which normally takes between one and two hours.

If you are unable to reserve a spot for the nighttime turtle walks, you can at least see the tread-like tracks still gouged in the sand early in the morning. Exhibit tanks feature live loggerheads along with green and leatherback turtles.

Call 407/627-8280 to make reservations for the turtle walks and to learn the center's current operating hours. The Marinelife Center is located on US 1; take exit 57 on I-95 in Palm Beach Gardens and go east on SR 786. After reaching US 1, travel north for about three miles; look for the center on the right.

CORKSCREW SWAMP SANCTUARY

After the first section of boardwalk, you'll be in one of the shadiest places in Florida. However, this bald cypress forest is notable for more than its comfortable climate: it is the largest remaining subtropical stand of old growth bald cypress anywhere in the world. As such, the trees hold a rich variety of native orchids, ferns, and bromeliads that are eminently photographable every day of the year.

Corkscrew Swamp Sanctuary, owned and operated by the National Audubon Society, is also world famous for its winter colony of nesting wood storks (the largest nesting colony in the United States). February is usually the best month to photograph the storks on their nests. You'll need a tripod and a long lens for the best possible pictures.

The rest of the year, the two-mile boardwalk will take you over and through a tremendous range of habitat, including wet prairie, marsh, and pinelands. In spring and fall, you should see migratory warblers and other songbirds. But don't look only skyward: gators, limpkins, river otters, and turtles are present every month. Incidentally, you won't have a big problem with mosquitoes thanks to the resident schools of mosquito fish that dine on the annoying bloodsuckers.

Operating hours vary seasonally: from 7 AM to 5 PM December through April; From 8 AM to 5 PM May through November. The swamp is located off SR 846 between Ft. Myers and Naples; look carefully for the sanctuary signs. Call the sanctuary office at 813/657-3771 for complete information

SIX-MILE CYPRESS SLOUGH PRESERVE

The best way to get close to animals is with a photo blind, something that's furnished for you on this 1.2-mile boardwalk trail overlooking a natural animal corridor. In addition, there are two observation towers to enhance your view of these 2,000 acres located just south of Ft. Myers.

In the traditional dry season from October to June, you'll find lots of animals concentrated around the so-called flag ponds: wood storks, snowy and great egrets, white ibis, and tri-colored herons. Year-round you might find ubiquitous gators, wild turkeys, raccoons, skinks and gray squirrels. Pileated woodpeckers and red-shouldered hawks are seen fairly often.

To locate the slough, take exit 22 off I-75 south of Ft. Myers and go west one-half mile to Six Mile Parkway. Turn left (south) and go three miles to Penzance Crossing. Turn left onto Penzance; the preserve is another tenth of a mile on the right. Call the county park office at 813/432-2004 for complete information.

SHARK VALLEY

Just the name of this area is enough to make you want to visit—but don't expect to see any sharks. Instead alligators and wading birds make this a photographer's dream. The entrance (thirty miles west of Miami) is at the northern end of Everglades National Park and therefore far removed from the coast. The site takes its name from the Shark River Slough which runs through here.

There are several unusual options to access Shark Valley. A paved road penetrates fifteen miles into sawgrass plains. You can either walk it, rent a bicycle, or take a two-hour tram tour. For photography, the best way is to walk or bike the road.

At the end of the pavement is an observation tower, offering a wonderful panoramic view of the region. The road is a loop, so you return by a totally different route, which effectively doubles your photo opportunities.

Gators are quite common, including young hatchlings: in fact, you'll have to be careful not to walk on the babies that may be obscured by the grass at the side of the paved trail.

The park opens at 8 AM, and the tram rides begin at 9 AM. It can get crowded quickly in winter months, so you need to arrive early. If not, be content with knowing that the animals have become accustomed to the tram and apparently don't view it as a great intrusion (say, like a train blowing its whistle at 1 AM outside your window).

It gets very hot in summer; January and February are generally considered prime months. Call ahead if there have been unusually heavy rains: during periods of high water, the trail is sometimes closed to human traffic in order to provide dry, high ground for the animals.

To reach Shark Valley, take US 41 west of Miami. The entrance is across from the Micosukee Indian Village (another photo op). Shark Valley has its own phone number: 305/221-8776.

LIGNUMVITAE KEY STATE BOTANICAL SITE

You'll see far more than plants and trees on this 280-acre gem of an island, which can be reached only by boat. You'll have plenty of bird species to shoot, but, perhaps most unusual of all, are the tiny tree snails unique to the Keys.

At one time, these snails were more highly prized than escargot. Collectors around the world coveted these shells, and enterprising locals were more than happy to provide them. Similar to the finches Darwin studied in the Galapagos, these shells were different from key to key. The shells varied in color and in color pattern on each island.

After gathering their booty, shell collectors routinely set fire to an island in order to increase the rarity—and selling price—of their shells.

The result is that Lignumvitae Key, which never suffered from such a senseless fire, contains one of the last virgin hammocks in the Keys. The snails here are quite spectacular: they bear cream-colored shells with bands of red and green. You will need a closeup lens (and probably a strobe) for frame-filling portraits of the two-inch-long creatures.

At the same time, you will be surrounded by some remarkable vegetation. The lignumvitae tree is supposed to live a thousand years. Like the rest of the foliage, it is of Caribbean origin, brought to the Keys by wind and wave.

Ranger-led tours are conducted on the island Thursday through Monday at 10:30 AM, 1 PM, and 2:30 PM—if you can get there. If the state-run boat is not operating, you will need to hire a boat from a local marina, and the ranger must be notified to meet you at the docks. For complete information call 305/664-4815.

NATIONAL KEY DEER REFUGE

The tiny Key deer is not much larger than a medium-sized dog. Once plentiful throughout the Lower Keys, the deer are now found primarily on Big Pine Key and adjacent No Name Key. Some deer also live on surrounding islands that have a good supply of fresh water. Only Big Pine and No Name keys can be reached by auto.

The Key deer population is quite small, estimated between 250 and 300 animals. It is not likely to grow much larger since the deer must share their refuge with considerable auto traffic, which kills over a hundred animals a year. Contributing to the deaths is the illegal practice of hand-feeding the deer, which lures the animals to the sides of the roads. Once the deer have become accustomed to traffic, there is a greater likelihood of collision with automobiles. The federal government is in the process of buying more land to expand the habitat, which consists of several kinds of tropical forest and a rare tree cactus hammock.

The first time you see a Key deer is memorable. They grow only 24 to 32 inches tall and weigh between 45 and 75 pounds—they truly are tiny! A newborn fawn weighs only between two and four pounds, and its hoof is the size of your thumbnail.

The best time to see deer is early and late in the day along Key Deer Boulevard. The deer are most concentrated near the road's dead end. At night, the best place to spot the deer is on barely inhabited No Name Key.

Another possible photo spot at dawn and twilight is the Blue Hole, an old quarry that is the largest body of freshwater in the Keys. It not only attracts the deer but also birds, gators, and turtles. In addition, you can hike through nearby Watson's Hammock with its forest of gumbo limbo, guava, acacia, poison wood, and strangler fig.

The 8,000-acre refuge is located in the Lower Keys, 128 miles southwest of Miami and 30 miles northeast of Key West. The refuge office, located in a shopping center off Key Deer Boulevard, is open from 8 AM to 5 PM. It has a good brochure describing Key deer habits. Call the office at 305/872-2239 for complete information.

GENERAL TIPS

Animals tend to move more at the same times when the light for photography is best: early and late. Your best pictures typically will be when the sun is fairly low in the sky. I try to limit my shooting to the first three hours after sunrise and the last two before sunset. Of course, that's not always practical and possible.

If I'm shooting around water during the day, I often use a polarizer; especially in the Keys. A polarizer removes the glare from the water's surface and makes it look more transparent.

The clearest blue skies usually appear right after a cold front, which cleans the air and makes everything seem sharper and crisper. March and early April, when the foliage is just getting its leaves, is another excellent period.

What

Fujichrome film does well in Florida regardless of the time of day. Kodachrome, I feel, loses too much of its punch in bright sun. I reserve it for early morning and late afternoon shooting, if at all.

Anticipate very dark conditions on swamp boardwalks. It may not even be possible to take photos without a tripod or a strobe.

For saturated color, even when using flash, I like to underexpose at least a third of an f-stop, as much as two-thirds in the middle of the day.

4

Biking Treks:
Three Overnight Adventures

Here's your chance to choose a weekend cycling trip in the Everglades and Keys or a six-day trip through either Central Florida or The Panhandle

Florida's Department of Environmental Protection has mapped out extended bicycling trips in three different sections of the state. If you cycle all three routes, you'll understand why Floridians say Florida is really three different states. These itineraries and the landscape they lead you past illustrate that to a tee. (Other cycling opportunities are listed in Appendix H. See also Chapter 18, Other Everglades Outings.)

Although the following routes are designated bicycle tours, you'll encounter cars and trucks occasionally; traffic may get quite heavy in parts. The trails use only a few roads that have bike paths or other facilities dedicated exclusively for cyclists.

Each tour is intended to cover between forty to sixty miles a day. The evenings are spent in a public park or campground.

Although some areas have shade, it's best to set out with the idea that you'll be in direct sun most of the day. That means bring sunblock and plenty of liquids. There is no stream, river, or canal in Florida that is considered safe to drink from. Carry plenty of water plus a purifier for backup. Convenience stores can be very scarce.

The only ability required to make any of these trips is the stamina to travel at least fifty miles a day on flat terrain in possible high humidity (depending on time of year). Knowing how to pack light but completely for extended trips is also important. A checklist at the end of this chapter details what you should plan to take.

EVERGLADES TO KEY LARGO AND RETURN (101 MILES TOTAL)

A two-day trip through the Everglades and Upper Keys. You'll overnight in one of the world's most famous snorkeling and diving spots. You may want to turn the one overnight into two. Make camping reservations well ahead of time.

Day 1: from the Chekika Ranger Station in the Everglades to John Pennekamp Coral Reef State Park in Key Largo.

Day 2: return to Chekika Ranger Station. Once out of the Keys, much of the return is through new territory.

What to Look For: This ride, well south of crowded Miami and its far-flung environs, is best made on a weekday to avoid the heavy weekend traffic of sportsmen who crowd into the Keys on Friday evenings and Saturday mornings, then clog U.S. 1 as they return to Miami late Sunday afternoon.

The ride starts in one of the nation's most unusual and most fragile ecosystems, the great river of grass known as the Everglades. The largest remaining subtropical wilderness on the U.S. mainland, this region offers some of the best overall wildlife viewing in all of Florida.

The route also passes through the rich fruit and vegetable farming area of the Everglades where the roads, except for the produce trucks, are still fairly quiet. The trip ends at the northern edge of the Upper Keys at Pennekamp State Park, one of the world's most famous snorkeling and diving spots.

One of the more remarkable sights here is the tremendous number of air plants rooted to the trees. They are attached to the skinny cypress trunks and branches, one after another, like decorations on a Christmas tree. They are nonparasitic and use their roots only as anchors.

Much of the other Glades vegetation is more akin to that of the Caribbean than North America. One of the best obvious examples of West Indian foliage is the gumbo limbo tree with its reddish bark and twisting branches. And, of course, there are the hundreds (thousands, actually) of alligators, the animal which epitomizes the Everglades for most people.

The Glades is mostly a huge expanse of sawgrass that grows in water only six inches deep. The highest spot is only eight feet above sea level, which illustrates how little the land has risen since it emerged from the sea only 6,000 to 8,000 years ago. This subtropical Great Plains is able to richly support snakes, insects, and fish. In turn, these animals nourish one of the world's great concentrations of birdlife.

Archaeologists say that at least three different Indian tribes lived in the Everglades before the present day. Most of the Indians you see in the Everglades today are descendants of the Seminoles who moved into the area quite late, in the 1800s. They remained free here only because the land was considered so inhospitable that no one else wanted it.

In the Upper Keys, you'll see mangroves the size of trees. Mangroves are easily distinguishable by their prominent root system, which acts as a barrier against storm erosion. Unfortunately, mangroves harbor all the mosquitoes in the world, but the insects are most active near twilight, and you should be at Pennekamp Park well before then.

Day One

Directions Southbound from Chekika to Pennekamp Park

Mi. Summary

00.0 Chekika Ranger Station Entrance. Turn R onto SW 237 Ave.

00.6 Turn L onto Richmond (SW 168 St).

04.6 Turn R onto SW 197 Ave.

05.8 Speed bumps, canal crossing.

06.0 Turn L as pavement curves left and becomes SW 192 St.

06.3 Turn R onto SW 194 Ave. after passing Caribbean Tree Farms.

08.8 Turn R onto Silver Palm Dr. (SW 232 St).

11.0 Turn L onto SW 217 Ave.

14.4 Homestead General Airport.

18.0 Turn L onto Palm Dr. (West Palm Ave.).

21.0 Robert's Fruit Market. This place is noted for its Key lime milkshakes. Definitely worth a try.

21.5 Convenience Store.

22.0 Turn R onto Krome Ave. (SW 177 Ave.).

22.8 Turn R onto US Highway 1.

23.0 Turn L onto Card Sound Rd. (Old Dixie Highway). Card Sound Road is a toll road seldom used by people traveling into the Keys because it is not a direct route. The toll does not apply to cyclists. For the most part, this

is an undeveloped stretch. It is a narrow road with a narrow shoulder bordered on the right by a guard rail and a canal.

26.6 Pass the entrance to the Florida Rock and Sand Company on the right.

27.2 Pass a tall microwave relay tower on the right.

31.7 Pass a second, shorter microwave relay tower on the right.

33.6 Pass a small crab shack where live blue crabs are for sale.

33.9 Pass a small marina on the right.

34.0 Pass a small restaurant bordering the canal on the right.

34.5 Pass through the toll booth. Bikes are free.

34.9 Cross a very high bridge spanning the water. The top provides a good panoramic view of the mangroves that you will be passing on your right.

35.9 Cross a short bridge.

36.2 Cross over another short bridge.

36.9 Cross a third short bridge.

37.9 Cross your last bridge, another short one.

38.7 Encounter a tall chain-link fence on both sides of the road designed to protect the endangered saltwater crocodile.

39.5 Road dead-ends. Turn right onto

State Road 905. Dirt road shoulder becomes much wider and tall trees begin bordering both sides of the road, preventing any scenic views to the right or left.

39.9 Chain-link fence on the left side; continues on the right.

40.2 Chain-link fence ends on the right. Dirt shoulder becomes much wider. Road is bordered on both sides by tall trees which make scenic views impossible.

41.6 On the left, the first in a series of paved turnoffs that will occur sporadically until US 1.

43.2 Pass a road on the right where trucks often enter.

45.3 Pass a short, white concrete fence on the left.

48.3 Pass Key Largo Hammock State Botanical Site on the left. Note: This is a possible side trip. This is the largest remaining stand of tropical hardwoods in the entire United States. Two narrow paved paths make ideal bike trails for exploring the site. At the entrance pick up a brochure, which identifies the different trees.

48.9 Card Sound Rd. joins US 1.

49.4 Keys Visitor Center located in shopping center on the right.

51.2 Pass the Caribbean Club on the right. This is where some filming was done for the classic Humphrey Bogart–Lauren Bacall movie *Key Largo*.

51.7 Arrive entrance to John Pennekamp State Park; on the left.

Day Two

Return from Pennekamp to Chekika Ranger Station

Mi. Summary

00.0 Pennekamp Park entrance; turn R and go north on Card Sound Rd. by bearing to the R when US 1 veers L. This is a repeat of Day 1.

28.7 Turn R onto US 1.

28.9 Turn L onto Krome Ave. (SR 997 North). Pass Farmer's Market, Florida Pioneer Museum.

32.7 Turn L onto Avocado Dr. (SW 296 St.).

34.7 Turn R onto Richard Rd. (SW 197 Ave.).

36.7 Turn R onto Bauer Dr. (SW 264 St.).

37.7 Turn L onto Redland Rd. (187 Ave.).

38.7 Turn L onto Coconut Palm Dr. (SW 248 St.), pass Fruit and Spice Park, an interesting place to walk around.

39.2 Turn R onto Tower Rd. (SW 192 Ave.).

40.2 Turn L onto Silver Palm Dr. (SW 232 St.).

40.5 Turn R onto SW 194 Ave. (Comfort Rd.).

43.0 Turn L onto SW 192 St.

43.3 Turn R onto SW 197 Ave.; pavement curves right, crosses canal.

44.7 Turn L onto Richmond Dr. (SW 168 St., unmarked "T" intersection). Cross canal and go to roads end.

48.7 Turn R onto SW 237 Ave.

49.3 Turn L into Chekika Ranger Station. The trek ends here.•

FLORIDA SPRINGS BICYCLE TOUR (327 MILES TOTAL)

Six days through the best of Central Florida. Where possible, make your camping reservations in advance.

Day 1: Paynes Prairie State Preserve near Gainesville (904/466-3397) to Gold Head Branch State Park, Keystone (904/473-4701). Distance: 63 miles.

Day 2: Gold Head Branch State Park to Olustee Battlefield State Historic Site, Osceola National Forest, and the campsite at Ocean Pond Campground (904/752-2577). Distance: 67 miles. Note: Ocean Pond Campground does not take reservations.

Day 3: Olustee Battlefield to Stephen Foster State Folk Culture Center at White Springs (904/397-2733). Distance: 30 miles. Note: camping arrangements must be made in advance.

Day 4: Stephen Foster Center to O'Leno State Park near High Springs (904/454-1853). Distance: 47 miles.

Day 5: O'Leno State Park to Manatee Springs State Park near Chiefland (904/493-6072). Distance: 58 miles.

Day 6: Manatee Springs State Park to Paynes Prairie State Preserve. Distance: 63 miles.

What to Look For: The prettiest times of year for this trip are in spring (March or April) and fall (October and November) when bouquet after bouquet of pastel wildflowers create an endless roadside ribbon.

If you cycle here during warm months, take heart in knowing that every day you will either visit or pass a 72-degree blue water spring whose cool temperatures normally revitalize even the weariest cyclist. You don't even need to carry snorkel gear to realize that the water in the springs of Central Florida is even clearer than that of the Keys.

In addition, you'll pass under great oak trees with their long Rip Van Winkle beards of Spanish moss, through rural farmland and postcard-perfect horse farms, and beside dark and brooding cypress swamps. You'll also visit several small towns where people live at a more relaxed, friendlier pace than in the heavily touristed areas.

This route, passing by or through ten state parks as well as the Osceola National Forest, is equally spectacular on the roadway. The available activities (hiking, fishing, tubing, snorkeling, and interpretive centers/nature trails) are so numerous along the route you may wish to prolong your tour. That's easily done by staying at private campgrounds or motels, which could chop some of your days into shorter, thirty-mile segments.

Most of the roads are rural, though you will have to contend with trucks and traffic in some parts.

Your starting point at Paynes Prairie is just nine miles south of Gainesville on US 441 (exit 73 on I-75).

Paynes Prairie: In the late 1600s, this huge, 18,000-acre basin created thousands of years ago was the largest Spanish cattle ranch in Florida. It was named after King Payne, a Seminole chief.

This is the only state land in Florida where you'll see bison roaming wild. Before being overhunted, bison were indigenous to the region, so the state has introduced a small herd into a 6,000-acre area. Other animals common here are white-tailed-deer, ibis, wild turkey, alligators, hawks, egrets, and pileated woodpeckers. This is also one of the most important wintering grounds of the sandhill crane, a bird that ranges between three and four feet tall.

For a period of ten years, between 1881 and 1891, Paynes Prairie turned into a lake when nearby Alachua Sink clogged up. The water was deep enough for paddle-wheel steamboats to forge an important new trade center. Then the water disappeared, almost literally overnight.

Day One
Mi. Summary

00.0 Park entrance.

00.3 Turn L onto US 441.

02.4 Turn L onto CR (County Rd.) 346.

07.6 Turn R onto CR 325.

11.6 Arrive at Cross Creek, the Marjorie Kinnan Rawlings State Historic Site. Rawlings, who won the Pulitzer Prize for her novel *The Yearling*, lived at this old-fashioned homestead for several decades. Tours are given every half hour. Open 9 AM–5 PM daily except Tuesday, Wednesday, and major holidays; (904/466-3672). Some of the nearby restaurants specialize in turtle, gator tail, cheese grits, and other items that were once a regular part of the Florida cracker diet; expect big-city prices.

16.1 Turn R onto US 301, a four-lane stretch often carrying heavy auto and truck traffic.

18.6 Turn L onto CR 318 in the town of Citra.

30.9 Turn L onto CR 315.

31.2 Go R at the Y intersection and stay on CR 315. Your first spring, Orange Spring, is on the L.

42.2 Cross SR (State Rd.) 20 at Interlachen.

49.6 Cross SR 100 at the town of Grandin.

55.5 Turn R at T intersection onto CR 315C.

60.5 Turn L onto SR 21, which often has heavy truck traffic.

63.2 Turn L into Gold Head Branch State Park.

Gold Head Branch State Park: This 1,562-acre park was named in honor of the gold panning once done here. Little gold was found.

The most interesting natural feature is the ravine trail, a mile-long walk that goes along the upper ridge. A boardwalk takes you down into the ravine, which is far cooler and more moist than the dry scrublands and pine forest that comprise the upper landscape. Fishing is available in several lakes.

Day Two

Mi. Summary

Mi.	Summary
00.0	Park entrance.
00.1	Turn R onto SR 21; remember the truck traffic.
10.4	Turn L onto SR 16.
16.1	Pass Camp Blanding.
16.9	Turn L onto CR 16A (Kingsley Lake Dr.).
18.3	Turn L onto SR 16.
18.9	Turn L onto SR 230.
25.8	Turn R onto Walnut St.
26.4	Turn L onto SR 16 (Brownlee St.).
26.5	Cross US 301.
26.8	Turn L onto CR 229.
33.4	Cross CR 225.
34.2	Stay on CR 229 by turning R and bearing R at the Y intersection.
38.5	Cross SR 121 (Main St.) in the town of Raiford.
38.7	Road (Central Ave.) bends L.
38.9	Road (now Raulerson Rd.) bends R.
44.6	Continue on CR 229.
52.1	Overpass at I-10.
52.7	Bear L after overpass; head toward Sanderson (restock here).
53.3	Turn L onto US 90, where auto traffic also increases.
60.0	Olustee Battlefield Site. Florida's largest Civil War battle took place here on February 20, 1864. Casualties in the half-day battle were enormous: 946 on the Confederate side, 1,861 on the Union.
61.4	Turn R into Osceola National Forest.
65.3	Turn L into Ocean Pond Campground.
66.3	Reach lake campsites.

Ocean Pond/Osceola National Forest: The camp setting in this 157,000-acre national forest, which is made up mostly of pine flatwoods, is perfect. You won't be camping at a small pond: the lake is called "Ocean" because of its large size. If you've brought a pack rod, this is the place to use it, night or day.

Look for blueberries and blackberries in late spring. If you spot a ponderous, slow-moving tortoise, you'll have made acquaintance with the gopher tortoise. It gained its name from the fact that it burrows and lives underground, just like a gopher.

Since many of the next day's roads lead through Osceola National Forest, you might want to avoid arriving here on a weekend during hunting season, which lasts from the middle of November to the third weekend in January.

Day Three

Mi. Summary

00.0 Turn L onto the entrance road.

00.9 Turn L onto CR 250A (not marked).

01.6 Overpass at I-10.

04.2 Turn L onto CR 250 (not marked).

13.0 Pass Osceola work center.

15.2 Cross US 441; road now becomes CR 25A.

18.3 Turn R onto US 441.

18.4 Turn R onto CR 131.

19.7 Falling Creek; waterfall on the right.

19.8 Falling Creek Church. Well over a hundred years old, the wooden church is made of heart pine, which is termite resistant.

23.2 Turn L onto CR 246.

26.4 Turn R onto US 41.

28.7 Enter town of White Springs.

29.6 White Springs springhouse, once a lavish spa.

29.7 Turn L into Stephen Foster Folk Culture Center.

Stephen Foster Folk Culture Center: Camping here is available at the group camp site only if you make advance arrangements. The center is located on the banks of the Suwannee River, which composer Foster made famous in his song "Old Folks at Home." Foster, however, relied heavily on his imagination since he never saw Florida or the Suwannee River. However, the plantation-style visitor center does contain the desk on which he wrote the song and a piano he frequently played. A stately carillon in front of the center plays his music on the hour and half hour.

Local crafts are displayed as part of the Folk Culture Center's effort to keep alive Florida's folk culture. A big celebration is held every Memorial Day Weekend when as many as 10,000 people attend the handicraft exhibition.

Day Four

Plan on leaving early this morning so you can spend several hours at Ichetucknee Springs State Park (mile 32.7).

Mi. Summary

00.0 Park entrance.

00.1 Turn R onto US 41.

00.2 Turn R onto SR 136.

00.3 Cross the Suwannee River.

03.3 Overpass at I-75.

04.0 Turn L onto CR 137.

10.1 Arrive town of Wellborn.

10.2 Cross SR 250.

10.9 Cross US 90.

15.4 Cross CR 252.

22.2 Turn L at T intersection onto CR 137/SR 240.

22.7 Turn R onto CR 137.

23.3 Cross SR 247.

28.7 Turn L onto Bomar Rd. Follow signs to North Entrance of Ichetucknee Springs.

32.7 Ichetucknee Springs State Park. This is a very beautiful spot for swimming, picnicking, or renting a huge inner tube (outside the park) to float 3.5 miles down the narrow, winding, 72-degree spring-fed river. A shuttle will bring you back to your starting point.

32.8 Continue straight as road becomes CR 238.

36.5 Turn R onto SR 47.
38.6 Turn L onto US 27 in the town of Ft. White.
38.9 Turn L onto SR 18.
42.9 Cross CR 131.
45.2 Turn R onto US 441.
45.7 Turn L onto park frontage road.
46.5 Turn L into O'Leno State Park.

O'Leno State Park: A wonderful old suspension bridge crosses the Santa Fe River, a tributary of the Suwannee. Then, at what looks like an earthen dam, the river literally disappears at a place called River Sink. The Santa Fe flows underground for the next three miles, showing itself only occasionally in the form of small pools.

O'Leno was once a thriving area, with its own general store and boasting the southernmost point of the telegraph line in Florida. When the railroad bypassed it, the town died shortly after 1900. Today, there is nothing but 6,000 acres of wilderness.

Day Five

You'll be passing close to quite a few springs today, all of which have entrance fees.

Mi. Summary

00.0 Park entrance.
00.3 Turn L onto frontage road.
00.5 Turn L onto US 441.
04.8 Santa Fe River.
06.7 Enter town of High Springs, with many small restaurants and antique and gift shops.
07.5 Turn R onto Main St.
07.8 Cross US 27 and SR 20.
08.3 Turn R onto CR 340.
11.4 Poe Springs County Park; good place for a swim.
12.7 Blue Springs; another good place for a swim.
14.7 Ginnie Springs. This is a large water-oriented recreation area

with canoe rentals, scuba sales and rentals, and camping. The main cavern is one of the state's most popular snorkeling and cavern dives.

16.7 Cross SR 47.
19.5 Begin crossing of Wacasassa Flats.
25.0 Cross US 129.
27.6 Turn L onto CR 341A (not signed); last paved road on the L before Suwannee River Bridge.
33.7 Pass Sun Springs Rd.
34.7 Turn L onto CR 232.
35.7 Road curves L.
37.2 Hart Springs County Park.
39.8 Turn L onto CR 334 (not signed or paved).
40.8 Pavement resumes, cross CR 341.
41.3 Pass CR 344A.

42.3 Turn R onto CR 313.

43.8 Turn L onto SR 26.

44.3 Turn R onto CR 341; first paved road on R.

49.7 Cross CR 346.

51.7 Cross US ALT 27 and US 98/19.

52.0 Chiefland shopping center; restock.

52.3 Turn R onto CR 320 (NW 19th St.).

58.0 Manatee Springs State Park.

Manatee Springs State Park: The large spring basin in this 2,075-acre park is a delight to swim in. Crystal clear water gushes out at the rate of 81,280 gallons every minute. If you doubt this statistic, try swimming against the current at the mouth of the spring.

A boardwalk follows the spring run out to the Suwannee River. During cold spells, manatees sometimes visit the run. Look and listen for the brown bird with white spots called the limpkin, which feeds primarily on apple snails.

Day Six

This final day offers some rougher riding situations on unpaved roads. You will be passing over the Ocala Limestone Plateau which, like the Kentucky Bluegrass Plateau, has some of the nation's best pastureland. Understandably, this is also excellent horse country with many scenic horse farms.

Mi. Summary

00.0 Join CR 320 at park entrance.

05.8 Turn L onto CR 341.

06.1 Turn R onto CR 320 (just before US ALT 27; not signed).

06.2 Cross US ALT 27 and US 98/19.

07.2 Cross CR 321.

08.5 Cross US 129.

11.0 Cross CR 319.

14.6 Turn R onto CR 339.

18.1 Turn L onto US ALT 27; beware of traffic.

19.6 Turn L onto CR 32 in Bronson.

21.0 Turn R onto CR 337.

21.9 Cross SR 24.

22.2 Levy County Courthouse.

22.3 Turn R onto Picnic.

22.4 Turn L onto US ALT 27.

22.5 Turn R onto CR 337 (Pennsylvania Ave.).

25.6 Turn L onto CR 316.

38.2 Turn L onto SR 121.

41.6 Cross US 41N; continue on 316C.

42.0 Turn L onto unsigned rough road that becomes Main St. in the town of Williston.

43.0 Turn R onto US ALT 27.

44.0 Turn L onto CR 318.

46.3 Pass Betty Crocker's "One Potato, Two Potato" horse farm.

52.3 Turn L onto CR 329.

59.4 Underpass at I-75.

60.6 Turn L onto CR 234 in downtown Micanopy, another antique center.

61.0 Turn L onto US 441; beware of traffic.

62.4 Turn R into Paynes Prairie State Preserve. The trek ends here. •

SEVEN HILLS TO THE SEA (283 MILES TOTAL)

Hills? In Florida? Seven Hills to the Sea sounds more like the name of a Chinese dish than geographic reality. But, yes, Florida does have hills. True, compared to other states, they may be more like molehills, but they fit the proper definition: mounds of earth that slant up and down.

Actually, this loop ride takes its name from the seven hills on which the capital city of Tallahassee is built. In the interest of truth, you should know the route begins south of the city, therefore south of the hills. You will encounter hills twice, but they won't be on land. They top two high bridge spans. Florida is incredibly flat, from end to end.

This tour loops just west of what is called the "Big Bend," where the Florida Panhandle joins the peninsula. Not many visitors are aware of it, but this is the region with the state's best beaches. Not only is the sand squeaky clean and sparkling white, the area is relatively uncrowded. It's too far to drive to from Tampa and Orlando for just a two- or three-day vacation; most weekenders are actually from Georgia or Alabama.

These roads stay close to the coast, so you'll also be passing through the region from which the state gets some of its finest seafood. Plan to sample the smoked mullet, fresh shrimp, and oysters, which are never better anywhere else.

The hodgepodge of terrain here—clear springs, sandy coastal plains, red clay hills, and thick swamps—only reinforces just how different the Panhandle is from Central and South Florida.

Day 1: Wakulla Springs State Park near Tallahassee (904/222-7279) to Ochlockonee River State Park, Sopchoppy (904/962-2771). Distance: 28 miles.

Day 2: Ochlockonee State Park to St. George Island State Park (904/670-2111). Distance: 47 miles.

Day 3: St. George Island State Park to St. Joseph Peninsula State Park, Port Joe (904/227-1327). Distance: 45 miles.

Day 4: St. Joe Peninsula State Park to Dead Lakes State Recreation Area, Wewahitchka (904/639-2702). Distance: 53 miles.

Day 5: Dead Lakes State Recreation Area to Torreya State Park, Bristol (904/643-2674). Distance: 47 miles.

Day 6: Torreya State Park to Wakulla Springs State Park. Distance: 64 miles.

Wakulla Springs State Park: It's a good thing the first day is so short, because you'll want to enjoy Wakulla Springs in both the evening and morning light. This park is truly extraordinary. The huge spring bowl spews forth 1.2 billion gallons of water daily, making it one of the largest springs in the world (Florida's Silver Springs near Ocala is the largest). Wakulla also is one of the deepest springs.

Amazingly diverse wildlife surrounds the spring boil and its run: wild turkey, white-tailed deer, limpkins, herons, and egrets. The alligator population is huge. There are so many resident gators, in fact, it's not safe to snorkel except in one very confined area. The best way to experience the spring is from one of the jungle boat trips, enjoying an outstanding view of the spring run and an amazing amount of wildlife.

The park's restaurant is good and reasonably priced. The lodge, built in 1937, is still decorated in 1930s-style furnishings. This is an ideal point to overnight at the beginning and end of your journey.

Day One

Mi. Summary

00.0 From Wakulla Springs State Park, turn L onto SR 267.

00.1 Cross SR 61.

01.0 Turn left onto CR 365, the first paved road after crossing SR 61.

04.9 Go L, then R across SR 61 to stay on CR 365 (Old Sheel Point).

09.0 Cross US 98 and continue on CR 365.

10.2 Stay on CR 365 at Y intersection; bear R.

11.7 Go L onto CR 375 (Jim Crum Rd.).

15.4 Turn L onto US 98; this is the main coastal highway and traffic on weekends and during hunting season is often heavy.

16.3 Enter town of Medart.

16.8 Go R onto US 319 when road forks.

22.5 Enter town of Sopchoppy; stay on US 319.

23.2 Go L at intersection with CR 375 and stay on US 319.

25.9 Cross Sopchoppy River.

27.5 Enter Ochlockonee River State Park.

Ochlockonee River State Park: Pronounced O-Clock-nee, this little-known park has an outstanding pine forest. The river eventually flows into the Gulf of Mexico about five miles to the south. If you fish here, you could catch both fresh and saltwater species.

The number of campsites here is quite limited, so make sure to have advance reservations. Take time to explore the pine forest as well as around the grassy ponds and the swampy areas, all of which hold a good deal of wildlife: fox squirrel, deer, bobcat, and the red-cockaded woodpecker.

Day Two

Mi. Summary

00.0 Return to US 319 and turn L.

00.7 Pass over Ochlockonee River into Franklin County.

03.6 Pass fire tower.

06.1 Go R onto US 98 and 319.

06.6 First view of the Gulf of Mexico.

10.7 Enter Lanark Village.

11.1 The island you see here is known as Dog Island.

14.8 Turn L at fire tower onto SR 30A.

16.1 Enter town of Carabelle.

16.5 Go L onto US 98.

17.4 Cross Carabelle River Bridge.

19.0 Pass Carabelle Beach.

29.0 Pass SR 65.

32.2 Enter town of Eastpoint.

33.1 Turn L at Suwannee Swifty convenience store onto unmarked road; this is a back way to St. George Island without all the traffic.

33.8 Go L on unmarked road; bear L to the bridge.

33.9 Toll booth to enter St. George Island.

38.4 Arrive St. George Island.

38.8 Go L at sign for state park.

43.1 Enter St. George Island State Park.

47.1 Arrive at park camping area.

St. George Island State Park: Before 1965, you could reach this barrier island in the Gulf of Mexico only by boat. That's why almost half the island has been saved as an undeveloped state park. Riding to the campground along the paved road, you'll pass strand after strand of golden sea oats growing atop sparkling white sand dunes. This is a spectacular area, with nine miles of absolutely pristine beach for walking. This is a good place to see birds in winter. Biting flies in summer can be a problem.

Day Three

Mi.   Summary

00.0 Leave state park entrance.

04.3 Go R onto road leading to bridge.

04.7 Begin ride on bridge across St. George Sound.

09.2 Toll booth.

09.3 Turn L onto CR 65.

09.4 Go L at stop sign on unmarked road.

10.4 Go L onto US 98.

12.4 Begin crossing 3.1-mile Apalachicola Bay bridge; this is one of your two hills.

15.5 Enter town of Apalachicola, famous for oysters.

15.6 Stay L to remain on US 98.

16.6 Go R onto 25th St.

18.6 Go L at stop sign at T intersection.

18.8 Go R onto US 98.

23.7 Turn L onto SR C-30.

28.1 Island in distance is St. Vincent National Wildlife Refuge, which can be reached only by boat.

30.5 Reach Gulf County.

36.3 Go L onto CR C-30E to Cape San Blas.

45.1 Arrive St. Joe Peninsula State Park.

St. Joe Peninsula State Park: Again tonight you'll camp on another beautiful spot that fronts the Gulf of Mexico. The 2,516-acre park is a long skinny peninsula which attracts many kinds of shorebirds year-round. In the fall, this is one of the best places in Florida to watch the annual hawk migration. September and October are normally the best months, but weather always plays an important factor. You have the chance to stay indoors tonight if you've made reservations for a rental cabin; this is one of the few state parks that offers them.

Day Four

Mi. Summary

00.0 From park entrance go straight on C-30E.

09.7 Go L onto C-30.

14.3 Good view of St. Joe Bay.

16.4 Go L to return to US 98, the main coastal road.

17.5 Enter town of St. Joe; stay on US 98.

25.5 Arrive St. Joe Beach (Beacon Hill).

28.1 Go R onto CR 386 (Overstreet Rd.).

33.8 Cross Intracoastal Waterway.

48.0 Go L onto SR 71.

48.2 Arrive town limits of Wewa Hitchka.

49.3 Cross SR 22.

51.8 Go R to Dead Lakes State Recreation Area.

52.3 Enter park.

53.1 Arrive campground. Dead Lakes State Recreation Area: Despite the unappetizing name, this is an excellent freshwater fishing area. The lakes (really part of a flooded swamp) take their name from the thousands of bare trees that were killed when the lakes were formed. Again, campsites are limited. This is another good birding area because of the marshy conditions.

Day Five

Mi. Summary

00.0 Depart park entrance.

00.5 Go R onto SR 71.

04.8 Arrive Calhoun County.

07.5 Intersection with SR 73; remain on SR 71.

13.0 Reach Chipola River.

15.1 Go R onto CR C-275.

17.5 Go L onto CR C-69.

26.3 Pass Calhoun County Correctional Institution.

27.6 Turn R onto SR 71.

29.0 Turn R onto SR 20 in Blountstown (E. Central Ave.).

30.6 Narrow, crowded 1.6-mile-long bridge over Apalachicola River; taking a ferry across is preferable.

32.9 Arrive town of Bristol.

33.5 Go L onto SR 12.

36.5 Arrive Robert Brent Wildlife Management Area.

37.4 Go L onto CR 270.

45.4 At T intersection, go L onto S-270.

46.5 Reach cattle guard at entrance to Torreya State Park.

Torreya State Park: Because of the dramatic landscape, including a 150-foot bluff overlooking the Apalachicola River, many consider this the most spectacular of all Florida state parks. One thing is for sure; it doesn't look like Florida. If you're interested in plants, you have the opportunity to see as many as 100 rare species that grow only in the park. One of them is the torreya, or yew tree, the largest bigleaf magnolia in the United States which is said to grow only inside Torreya Park. An attorney in the nearby town of Bristol was so overwhelmed by the landscape he became convinced Torreya Park was actually part of the biblical Garden of Eden.

Day Six

Lots of turns and road changes this last day. Follow directions carefully. A long day, too, covering almost 65 miles.

Mi. Summary

00.0 Leave state park entrance.

01.0 Go straight on C-1641.

02.6 Turn L at T intersection; follow sign to Chatahoochee.

03.1 Turn L onto unmarked road; continue straight.

06.4 Arrive Gadsden County.

08.7 Go R at Y intersection; do not follow sign to Chatahoochee.

09.1 Continue straight on CR 270 (road joins from the left).

10.5 Pass CR 269.

11.9 Enter town of Sycamore.

12.8 Cross CR 379.

13.6 Stay on CR 270 at angle intersection with CR 483.

13.8 Pass Greensboro Elementary School.

15.3 Go R at T intersection and stay on CR 270 (Ernest Rd.).

15.5 Go L to stay on CR 270 at intersection of Jackson and Selman; cross railroad tracks.

15.6 Turn R onto SR 12 (Green Ave.).

16.1 Cross railroad tracks.

16.5 Go straight when road from right intersects; cross bridge.

16.8 Pass CR 379.

18.0 Go L onto CR 65-D.

18.4 Cross railroad tracks.

20.1 Go R onto CR 65-A at T intersection.

23.7 Go R onto SR 65 at T intersection.

24.9 Go L onto CR 65-B.

30.4 Go R onto SR 267.

31.0 Pass CR 65 intersection.

37.9 Arrive Liberty County.

38.3 Go L onto SR 20.

40.3 Enter Leon County at Ochlockonee River Bridge.

41.5 Pass CR 375 and Smith Creek Rd.

41.8 Go L onto SR 267.

56.2 Enter Wakulla County.

60.6 Cross US 319.

63.8 Cross SR 61.

63.9 Turn R into Wakulla Springs State Park. The Trek ends here.•

TIPS FOR LONG TRIPS

• Place all the packs on your bicycle and none on your back. All equipment on a bicycle tour is usually carried in panniers or saddlebags on front or rear carriers, and a handlebar bag. Carrying weight on your back shifts your center gravity and makes cycling more difficult.

• Pack the weight low and evenly on both sides for maximum stability. You might want to practice before setting out: braking distance increases, and your balance may be quite different.

• In Florida, it's a good idea to start cycling early to avoid heat and traffic. Do not travel at night. Most serious bicycle accidents happen at night.

• Bicycles are considered vehicles in the state of Florida. Therefore, cyclists have all the rights and responsibilities of other vehicle drivers.

• Florida law requires that all cyclists always wear a bicycle helmet (ANSI or SNELL approved) while riding.

• Wear bright colors so automobile drivers can see you. Brightly colored packs will help, too.

• At railroad tracks, slow down and make sure your wheels are at right angles to the tracks. Tracks often are at sloping angles to roads. Bicycle tires can slide parallel to the track, which can throw the rider.

• Carry plenty of water and high-energy snacks. Two water bottles mounted on the frame of the bicycle are suggested.

EQUIPMENT:

• Multigeared bicycle with 'drop' handlebars.
• Handlebar bag or day pack with instant access to tire repair kit, snack food, first aid kit, etc.
• Tire pump.
• Basic tool kit: 6" adjustable spanner, screw drive tire irons, pliers, tire repair kit, and spare tube.
• Bike lock.
• Cycling gloves.
• Sunglasses.
• Sunscreen spf 15 or above.
• Lip balm (with sunblock protection).
• First aid kit and sewing kit.
• Small plastic bags for repacking food and carrying incidentals.

For Camping:

• Tent, waterproof and bug proof.
• Sleeping bag or sheet, depending on season.
• Foam or air mattress.
• Ground cloth.
• Small stove and fuel.
• Cooking gear, dishes, and utensils.
• Insect repellent.
• Flashlight.
• Garbage bags for packing dirty/wet clothes.

Clothing:

- 3 pair shorts (2 pair cycling shorts).
- 1 pair long pants.
- 3 short-sleeve shirts.
- 1 long-sleeve shirt.
- 5–7 pair socks.
- 5–7 pair underwear.
- Warm sweater, jacket, even long johns for sleeping if traveling during cooler seasons.
- Windbreaker and/or rain gear.
- Swimsuit.
- Towel and toilet articles.
- Comfortable shoes for cycling and for camp.

When

No doubt about it, the best time for a Keys cycling trip is in winter. Central Florida cycling is good from November until May. The Panhandle starts cooling down about a month earlier, in October.

Where

For additional cycling opportunities in other parts of Florida, see Appendix H and Chapter 18, Other Everglades Outings.

5

Snorkeler's Guide
to Freshwater Springs

The numerous springs and clear lakes throughout Central and North Florida are one big fishbowl, and all it takes for a look inside is a simple four-piece swimming outfit: mask, snorkel, and a pair of fins.

Snorkeling (also called skin or free diving) is easier than walking. All you do is stay face down in the water and paddle at leisure. Your rubber air tube extending above the waves will allow you totally to forget your dependence on the surface and concentrate instead on the fascinating terrain below.

I've been a snorkeler longer than I can remember. My parents claim I started exploring the bottom of bathtubs when I was an infant. I don't doubt it since curiosity about aquatic life seems almost instinctive. Give a mask and snorkel to any young child and he or she will sightsee in the shallows for hours. It seems to matter little how much they see or how far they explore. The ability to conquer another world and remain freely in this new habitat is reward enough.

Florida enjoys the nation's (perhaps the world's) best freshwater snorkeling thanks to the Floridan aquifer, the vast underground river that flows beneath the top half of the state, creating the most extensive system of underwater caves and tunnels in the entire United States. In many places, this river breaks through the ground to form a spring and its own river, called a spring run.

Although the term *spring* is likely to evoke an image of a tiny fountain of water bubbling up out of the ground, some of Florida's springs pour from a tunnel whose mouth may be 60 to 100 feet across. Some produce full-grown navigable rivers many miles long.

In addition to the scores of lesser springs, Florida contains seventeen springs of major magnitude, more than any other state. A major spring is one whose average discharge is at least 100 cubic feet per second, or 64.6 million gallons daily.

Although quite a few divers have died inside spring tunnels, it doesn't require any special skill, strength or daring to explore the open waters of the spring bowl and spring run. However, actual penetration with scuba into the cave system definitely is a dangerous business that should not be attempted by anyone who hasn't received special cave diving certification.

Scuba divers have only one advantage over snorkelers: they can stay under water for extended periods while snorkelers have to breathe on the surface at least every minute or so. Otherwise, snorkelers can do anything scuba divers can, but with no risk.

You can simply float placidly on the surface or continually plunge downward for close-up inspection of the bottom. It depends on the amount of effort you want to expend and the type of view you want. For a good wide-angle view of everything going on below, floating is all the activity that's required. For a one-to-one, mask-to-fish-eye confrontation, you normally need to swim down a few feet to fish level.

Besides sightseeing and fish watching, snorkelers can treasure hunt for lost jewelry, prehistoric shark teeth, or Indian artifacts. Or they can take the ultimate underwater memorabilia: photographs.

Many springs are so populated with fish life and other interesting sights that an underwater camera is well worth the investment. Whether you outfit an existing camera with an underwater housing or purchase one of the inexpensive amphibious units like the Minolta Weathermatic-A, you'll probably be amazed at how well pictures taken in shallow spring water turn out.

All it takes for a look inside is a mask, a snorkel, and a pair of fins.

The number of springs where you can try out your camera equipment is truly amazing: in Central Florida alone you can find well over a dozen springs that daily gush forth millions of gallons of vodka-clear water. North Florida has even more. Besides clear water, all springs have another common characteristic: cool water. Their water temperature is a constant 72 degrees, making them perfect for swimming on the hottest summer days. Many are located in or near state parks or a national forest, which also makes them ideal picnic and camping sites for an extended weekend trip.

You'll note that in many places scuba divers share the springs with snorkelers. Although you may feel you're missing the spectacular sights, it's simply not so. Most tunnels are simply large limestone passages, very dark, very monotonous. They do not have the stalagmites and stalactites found in many dry tunnel systems throughout the Southeast. There's considerably more to see in the open, sun-lit spring areas.

As the old joke goes, what do you see in underwater caves? Wet rocks. Also, scuba divers are not allowed in many of the places snorkelers are.

Following are some of the most popular and accessible Florida springs. Most are either commercially operated or owned by the state or county and charge admission fees.

PANHANDLE AREA

Vortex Spring: (Near the town of Ponce de Leon, just 4.8 miles north off I-10's Exit 15.) With a maximum depth of fifty feet and a head pool extending 200 feet across, this is a popular spot for instruction and check-out dives, and the run is good for snorkelers. With almost 400 acres of woodlands surrounding the spring boil, Vortex claims to be Florida's largest commercial dive operation. Overnight accommodations include campsites, dormitories, and efficiency rooms. The spring pool is home to at least eighteen different species of fish, including huge hybrid Japanese goldfish. A fully stocked dive shop with air fills is on site. Water clarity is usually affected by rain runoff for only a day or two. Call the Vortex dive shop at 800/342-0640 or 904/836-4979.

Morrison Spring: (Also near the town of Ponce de Leon, just four miles south off I-10's Exit 15.) Considered one of the best spring dives in the state, the large basin is also excellent for snorkeling. Striking moss-draped cypress trees border the basin, which contains two different cave openings. Do not try to swim into them. The spring run travels a half mile into the Choctawhatchee River. For more information, call 904/836-4223.

Cypress Spring: (Seven miles south of I-10's Exit 17 near the town of Vernon.) This is a spectacular spring with a 150-foot-wide basin. It's only twenty-five feet deep to the narrow cavern opening, but the flow makes it impossible to enter.

Besides grassy areas, there are quite a few old trees that house largemouth bass and other species. Camping, canoes, and a concession stand are available. For more information, call 904/535-2960.

Merrit's Mill Pond: (Located just outside the city of Marianna.) The main spring is known as Blue Springs. As you'll see, the term *blue* crops up frequently in spring names; this is not surprising considering water color in the deeper springs.

The various springs and the five-mile-long spring run offer lots of different snorkeling and scuba opportunities. The pond itself averages fifteen feet deep, but snorkeling only is permitted in the head pool. Both snorkeling and scuba are an option virtually everywhere else. Rent a canoe and stop at the different sites, including Twin Caves, Shangri-la Spring, Indian Washtub, Gator Spring (not only might you see a gator but also turtles). Snorkeling here is free.

Wakulla River: Wakulla Springs, just south of Tallahassee, is one of the deepest springs in the world, but it is virtually closed to swimmers and snorkelers because of the boat tours and the large gator population. Well outside the park, you can snorkel in the spring-fed, sand-bottomed Wakulla River, one of the prettiest rivers in allof Florida. Fossils are sometimes found along the bottom, and manatees like to visit the river mouth during the summer. No dive shops are nearby, but canoe rentals are available where US 98 crosses the Wakulla River. For more information, call 904/925-6412.

Wacissa River Springs: (Exit 32 off I-10 near Tallahassee, go 10.5 miles on SR 59 to reach the spring.) More than a half dozen different springs form the headwaters of the river, and each can be visited by small boat or canoe. The Wacissa also joins the Aucilla River to create a fourteen-mile-long canoe run. You need to bring your own boat to explore this site; the nearest dive shop is in Tallahassee. A public boat ramp is provided.

Ichetucknee Springs State Park: (Exit I-75 at SR-47 and go south for twelve miles on SR-47 to SR-238. Turn right onto SR-238 and follow road to park entrance.) This is an extremely popular spot for snorkelers, nature lovers, and those who like to watch the world go by from an inner tube. The three-hour river float passes through unspoiled woodlands that line the banks. Several springs feed the river, which is always crystal clear. Because of the distance and the cool water temps, a wet suit is definitely necessary. Once you start out, there's no turning back against the current. A tram operated by the state park is available to transport you back to your starting point between Memorial and Labor Days. Outside of that time period, you will need to arrange your own return; the easiest way is to drive two cars.

The float is divided into a northern section (1.4 miles) and a southern section (1.7 miles). The number of visitors is regulated to a maximum of 3,000 daily on a first-come basis. Arrive early on summer weekends or you may not get in. Blue Hole Spring, located inside the park, is restricted to certified cave divers. For complete information, call the state park office at 904/497-2511.

Ginnie Springs: (From US 41, go west onto SR-340 for just over 6.5 miles to a graded road on the right with the Ginnie Springs sign.) This is an excellent dive resort with camping, air station, and rest rooms. It includes several springs on the banks of the Santa Fe River. Ginnie Springs itself, the favorite, has a sand bottom loaded with eel grass and a cavern that widens into two separate rooms. Do not try going inside the cavern or any other opening here. For more information, call 800/874-8571 or 904/454-2202.

Blue Springs/Santa Fe River: (Situated near High Springs, take US 41 to SR 340 for 4.5 miles to the entrance sign.) Another commercial operation, but it permits snorkeling only. You'll find lots of tame bream that like to be fed and good plant life. A small cave opening sits at the twenty-five-foot bottom. Just east is Naked Springs, where supposedly in times past people too poor to own bathing suits swam naked; sounds like just another excuse for good old-fashioned skinny dipping. Camping is available.

Santa Fe River: When rain is scarce and the river drops, this is one of the best places in the state to find fossils. Several springs—Big Awesome, Little Awesome, Trackone Siphon, and Myrtle's Fissure—line the Santa Fe from Ginnie Springs to SR 47. In dry periods, the brown tannic water created by the cypress trees lining the riverbanks is partly replaced by the clearer spring water, an ideal time as visibility grows to as much as forty to sixty feet. Fossils and Indian artifacts are commonly found on the bottom along this route. Be sure and display the diver's flag on an inner tube or your canoe if you decide to make this float, a distance of about two miles. Consider a wet suit a necessity.

Manatee Springs: (Near Chiefland, take US 19 to SR 320 and follow the signs to the state park.) Named for the manatees that formerly wintered here, but few manatees visit anymore. No one knows exactly why. If you want to see manatees, go to Crystal River (see below). The large basin of Manatee Springs issues 96 million gallons of water daily down a half-mile-long, cypress-banked run. Snorkeling is restricted to the basin proper and the first 200 feet of the run. You'll see lots of fish and aquatic plants. Also inside the park is Catfish Sink, sometimes not worth the bother because of its green algae cover. Complete information is available from the park office; call 904/493-6072.

CENTRAL FLORIDA REGION

Rock Springs: (Take Hwy. 441 into Apopka, just north of Orlando, until you come to the sign on the right directing you to Rock Springs. Follow this road until it dead-ends, then turn right again, go less than a half mile and Kelly Park will be right in front of you.) Rock Springs flows from a cave located at the base of a limestone cliff. Past fatalities here have resulted in a grating being put in place to keep swimmers from entering the partially air-filled cave. However, you still have the benefits of the 1.5-mile-long spring run, which has a bright sand bottom, natural foliage along the banks, and plenty of fish and turtles for viewing. The creatures tend to hide during periods of heavy use, so the most interesting time to visit is during early morning, late afternoon, and weekdays. Snorkelers also have to share the run with people navigating the swift-flowing water in over-sized inner tubes. The tubers have the legal right-of-way. Keep your eyes open and stir the sand if you float the spring run. Sizable prehistoric shark teeth have been found here.

Kelly Park itself is another favorite picnic area, but you can camp here overnight if you wish. For more information, call 407/889-4179.

Blue Spring: (Take the marked exit off I-4 going toward Daytona; in Orange City, turn left on French Ave. and follow the signs to the park.) The spring boil here is huge and issues 121 million gallons of water a day. You can snorkel in the area around the spring as well as the half-mile-long run (which empties into the St. Johns River) except during winter months when the manatees are present. You'll see lots of fish here throughout the year, including largemouth bass, catfish, gar , and tilapia. Picnic facilities, camping, and canoe rentals are also available. For more information, call the park office at 904/775-3663.

Alexander Springs: (Located in the Ocala National Forest. Take US 441 to its intersection with St. Rd. 19 at Eustis. Turn right at the overpass and follow St. Rd. 19 for about fifteen miles to St. Rd 445. Turn right and follow the signs to the recreation area.) The spring basin, one of the state's largest, can hold a platoon of snorkelers and divers, which it often does on weekends when training classes are held. However, there is always enough empty water away from the beachfront access or the area around the cave, located twenty-seven feet down. Alexander Springs is home to numerous largemouth bass and panfish. Don't be surprised to see ocean-going mullet swimming about, too; they enter via the fifteen-mile-long spring run that empties into the St. Johns which, in turn, empties into the Atlantic. Picnicking, canoe rentals, and camping are all available. For complete information, call 904/669-3522.

Silver Glen Springs: (Also part of the Ocala National Forest, the recreation area is located on St. Rd. 19 about six miles north of the St. Rd. 19-St. Rd. 40 intersection.) This spring is one of my favorites because of the thick grass beds interspersed with a white sand bottom and loads of fish. The shallow water and reflected light off the bottom make the spring basin superb for underwater photography. Look for largemouth bass and, in the fall, schools of striped bass, near the main spring. The half-mile spring run leading to Lake George has dangerous boat traffic on weekends. Even the rest of the time the run should not be attempted unless you are beside a canoe or boat of your own. For more information, call 904/685-3990.

Salt Springs: (A commercial campground and recreation area in the Ocala

Forest, Salt Springs is located on SR 19 in the town of Salt Springs.) You have three spring boils to snorkel around and a five-mile run which leads to Lake George. Gators along the spring run have sometimes been curious, and they are not afraid of people. The time they are most likely to bother a snorkeler is during the spring-time mating season. Don't take any chances—leave the water anytime you see an alligator here or anywhere. For more information, call 904/685-2048.

Crystal River: (Near the town of Crystal River on the Gulf Coast on US 98.) In the past, Crystal River has offered the finest freshwater snorkeling in Florida, and it generally was considered the best freshwater snorkeling area in the entire world. Unfortunately, the water clarity in some areas is greatly reduced because of runoff, but some of the smaller springs in isolated pockets are still crystal clear. The snor-keling activities are varied, and it would take a chapter devoted to Crystal River to discuss them all. A boat is necessary to visit any of the worthwhile springs. Sturdy john boats with small outboard engines can be rented from Crystal Lodge Dive Center (904/795-6798); Plantation Inn (904/795-5797); and Port Paradise Dive Shop (904/795-3111). Rentals are by the hour or the day; weekend reservations for when the manatees are present should be made several weeks in advance.

There are thirty known springs near the headwaters, called King's Bay, but only eight are of interest to snorkelers. The most important and most popular is King's Spring, located just south of Banana Island. The spring measures seventy-five feet across and drops to as much as thirty feet. Crystal River's other major springs are located in canals connecting with King's Bay. None are dived as much as King's Spring itself, so they should offer more solitude on crowded weekends.

When anchoring at King's Spring, never motor across or stop over the springs: you could hit a diver. Instead, stay on the rim of the spring in the four-foot shallows. Both fresh- and saltwater species including largemouth bass, bream, snook, mullet, redfish, trout, sheepshead, gar, tarpon, and snapper visit the spring. The variety is truly incredible.

Even more spectacular and unusual, in winter months a large herd of manatees seek refuge in the area, and it is often possible to approach the creatures closely for pictures. However, you must remember these are an endangered species under strict protection, and there are harsh penalties levied against anyone thought to be harassing one of the animals. So, never chase a manatee, much less attempt to ride one: if you want pictures, let the manatee come to you. Despite their large size, they are quite harmless.

Two other springs, Grand Canyon and Mullet, are located near King's Spring. Grand Canyon is simply a thirty-five-foot-long crack in a rock that drops to a depth of twenty feet. Mullet's Gullet, which has several small springs, is another clear shallow area excellent for photography. For complete information on the area, call the Crystal River Chamber of Commerce: 904/795-3149.

Rainbow River: (Near the town of Dunellon on Florida's West Coast, above Tampa.) This clear-water river runs for 5.5 miles before emptying into the Withlacoochee River. The headspring is located within the boundaries of a tourist attraction, off-limits to land visitors, but it is only 1.25 miles upriver from the nearest boat launch to the spring basin. Depths are shallow, only seven to thirty feet. It's a superb setting for underwater photography. Many snorkelers like to float with the current back to the boat ramp. For camping reservations and more information, call the Rainbow Springs State Campground: 904/489-5201.

Who

The following dive shops can supply you with the latest, up-to-date information about snorkeling in their area or the springs in general.

American Pro Dive
715 SE Hwy. 19,
Crystal River, FL 34429
800/291-DIVE, 904/563-0041
Fax: 904/795-4119

Birds Underwater
8585 N. Pine Needle Trail
Crystal River, FL 34428
904/563-2763

Branford Dive Center
US 27 and Suwanee River
Branford, FL 32008
Mailing Address: PO Box 822
Branford, FL 32008
904/935-1141
Fax: 904/935-1141

Crystal Lodge Dive Center
525 NW 7th Ave.
Crystal River, FL 34428
904/795-6798

Devil's Den, Inc.
Route 3, Box 23-DD
Williston, FL 32696
904/528-3344

Ginnie Springs Resort
7300 N.E. Ginnie Springs Rd.
High Springs, FL 32643
904/454-2202
Fax: 904/454-3201

Hal Watt's
40 Fathom Grotto
9487 NW 115th Ave.
Ocala, FL 32675
904/368-7974, 407/896-4541
Fax: 407/896-4542

Plantation Inn Marina
9301 W. Fort Island Trail
Crystal River, FL 34429
Mailing Address: PO Box 1093
Crystal River, FL 34429
904/795-5797
Fax: 904/795-1368

Steamboat Dive Inn
Corner US Hwy. 27 and 129
Branford, FL 32008
Mailing Address: PO Box 1000
Branford, FL 32008
904/935-2283, 904/935-3483
Fax: 904/935-1471

Coral Reef Scuba
2020 N. Point Blvd., Unit 8
Tallahassee, FL 32308
904/385-1323
Fax: 904/385-3910
and

1362 Lake Bradford Rd.,
Tallahassee, FL 32304
904/576-6268
Fax: 904/574-6339

Talley's Pro Dive
PO Box 124
Crystal River, FL 34423
904/795-2776
Fax: 904/563-0295

Vortex Springs, Inc.
Route 2, Box 650, Hwy. 81 N.
Ponce De Leon, FL 32455
800/342-0640, 904/836-4979
Fax: 904/836-4962

What

Although the technique of snorkeling is easy, selecting the proper equipment for it is not. The problem is most snorkeling gear tends to look alike, and so many people are tempted to invest as little as possible. That is a serious mistake. Cheap, poorly fitted equipment can make snorkeling almost unbearable, causing foot blisters, mask squeeze, and possibly even mouth sores.

For example, the snorkeling gear you find in most drug stores is fine for kids paddling around a swimming pool, but it's nothing you want to use in open water where it's a bit difficult to continually dump the ocean out of a leaky mask or keep standing on the bottom to adjust a too-tight fin.

Snorkeling gear should be selected with the same care you would use in finding the best restaurant in a strange town. In both instances you're working in unfamiliar territory and the total tab is likely to be about the same. A good quality snorkeling outfit will cost between $75 and $150; if that seems a bit much, remember you're talking about an investment that should last at least five to ten years, longer with proper care.

In putting together your first snorkeling outfit, you should seek professional advice to obtain a good custom fit. You need to visit the nearest pro dive shop. Florida is filled with such stores, so you can stock up on gear almost at a moment's notice.

Of all the items, the mask is the most important. It is your "looking glass" into what divers call "innerspace," and as such should provide a picture as clear and problem-free as the one supplied by your TV set. A mask needs to be fitted to your face with the same precision as a pair of glasses. It's done by holding a mask against your face without using the strap.

Inhale slightly through your nose and let go of the mask. If the mask fits properly, it will seal so securely there aren't any open spaces anywhere on your face. Don't accept any other test: not even the tightest strap will stop an overly large mask from leaking. On the other hand, don't buy a mask that's too small.

If a mask seals properly, try it on with the strap. If it feels uncomfortable, try another. If a mask is too small for you, the strap is apt to dig the mask skirt into your face, gouging it like a cookie cutter.

Perhaps the most common complaint among new snorkelers is their cheap fins which create large welts and blisters. They deserve what they get; a pair of fins should never be purchased without seeing whether they fit, just as with a pair of shoes. The only store where you're likely to find the perfect fit keeps its fins in shoe boxes__and not sealed in plastic—a pro dive store.

The snorkel is your simplest piece of equipment and it won't cause any problem unless you select the wrong design. Snorkels come in many shapes and sizes, and the rule of thumb is the less there is to them, the better. The snorkel base should have a normal U-shape without any fancy curves. If the angle is too sharp, it will be difficult to expel water. Also, a snorkel should be open-ended so you can quickly blow out the water after you swim to the bottom.

Another advantage of shopping at a pro dive store is they'll usually let you exchange your merchandise if it doesn't perform or feel just right after you test it. You'll need the original packaging for exchange, and you should also verify the exchange policy at time of purchase.

When

Winter is always a good time to dive the springs, especially for those normally interested only in diving saltwater, since serious wave action may be kicking up too much rolling in the ocean for a comfortable offshore trip. Since most springs are in the Panhandle and North and Central Florida, quite a few of the divers are from neighboring states, particularly Georgia and Alabama. However, the springs are also close enough for a long weekend from such east coast states as the Carolinas and even Virginia, Tennessee, and Louisiana. Serious, prolonged rains can sometimes impact springs near the Suwannee and Santa Fe rivers, when the rivers overflow and darken the top layer of water. This is rarely a problem at places like Vortex, Alexander Springs, and others that are isolated ground holes fed by water that is always clear.

6

The Best Thrill Rides
in Central Florida

Why is it we sometimes like to scare ourselves silly?

As a youngster, I walked at night through a particular graveyard (cemetery sounds too refined) to deliberately give myself the creeps. It wasn't a daily or week-ly ritual: I did it only when I got really bored, or when I couldn't settle down long enough to study for a test.

Nothing like a stroll among the dead, half scared out of my wits at every shuf-fling or scraping sound, to put the world in better perspective.

Yet this particular graveyard wasn't all that far from a main thoroughfare. If something bad really came after me, I figured I could run faster than any ghoul or mummy, which were never depicted as all that agile in the movies. And a big plate of spaghetti with extra garlic bread always eaten ahead of time was certain to keep any vampire away.

Controlled, safe thrills, that's what I was inventing for myself. Unfortunately, you can no longer walk around graveyards at night without attracting the attention of the police or a psychiatrist. These days the only socially acceptable ways to scare yourself silly are at horror shows and theme parks, where we actually pay to inflict terror on ourselves.

Why do we do it? Is it a game of make-believe where we imagine we're looking death square in the face and spitting in its eye? Or is it a primal need to feel the occasional adrenalin rush, a built-in addiction resulting from the millions of years our ancestors ran from saber-toothed tigers and big hairy mastodons?

I don't pretend to know.

But I can tell you where the best collection of hair-raising, gut-wrenching, holler-till-you're-hoarse rides are in the theme parks of Central Florida, the worlds number one vacation destination.

I've rated them by a scream factor of 1 to 6: like whitewater rapids, a 6 is impossible. A 1 would be a kiddie carousel. The Magic Kingdom's Alien Encounter, which is quite scary for many people, is a theater experience rather than a ride, so it doesn't qualify.

BUNGEE JUMPING

None of the major theme parks allow bungee jumping, so look for bungee jumping billboards near the major tourist areas like Kissimmee, South Orlando, or Daytona Beach. I was not about to attempt this myself, but Jim Poppino of Mims, FL, tried it when he was a journalism major at the University of Central Florida. Here's how he described it in an article he wrote for my feature writing class:

"You stand up and look out. In the distance you can see Wet 'n' Wild. Nearby is a hotel where tourists stand on open balconies or behind closed windows and peer intently. You are the subject of their interest.

The man next to you is talking, giving precise instructions. He takes your left hand and places it on a metal rail. You do the same with your right hand and step forward.

The man says, "Three."

The metal rail is cool to the touch. A gentle wind makes the 60-degree air seem like 20. The wire cage rocks slowly, almost imperceptibly in the wind.

All is quiet, except the man next to you, and he says, "Two."

Someone probably told you not to look down, but you do anyway. You see your feet . . . and only the heels of those feet are resting on a solid object. Between your ankles you see a very small rectangle, about one inch by two. That is the inflated air bag. If anything goes wrong, you're supposed to land on that.

The man says, "One."

For a split second you grip the railings tighter, your knees stiffen, while your feet resist the gentle tug of the heavy thick cord that tie your feet to the cage like some kind of strange elongated umbilical cord.

The man says, "Go!"

Simultaneously you let go of both railings, extending your arms straight out from your body. You lean forward and feel your feet touch the cage for the last time as gravity takes over.

As you fall, literally headlong towards the ground, you see minute details as they slip out of your peripheral vision. Wet 'n' Wild is the first to slide by, closely followed by the small groups of people watching from the ground.

Meanwhile, you are aware of the ground rushing up, accelerating at thirty-two feet per second.

The air bag enlarges magically as you get closer. The force of the increasing wind dries your eyes. Your mouth is closed but the wind finds a way in and so your throat becomes thoroughly parched.

In two seconds, you have fallen ninety-six feet. In the next second, you and the ground could become one.

Snap!!

Instead of the soft plop of your body slamming into the hard earth, you are instantly whipped back. Your tongue, eyes, and the air in your lungs attempt to exit your body, forcibly. Your view of the ground is replaced by the wire cage as you reverse direction. Suddenly, you're hurtling upward as the elastic cord pulls you skyward and the cage looms bigger and bigger.

Gravity is a stubborn force, though. Just as it appears you will be able to reach out to grab the cage, gravity pulls you back with a subtle tug. Twisting around, you try to position your body but with little success. When you reach the end of the cord again, the reaction is not so violent, your response not so drastic. Within a few moments you are swaying gently under your own momentum; shortly, you will be on the ground.

That is what happens when you bungee jump, the physical equivalent of riding the tip of a bullwhip.

What compels grown adults like myself to pay money to strap on a giant rubber band and jump off suspension bridges, cranes, or any other object of considerable height?

"Peer pressure and curiosity," explains an employee of the bungee jumping operation. "People drive by and see the crane or the sign, or they just watch someone do a jump and decide to see what it's like for themselves. There is usually some pressure from friends if a group of people are jumping."

The fellow who jumped ahead of me—now a veteran of a single bungee jump—agrees. He also cites the age-old mountain climbing proverb: "Because it's there, that's why."

Another bungee jumper sheds a different perspective: "I like living on the edge."

Evidently a lot of people share the same feelings. A hundred people or more will bungee jump here on a good day."

Jim did the rating for this ride.

Scream factor: 5+

THE TOWER OF TERROR
Disney-MGM Studios, Orlando

Once upon a time, a long, long time ago, the wicked witch on the Snow White ride was as scary as Walt Disney World went. Then came Space Mountain (a ride that took ten years to develop); the Disney experience was never the same again.

The Tower of Terror is not for control freaks. The point of this ride is for you to have absolutely no control and no way out as your elevator plunges down thirteen stories at 40mph.

The drop is so sudden and swift that people who hang sunglasses around their neck have reported that the glasses floated almost shoulder-high as they plummeted toward—what? Death? Severe injury? How can anyone possibly survive this?

The free fall lasts only about two seconds, more than enough time to relive your life and make resolutions to your God about how-you'll-reform-and-be-good-for-the-rest-of-your-life-if-you-can-just-get-through-this-without-dying. Lord knows you'll never do this again, either!

Right?

Well, a lot of people do get back on the ride, expecting it to be less terrifying since they know what to expect. Guess what: it doesn't always work that way.

One Disney publicity employee who confronted terror in the tower more than fifty times said the ride disturbed him more each time he rode it. He even dreams about it.

This is a serious ride that leaves some people so limp they feel knee-walking drunk afterwards.

Scream Factor: 5

BACK TO THE FUTURE
Universal Studios Florida, Orlando

Both Shakespeare and modern suspense writers always mix comedy with their terror. A good laugh or a sigh of relief helps break the tension so you're set up for the next emotional turn of the screw. The designers of the Back to the Future ride take good advantage of this technique on what is easily Central Florida's best flight simulator.

For four minutes (an unusually long time for a theme park ride) your DeLorean automobile rockets through space and time trying to catch the evil Biff who has stolen a time flux converter from Doc Brown. If you don't apprehend Biff, the future of mankind could be destroyed!

The excitement is both visual and physical. You crash through signs and billboards, and even get swallowed by a dinosaur. Everything happens far faster than you can anticipate. Two huge seven-story OMNIMAX screens in front of you display the non-stop action, and your attention never wanders from them.

Your DeLorean (seating four in front, four in back) is small enough that the hydraulics can really whip you around. If you have a bad neck, heed the posted advisory and avoid this ride. (Contrast the limited seating on this ride to Disney-MGM's Star Tours, a flight simulator that seats as many as forty. That kind of mini-auditorium can't be maneuvered as rapidly as the DeLorean.)

As you prepare to exit the DeLorean, you may feel like a bottle of soda that's just had all the fizz shaken out.

Scream Factor: 4

BOMB BAY
Wet 'n Wild, Orlando

If the sudden drop in the Tower of Terror seems frightening, just wait until you try this one. Word has spread about the water slide called Bomb Bay, so you won't have to wait in line long. The experience is just too intense for a lot of people. Once you bomb out, you'll understand why.

First, you enter a bomb-like contraption that doesn't seem any larger than a phone booth. A voice tells you to cross your ankles and your arms to protect your limbs; at that moment, you might also want to make the sign of the cross.

You know that at some point the trap door floor beneath you is going to disappear. Like Wily Coyote, you're perched for a great fall . . . you just don't know when. You might want to grimace at the voyeurs down below who are enjoying your anxiety on a TV camera monitor.

GOODBYE!

You drop vertically for seventy-six-feet. You're plummeting at such speed that you never again come in contact with the slide behind you—because you're riding a sheet of water.

Your descent doesn't last long. Try to finish screaming before you hit the pool at the bottom so you don't swallow a lot of water. Either gagging, choking, or coughing after you've just screamed your lungs out is considered bad form. Inhaling chlorine also makes for a sorer throat.

Scream Factor: 5

DER STUKA
Wet 'n Wild, Orlando

Der Stuka, which probably translates as "weenie ride" in water park parlance, is a shorter, less terrifying water slide than Bomb Bay. For one thing, you know when you're about to shove off, because you're in control of when you hit the chute. However, this ride could cause you more problems than Bomb Bay if you wear contacts: on Der Stuka, water slaps your face so hard and fast your lenses could get washed out. If you wear contacts, close your eyes and pretend you're falling down a dark tunnel. That's what I had to do.

A word of advice for women: wear a one-piece bathing suit. Loose-fitting bikini parts have sometimes been torn off by the water force. The guys have enough trouble not losing their swim trunks.

On Der Stuka, you notice the slide behind you, and that feels like a reassuring pat on the back. That may not sound like much consolation, but it's actually a big one since you never feel like you're free-falling. As at Bomb Bay, you want to slide with your limbs crossed.

Scream Factor: 4

KUMBA
Busch Gardens, Tampa

Prefer a roller coaster for your kicks? Busch Gardens has three good ones: the Python, the Scorpion, and the Kumba, the newest and fastest. A python and a scorpion are naturally occurring jungle-related animals, but what is a Kumba? A mythical jungle beast that roars—loudly. So do many of the people who ride it.

Kumba one-ups the Tower of Terror with not two but three loooooong seconds of total weightlessness with a 360-degree loop, a separate 108-foot vertical loop, and a double corkscrew. That's a lot to undergo in a short, 2.38-minute ride. Even tough roller coaster veterans usually death-grip the thick restraining shoulder bars. The Kumba inspires few thoughts of joyriding with your hands in the air.

Scream Factor: 5

SPACE MOUNTAIN
Disney's Magic Kingdom

Believe you've outgrown your fear of the dark? I'll bet not when you're being tossed around like a Ping-Pong ball in a lottery drawing, without a clue to mark how far away or where the way out is.

Space Mountain, granddaddy of Orlando thrill rides, still generates enough respect that people routinely back out at the last moment. Perhaps it's the green warning lights and other special effects that create too much uncertainty about what could happen next.

So what if you have waited forty-five minutes in line? Matters of life and death need not be rushed into—they should be carefully considered, ideally from a respectable distance. A quiet spin instead on the Grand Prix Raceway kiddie cars might be called for to think this over.

If you see it through, as most people do, you'll be warped into a void as black as a satin blindfold. You'll barrel around at neck-snapping speeds that seem far faster than the actual 28mph, and you'll probably be crouching to avoid a metal beam—or something—which you know is waiting to decapitate you.

If you haven't ridden Space Mountain in a couple of years, it's time to go again. This ride holds up wonderfully well in the scream department. None of Disney's newer roller-coaster rides comes close to equaling it.

Scream Factor: 4+

AS MUCH FUN AS SCARY

The following rides will probably raise a neck hair or two, but they tend to be a lot more fun than any of the rides above because of their terrific special effects. Adding to their enjoyment is that none turns into an endurance contest where you have to fight to retain your wits and your lunch.

At Universal Studios: Jaws, Kongfrontation, and Earthquake are good fun. In all three, try to sit as far forward as possible. However, the back seat in Kongfrontation is also worthwhile since it puts you and old Banana-breath in fairly close proximity. Young children (and a lot of adults) love the Hanna-Barbera flight simulator.

At Walt Disney World: Big Thunder Mountain is enjoyable, even if fairly tame. The newer Splash Mountain is a typical flume ride where you might get wet at the end. Star Tours and Body Wars are pleasant but dated simulator rides. They both need a whole lot more shakin' goin' on.

Who

Wet 'n Wild, Walt Disney World, and Universal Studios are located about a half hour west of Orlando, off I-4. The exits are unmistakable thanks to all the signs. Busch Gardens is located in Tampa. Take I-4 west from Orlando and follow the signs. Bungee jumping operators go in and out of business with some frequency. Check the Yellow Pages not only in Orlando and Kissimmee but also in Daytona Beach.

What

All of the theme parks charge daily admission fees. One day each at Wet 'n Wild and Busch Gardens is probably sufficient. Universal Studios requires at least two days. At Disney World, you will need full-day admission to the Magic Kingdom and the Disney-MGM Studios. The most exciting thing in Epcot is the chance to dive the Living Seas; see Chapter 26.

When

Wet 'n Wild closes during winter cold fronts. All of the other attractions are open every day of the year, though operating hours change with the seasons. In summer and during holiday periods, all of the theme parks have extended hours into the evening. During other parts of the year, the parks usually close around 5 or 6 PM.

Why

Because they're there.

7

Ocean Kayaking
from the Keys to the Panhandle

The first time I tried kayaking was about as far away from Florida as you can get. It was in Central Asia, in the former Soviet Union. I was part of the first American group to attempt a descent of the Class IV-V Chatkal River.

Though I spent most of my time aboard a raft, I did have a chance to try out our one kayak in calm water. Unlike the sluggish raft, the kayak was all sports car. It was streamlined, fun to steer, and extremely maneuverable.

I'm not surprised that kayaks have become increasingly popular even in Florida, which is not known for its whitewater. But we have plenty of ocean and more and more people are appreciating that kayaks are much easier to use in the Gulf and Atlantic than canoes.

Wading birds and pelicans often nest in islands just offshore in many parts of South Florida, and kayaks are usually much less disturbing to them than canoes. The reason is that kayakers always hold their paddle blades well away from their craft, which permits even the newest kayaker to move silently.

Novice canoeists, on the other hand, often scrape their paddle against the canoe sides, and any additional noise the paddler makes while shifting gear or plunking the paddle on the bottom is magnified, since the inside of a canoe acts like a mini–echo chamber. That's why a fleet of inexperienced canoeists tends to sound like a bunch of bad drummers.

New kayakers also have a much easier time going in a straight line, maneuvering around islands and navigating through narrow channels, where first-time canoeists typically move forward like an undulating snake.

Florida's best kayaking is in the Keys and along parts of the Gulf of Mexico. Not only because the wave action is smaller compared to the Atlantic, but also the Gulf offers many small, isolated islets that you can paddle to hour after hour or day after day.

THE KEYS

If it seems like it would be boring to paddle only beside the Overseas Highway that links the Florida Keys, you'd be right. However, the Keys consist of several hundred islands, many of them are situated close together, and this creates superb kayaking opportunities. In Florida, such areas are referred to as "backcountry."

The Keys, which contain almost a thousand different islands, my favorite part of the state to kayak. I never quite know what will appear around the next island—or what might be in the middle of it, for that matter. It's possible literally to paddle through some mangrove islands thanks to the large tunnels created by the tangle of mangrove roots.

The wildlife viewing in the Keys is as good—and sometimes I think far better—as in nearby Everglades National Park, which juts into Florida Bay on the Gulf side. The one exception is the chance to spot alligators, which are generally absent in the Keys since they prefer freshwater, something the islands notoriously lack.

My last Keys kayaking trip was off Big Pine Key in the Lower Keys. The Gulf islands here are included in two national wildlife refuges: National Key Deer and Great White Heron. In some places, there is not only the possibility of spotting an endangered Key deer (the deer sometimes swim to the islands from the mainland) but also of seeing many different birds, including roseate spoonbills, osprey, great white egrets, and the uncommon great white heron. Bird watching is much more of a certainty.

My last kayaking trip was with Lost World Adventures, which provided a remarkable feel for the Big Pine Key area in just half a day. We assembled at the far end of the bridge that connects Big Pine Key with the smaller and less densely populated No Name Key. Crossing the bridge, I was treated to the rare and remarkable sight of Greek sponge fishermen from Tarpon Springs transferring their huge bales of sponges from a work boat to two dinghies that shuttled the sponges to shore. Once on land, the sponges would probably be taken to Key West and sold.

Bill Keogh, owner of Lost World Adventures, remarked that in his twelve years in the Keys he'd never seen a loaded sponge boat so closeup. It turned out to be just a prelude to the day's other remarkable sights.

We loaded the kayaks into the water, careful not to step on the bottom just off-shore. This caution wasn't to protect anything growing there—the bottom was barren—but to keep from sinking knee-deep into the soft mud. Because the bottom is soft in so many areas, it's never advisable to walk offshore without first testing the bottom with a paddle.

We shoved off and began hugging the narrow channel next to the mangrove shoreline. Although the islands are part of the Great White Heron Refuge, the mangrove trees were home to far more interesting birds—dozens of yellow-crested night herons, which feed most actively after dark. These herons, which have a remarkable yellow plume and a striking orange eye, allowed us to approach them quite closely, a wonderful chance for nature photography.

Although the birds captured most of our attention, the underwater flats surrounding the mangrove islands proved equally interesting once we took the time to look. To many people, the flats seem dead and unimpressive at first glance, yet they are very rich and prolific communities. The flats are the foundation of the aquatic food chain that many animals depend upon.

The area around No Name Key is populated with rich flats of turtle grass. Turtle grass provides shelter for many tiny animals including fish and snails, but stingrays, turtles, barracuda, and sharks also live in these grass meadows. Turtle grass flats are easy to identify, since the bottom appears to be covered in a dark carpet. Individual pieces of grass are flat and broad, similar to those used in many aquariums.

The grass flats are accompanied by regions of a pale mustard color, an area technically known as the hardbottom. The yellow-tinted surface mirrors the colors of the sponges and corals that thrive in the hardbottom. Sponge flats are always interesting to snorkel over, not only to see the sponges and small corals that cover the bottom, but also to look for the small lobster, young reef fish, and other animals that inhabit this environment.

Recent winter storm damage to the hardbottom was visible in the shallows beside the mangrove islands where many bucket-sized sponges lay on their sides. Storm surge had uprooted these sponges, which normally stay anchored to the hardbottom and other secure structures such as wrecks and coral reefs. Although they may look more like plants, they are true animals that survive by filtering water through their soft bodies. Though unanchored, most of the sponges were still very much alive and would probably remain so as long as they remained covered by water.

As fascinating as the land below and around us was, the trip's highlight was our disappearance into the heart of a mangrove island. The narrow channel tunneling into the island was not readily visible, and I could barely identify it even though I knew where to look.

We literally paddled inside the island, as red mangrove trees towered over us like medium-sized oaks. The twisted and intertwined roots, although a bizarre sight, were of impressive size. Many were thicker than my wrist, and all were shoulder-level when I paddled past them. The limbs interlocked to create a canopy that both drooped and soared anywhere from fifteen to thirty feet above us.

In this eerie but beautiful forest the bright blue sky and noontime sun were muted by a broken ceiling of small, oval-shaped green leaves. The sunlight that managed to penetrate the numerous thumb-sized openings dotting the canopy appeared like unnaturally bright blotches.

The silence around us was almost deafening. Hardly anyone talked. Human language would be too intrusive and too alien here. Bill, almost in a whisper, told me that if I thought this was an awesome sight, I should see it at night under a full moon. I suspect that by moonlight this tunnel would be spookier and more compelling than any horror-movie set yet devised.

The narrow and winding channel extended for perhaps a hundred yards into the island; however, I could be way off in my estimate since it was difficult to get any kind of normal perspective here. At the end of the tunnel, we clustered our kayaks together, looking about and talking quietly for almost twenty minutes. When it was time to depart, we left very reluctantly.

With the tide still dropping, we faced one of the more challenging aspects of kayaking in the Keys—not running aground. Many flats have almost no water at low tide, and if you're not careful, you could do some slogging through the soft bottom. This is where a knowledgeable guide like Bill comes in handy for staying afloat.

An unusual characteristic of the Keys is that on some days the difference between low and high tide is only a few inches. Local tide charts are helpful, but unusually high barometric pressure or strong winds sometimes produce unbelievably low tides. We experienced one of those times. The tide was still going out when it was scheduled to be returning. Fortunately, we made it back to the landing without much problem.

Since a number of cold fronts had recently passed through, the water was quite chilly, so we never took a snorkeling break. In summer, I always like to take along snorkeling gear to view all the activity on the flats. Snorkeling is something that many kayak outfitters include on guided trips, but you may have to supply your own equipment, so always check ahead.

If you rent a kayak and take off on your own through the mangroves, always be respectful of the birds, especially when they're nesting. It's always tempting to get a good view of a nest, but try to resist the impulse. Many bird species are sensitive to any sort of disturbance during the breeding season, especially just before or during egg incubation. If you accidentally scare a bird off its nest, try retreating a few hundred yards. The bird will usually return almost immediately.

It's important that the adults remain on the nest almost constantly not only to guard the eggs against predators, but also to protect the uncovered eggs or nestlings from the intense Keys sun. For this reason, always try and keep a couple of hundred feet away from any nests.

Bring binoculars, and you won't have the need to get so close.

Florida Bay Outfitters
104050 Overseas Highway
Key Largo, FL
305/451-3018
From half-day tours to 7-day wilderness trips into Everglades National Park. Full-day trips to Lignumvitae Key State Botanic Site and Indian Key Historic Site.

Papa Joe's Marina
Mile Marker 79.7
Islamorada, FL 33050
305/664-5505
Single and double kayaks rented by the hour.

Ocean Paddle South
2244 Overseas Highway
Marathon, FL
305/743-0131
Guided tours as well as single and double kayak rentals both here and at Bahia Honda State Park in the Lower Keys.

Reflections Kayak Nature Tours
P.O. Box 430861
Big Pine Key, FL
305/872-2896
Excursions into the adjacent Great White Heron National Wildlife Refuge as well as Everglades National Park.

Lost World Adventures
Box 431311
Big Pine Key, FL
305/872-1040
Four-hour guided tours into the Great White Heron National Wildlife Refuge, the Key Deer Refuge, and the Coupon Bight Aquatic Preserve.

Mosquito Coast Island Outfitters & Kayak Guides
1107 Duval St.
Key West, FL
305/294-7178
Four- to five-hour natural history tours from Geiger Key or Sugarloaf Key.

What

Reading the water depth is important in the Keys. Here's a good way to navigate through the shallows. Polarized sunglasses help the colors stand out:

Brown run aground,

White you might,

Green nice and clean,

Blue sail on through.

Pets are not permitted on either the Great White Heron Refuge or Everglades National Park islands. Camping, campfires, cutting of vegetation, littering, or collecting of any kind are prohibited on all refuge lands. The only Keys islands falling under the jurisdiction of Everglades National Park that are open to visitors are Little Rabbit, North Nest, and Carl Ross keys. A permit is needed to camp on any of these islands.

FORT MYERS AREA

Most people know Fort Myers as the winter home of Thomas A. Edison, one of the world's greatest inventors. However, what you might not know is that a string of barrier islands just offshore makes this one of the better places in Florida for kayaking. The barrier islands include such famous names as Sanibel, Captiva, Gasparilla, Cabbage Key, and Cayo Costa.

If you decide to take a few days paddling through these islands—they're all within sight of one another—you have a choice about where to spend the night. You can either camp near the water or sleep in some of Southwest Florida's finest waterfront resorts. It all depends on your inclinations—and your budget.

For instance, after some exploring around the Ding Darling National Wildlife Refuge, you could overnight at South Seas Plantation. It has about everything you can imagine, including outdoor hot tubs.

Another possible stay-over is Cabbage Key, which can be reached only by boat. It was the residence of novelist Mary Roberts Reinhart, and her home is now the Cabbage Key Hide-A-Way, a small inn. The Hide-A-Way's walls are papered with dollar bills—supposedly more than 10,000 of them at any one time—and everyone is invited to sign and leave one of their own. Among the more famous signatories have been former CBS news anchor Walter Cronkite and Florida balladeer Jimmy Buffet. Not surprisingly, neither of their signatures is on public display.

You might want to spend part of a day exploring nearby Gasparilla Island. Although the local pirate legends are increasingly being discounted as false, locals on Gasparilla Island enjoy exploiting the legend of their patron pirate, Jose Gaspar, who supposedly headquartered here in the early 1800s and left behind much buried treasure that never was found. Recent evidence indicates the entire Gaspar saga is the product of some public relation person's dream.

But Gasparilla Island doesn't need any hokum to make it notable. Rental bikes will take you through the old fishing village of Boca Grande, which claims to be home to the "World's Greatest Tarpon Fishing." Each spring and summer massive schools of the silver kings invade Boca Grande Pass, luring in anglers from everywhere. Trophy tarpon of a hundred pounds or more are on display at several places in Boca Grande.

Instead of Boca Grande, you may want to spend the evening camping at Cayo Costa, a barrier island regarded as one of Florida's most natural and beautiful. Many boats come here during the day, but most leave well before sundown.

Whether you're looking for a sea kayak rental, instruction, nature tours, or overnight paddling trips, one of the following outfitters serving the greater Ft. Myers area should be able to serve your needs.

Estero River Outfitters
209919 Tamiami Trail
Estero, FL 33928
813/992-4050

Daily river rental and sales. Also, off-river rentals for those who want to keep a boat several days. Sponsor a moonlight paddle the Saturday night closest to the full moon.

Gulf Coast Kayak Company
4882 Pine Island Rd., NW
Natlacha, FL 33909
813/283-1125

Two daily guided nature trips lasting four hours through the back bays and mangrove estuaries of Matlacha Pass Aquatic Preserve or Ft. Myers Beach with the Ostego Bay Marine Science Center (9 AM to 1 PM except Monday). Specialty tours include sunset bird-watching tours and moonlight trips two days before the night of the full moon. Camping trips are regularly scheduled to Cayo Costa State Park. Rentals available hourly or daily. Plans include establishing a paddling school.

Sanibel Sea Kayak
Wildlife Tours
Tween Waters Inn,
Captiva Island
Mailing address: Box 975
Sanibel, FL 33957
813/472-5161 (ask for marina)

Guided interpretive naturalist tours of Pine Island Sound, Gulf of Mexico, and J.N. Ding Darling Preserve. Species seen include osprey, bald eagles, dolphins, manatees, otters, herons, ibis, anhingas, wood storks, and many types of wading birds. Half-day trips leave at 8 AM and 1 PM. Maximum of six people per trip. Also sunset, full moon, and new moon excursions. Instruction available. Special programs for physically disabled persons.

Southern River Sports
4836 Bonita Beach Rd., SW
Bonita Springs, FL 33923
813/495-9496

Rentals and B.C.U. certified instruction for beginner through advanced paddlers. Three-hour tours available morning and afternoons. Also four-hour barrier islands interpretive lecture tours; full-day out-island paddles; and two-day, one-night mini-expeditions in the 10,000 Islands of the Everglades.

THE BIG BEND

Kayaking in Southwest Florida brings you into a lot of contact with civilization. If you prefer solitude and uncrowded camping experiences, try the Big Bend region south of Tallahassee. Unlike the Keys or Ft. Myers area, where it's easy to join organized weekend kayaking groups, Big Bend has not yet beeen populatd by outfitters.

This is a route of real adventure, with few places to provision along the way. If you come upon a store with food and drink, you'll be that much farther ahead. The island campsites are primitive with no facilities. Reservations are not taken for the designated land sites.

The following itinerary is a long one, far too much to tackle in less than a week. However, there are numerous places to take out, so the trip can be done in several segments instead of all at once. These places are highlighted in the text.

Mi. **Summary**

000.0 St. Marks Lighthouse: This is your launching point. Get permission to leave a car for an extended period, then drag your kayak into the Gulf and go left.

012.0 Aucilla River. After leaving the lighthouse, you'll pass beaches and hammocks, but soon the landscape changes to marsh grasses, mud flats, oyster bars, and plenty of empty water. The Aucilla River is easy to pick out both by its marker and, on weekends, the boat traffic. The river serves only as a location checkpoint. There are no accessible camping sites. Even though this is a freshwater river, it's saltwater for several miles upstream. Don't count on this as a place to filter/purify water.

It's possible to take out here at the boat ramp. For many people, twelve miles is probably long enough for one day.

021.0 Econfina River Campground: Good camping here, two miles upstream from the river entrance. After pushing this far, you're probably more than ready to call it quits for the first day. There's even an opportunity to stay in a motel at Econfina-on-the-River, which also has a small store.

028.5 Hickory Mound: Sometimes referred to as Smith-McCullen Creek. It can be shallow here at low tide. As part of a national wildlife refuge, Hickory Mound itself is off limits to camping. It is highly regarded among locals as a good crabbing spot in summer. In fall, it's one of the better areas for watching migrating birds and butterflies.

032.0 Little Rock Island: Located about a mile offshore, this tiny island covers only a few acres.

It's a delicate site, ecologically, and you're better off bypassing it completely in favor of Rock Island, just a few hundred yards away.

032.0 Rock Island: This is a nifty spot, several times the size of Little Rock Island. Approaching from the west, you'll find a pair of cuts in the lime rock where you can land and drag your kayak higher. From the artifacts that have been found here, it's obvious that Indians were well acquainted with the site. The camping area is just inland from your landing point. Do not fish here: the highly polluted Fenholloway River (Florida's only designated "industrial river") enters the Gulf not far from here.

036.0 Lower Fenholloway Boat Ramp. A mile upriver, you can take out if you've planned only a short trip. It's also possible to camp here, although locals sometimes use this as a place to party on weekends.

046.0 Spring Warrior Camp. Situated about 1.5 miles up Spring Warrior Creek. You can camp here and possibly get fresh water. It's possible to take out at the concrete boat ramp.

050.0 Yates Creek: Another boat ramp for taking out with a possibly shallow approach at low tide.

052.5 Adams Beach: Another possible take-out point situated at the end of a county road. For the next dozen miles or so, you'll be paddling by more built-up areas.

061.0 Keaton Beach. This Taylor County beach has a small park-like area right on the water with running water, rest rooms and picnic tables. This area was really clobbered by the so-called "Storm of the Century" in 1993. The landmark restaurant was destroyed. In its place is a small food stand. There's also a small bait store and a protected boat ramp if you decide to take out.

062.0 Hagen's Cove: It's unfortunate that camping isn't permitted here, since this place is a gem with an open grassy area, covered picnic tables, a chemical toilet, and a boat ramp for take out. Compared to nearby Keaton Beach, Hagen's Cove is never heavily used. There's also an observation platform for viewing wildlife, mostly wading birds and, in winter, migratory waterfowl. It's not a bad place to hunt for scallops, just offshore in the seagrass.

063.0 Piney Point: The vegetation here usually isn't cropped or maintained, so while camping might be possible, you'll have to work to fashion a comfortable site.

063.5 Piney Point II: Just go another

half-mile and you'll arrive at a nice camp site with a decent beach. There are also lots of cactus here, so don't wander around in the dark without a light.

065.0 Sponge Point. Besides being public land, this is a nice camping area that doesn't see a whole lot of traffic, even on weekends. A marshy area separates the point from the mainland, but it's quite walkable at low tide. This is the best camping location in the immediate locality.

068.0 Fishermen's Rest: Similar in terrain to Sponge Point. A good small camping area. Tall pines easily seen from the water are like a beacon.

071.0 Dallus Creek North: A small area with some real potential problems at low tide (assuming you don't like dragging your stuff through mud). The main thing going for this spot is that it receives little traffic.

073.0 Upper Dallus Creek: A boat ramp for possible take out. Also picnic tables, but camping is not permitted.

078.0 Steinhatchee: This area is turning into a popular, crowded weekend getaway. That means you'll find plenty of provisions, motels, and restaurants. You can stock up here and camp on a nearby spoil island.

078.5 North Steinhatchee Spoil Island: Spoil islands are created when rivers and creeks are dredged. This is an unusually large spoil island, covering between fifteen and twenty acres. It offers far more than barren, piled-up river bottom: trees and other vegetation have taken hold here to provide a very comfortable camping site.

079.0 South Steinhatchee Spoil Island: This is more like a traditional spoil island, just a big pile of ground. No reason to stop here.

079.5 Lazy Island: This is another possible site to set up before making a run to Steinhatchee for supplies. Nice shade and a good beach.

090.0 Bowlegs Point: The first good camping site after Lazy Island. Marshland separates the hammock of palms, pines, cedars, and hardwoods from the mainland.

092.0 Pepperfish Keys: Bowlegs Point is a preferable campsite. This is another small place overrun with cactus.

100.0 Horseshoe Beach: A fitting place to mark 100 miles into the trip, since this is a small fishing village where you can resupply and take out.

101.0 Horseshoe Beach Spoil Island: You probably want to camp here and commute to Horseshoe Beach for provisions. The best approach is from the north. The beach isn't particularly pretty but it's solid. Tides aren't as much of a problem here as at many other places.

103.0 Horseshoe Cove: Part of a county recreation area. Depending on the latest rules, camping may or may not be permitted. Between here and Shirred Island, many of the islands are privately owned and should not be approached.

109.0 Shirred Island: Another location connected to the mainland by marsh. You'll find an RV park and campground at the south end of the island, which you should have no trouble spotting from the water. Lots of oyster bars make low tide a problem.

111.0 Pine Islands: Big and Little Pine Island are the last camping areas before your arrival at the Suwannee River, only a handful of miles farther.

114.5 Cat Island: This was another Indian site. There's even a fairly large shell mound. Nothing may be disturbed.

116.0 Little Bradford Island: A popular boating spot with a narrow beach that could disappear with high tide. The adjacent channel is fairly deep and fast-flowing; low tide shouldn't present any problems.

118.0 Village of Suwannee: It's only two miles upriver from Little Bradford Island to the town of Suwannee. Salt Creek is the fastest way to get there. The county park has covered picnic tables and a boat ramp for take out. If you ask permission, you should have no trouble finding a place to camp.

Who

At the moment, you're pretty much on your own. You could contact one of the Panhandle canoe clubs (Appendix D) to try and form a group of kayakers. An excellent reference is *Sea Kayaking in Florida* by David Gluckman (Pineapple Press: Sarasota, FL), which goes into this route in considerable detail.

What

TIPS FOR LONG TRIPS
- Pack everything in waterproof containers.
- Pack the weight low and evenly in front and back for maximum stability.
- In summer, it's a good idea to start paddling early to avoid heat. Do not travel at night.
- Carry plenty of water and high-energy snacks. Your body needs a gallon of water a day.

EQUIPMENT:

- Spare paddle
- First aid kit
- Sunglasses
- Sunscreen 15 spf or above
- Lip balm (with sunblock protection)
- Small plastic bags for repacking food and carrying incidentals
- Toilet kit

For Camping:

- Tent, waterproof and bug proof
- Sleeping bag or sheet, depending on season
- Foam or air mattress
- Ground cloth
- Small stove and fuel
- Cooking gear, dishes, and utensils
- Insect repellent
- Flashlight

- Garbage bags for packing dirty/wet clothes and for hauling out garbage

Clothing:

- neoprene booties keep your feet warm and are good for walking in water
- 3 pair shorts
- 1 pair long pants
- 3 short-sleeve shirts
- 1 long-sleeve shirt
- 5–7 pair socks
- 5–7 pair underwear
- Warm sweater, jacket, and even long johns for sleeping if traveling during cooler seasons
- Windbreaker and/or rain suit
- Swimsuit
- Towel
- Comfortable shoes for camp

When

Anytime of year, though it can get quite hot in summer and very cold and choppy in winter. The Panhandle starts cooling down around October and doesn't start heating up again until April or early May.

8

Simple Saltwater Fishing:
in the Surf or from a Pier

One of my favorite ways to wake up is with my feet in the surf, casting a long rod and watching the first spokes of the sun appear on the horizon. No matter how long I've been up, it isn't until the first waves of surf roll over my feet that I'm fully awake: predawn water always feels refreshingly brisk, even in the middle of summer.

I like the simplicity of surf fishing. There's no boat battery to charge, no boat to trailer, no long lines at the ramp, and no boat to clean up afterward; it's uncomplicated, the way fishing was meant to be.

As much as I enjoy the sunrise and the predawn stillness, it's not long before I'm ready to feel a tug on the line and crank a fish through the surf. Since time and tide wait for no man, I've learned that the best way to catch fish is to set my alarm clock according to the moon.

This particular morning a friend and I are fishing the northern end of the Canaveral National Seashore near New Smyrna. It's Sunday and we've arrived early at parking area No. 3, which is often filled by 10 AM on weekends. And once the spaces here and at the other four designated areas are gone, anglers must go elsewhere since off-road parking isn't permitted anywhere on the national seashore.

Unlike the other end of the seashore at Playalinda, this is serious surf fishing territory. No surfboards or swimmers congest the waterline. Instead, a long line of sand spikes with rods jutting skyward marks the beach boundary, a willowy contingent that slowly retreats inland as the tide advances.

The bluefish are running, so action is sometimes frantic when a big fish bends a rod at a bizarre angle and its owner, who's been sitting patiently on a stool nearby, scrambles to retrieve it. Blues usually appear in October and last into December as they make their migration south for the winter.

Mullet strips are the preferred bait. Frozen mullet, as well as frozen sand fleas and shrimp, are available at a bait shop near the park entrance. The frozen mullet, however, become too mushy as they thaw. And mushy mullet usually don't stay on a hook well after it's cast several times.

Bill solves this problem for us by purchasing fresh mullet the day before at a seafood store. Fresh meat stays strong and firm no matter how many times it's hurled into the waves.

The fresh mullet also attracts the attention of a great blue heron standing quietly at attention about ten yards away. Gradually it stalks closer to see if we can be trusted. It should be the other way around. Once, when Bill turns his back, the bird strikes quickly, stealing most of one mullet from our cutting board. This is not a greedy bird; one partial mullet is enough since it never returns.

However, we anglers are experiencing a dilemma: what size hook to use. Most of the blues are running small, only two or three pounds. Bill's No. 1 hook is pulling in more fish, even an occasional whiting. My larger No. 3 is attracting plenty of hits but must be too big. Tired of waiting for the big one that never appears, I eventually switch to the smaller hook size and enjoy better success.

TIDES:

Every type of angling is based on the influence of the moon. Freshwater anglers fish according to the phase of the moon. Saltwater anglers do the same but express it differently: calling it "according to the tides." However you phrase it, tides are of particular importance in planning any Florida saltwater fishing trip.

I've always found the discussion of tides to be pretty cut and dry, a little on the academic side, so it's always struck me as kind of strange that tides were something anyone ever wanted to sing about. Yet it's been done, in the old ballad called "Ebb Tide." But if you're like me, you can't remember more than the first few words: "First, the tide rushes in . . . ."

However, for fishing purposes you need to forget those words because they don't describe an ebb tide; an ebb tide is exactly the opposite, when the water rushes out. It's not likely that it would happen, but anyone who schedules his fishing according to the song will get terribly fouled up. The changing of the tides is never ending, with the water level sometimes varying almost minute by minute. This is due to the tidal flow caused by the gravitational pull of the sun and moon. Being closer, the moon exerts more influence. The result is that twice every 24 hours the water leaves the bays and estuaries, moving away from the coast. And then, almost as soon as it's gone, it starts to return.

More than anything else, tides are the best predictors of inshore saltwater fishing, of where the fish will be and how they will move. Since the moon rises fifty minutes later every day, the tide can be counted on to follow suit. And an angler who fishes the same spot day after day must plan accordingly if he doesn't want to be left high and dry in lots of ways.

What the tide does is rearrange the distribution and availability of game fish food. For instance, at slack tide (when the water has stopped flowing either in or out), baitfish and crabs move close to the jetties, mangroves, and beaches where they can feed without being threatened by predatory species.

However, once the tide starts flowing again—in or out makes no difference—these baits get pulled along with the strong flow and no longer enjoy any protection. This is why fishing around any inlet or river is usually best the first two hours following a tide change. The game fish will be concentrated there, waiting to pick off every free meal that floats by.

On the other hand, during the periods of slack water—at the peak of either the high or low tides when the water stops flowing—the fishing is equally as dead because the free meal delivery service is temporarily suspended. For this reason, many anglers plan to arrive at their favorite spot right at the slack period so they can set up and take advantage of the lively feeding activity to follow.

But that's not all there is to tidal flow. Not all tides bring in or take out the same amount of water. Spring tides (a confusing name since they have no relationship to the time of year) are abnormally high tides that occur twice a month. They are caused by the combined pull of the sun and moon when the two bodies come in line with the earth. This happens at the full and new moons.

In many regions, spring tides trigger large-scale migrations of fish, luring them into bays and rivers in numbers much larger than normal. The wise angler knows this and is sitting (or floating) there, ready.

At the opposite end of the tidal scale are the neap tides, lower than normal tides. They also occur twice a month, at the first and third quarter moon phases. Neap tides generally ruin bank and shore fishing because they can leave lots of exposed bottom (which may be too soft to walk on) between the angler and the fish.

At the same time, neap tides can generate the best fishing of the month in channels and inlets. With the water level sharply reduced, bait fish are forced to crowd together. Fish like mackerel, bluefish, and stripers will sometimes go wild at such times.

In a nutshell, this is what tides mean to the angler. When there is a quarter moon, the tides are at their lowest. At the full and new moons, the tides have their greatest flow. Tides repeat themselves roughly every two weeks. Conditions are directly opposite from one week to the next: if it's high tide at noon the first Sunday of the month, it will be low tide the second Sunday, back to full on the third Sunday, and low again on the fourth.

Consequently, depending on the locality, you can experience a week of good fishing (high water) followed by one that's mediocre. But that doesn't necessarily have to follow if you fish the terrain accordingly. The tide level that makes one place poor may make another a hot spot.

Of course it's only a general rule and not mandatory that there be two daily highs and lows in every locality. In certain parts of the Gulf of Mexico, there is only one high and one low, or the water shift is so small there appears to be none at all.

And the amount of water moved out also varies from place to place. The level may fall just two or three feet in one spot and perhaps six to seven feet just a few miles away. This is mostly the result of vastly different bottom contours.

In fishing the tides, you should keep in mind that good fishing is often determined more by wind than tides.

Breaking waves carry a tremendous energy. Every shore fisherman who's tried to stand in heavy surf can testify to that. Sometimes the wave power is so strong you have to retreat to shore.

That power is also hurling pushing, bait fish, mollusks, and shells toward land. And large game fish that normally stay far offshore will often travel in close to take advantage of all the dislodged food.

Wave action is particularly important for surf fishermen; the rougher it is, the better the fishing is usually. This is one of the reasons why the first storms of the fall not only mark the change of seasons but also herald the fish migrations along the Atlantic Coast.

So while time and tides may wait for no man, a smart angler will take advantage of both.

TIDE GLOSSARY

These days it seems like everything has its own specialized vocabulary. The language of tides is an old one, developed over the decades, and there's a term to aptly describe almost every condition.

Tide: The rise and fall of the earth's waters, caused mainly by the position of the moon relative to the earth.

New Moon: No moon to be seen, or only a small sickle of light is visible. A period of spring tides.

First Quarter Moon: When the moon is at right angles to the sun and earth. Marked by little rise and fall of water. Only a quarter of the moon is visible. Neap tides.

Full Moon: When the sunlight is fully reflected off the moon's surface. Spring tides.

Third Quarter Moon: The moon is again at right angles. Neap tide.

High Tide: When water level reaches its highest point depending on the moon phase.

Low Tide: When water falls to its lowest level.

Flood Tide: When the tide comes in, also called a rising tide.

Slack Tide: When the water has stopped flowing; occurs at the end of both high and low tides.

Half Tide: Approximately three hours after the high or low tide, the midpoint in the tidal flow.

Ebb Tide: When the tide is falling.

Spring Tide: A rise and fall of the tides occurring roughly every two weeks in most areas.

Neap Tide: A small rise and fall of the tides occurring every two weeks.

Diurnal Tide: Only one low and one high tide occur daily.

Semi-Diurnal Tide: Two high and two low tides occur each day.

Florida surf fishing offers an ever-changing smorgasbord, the size and type of fishing varying according to the time of the year: bluefish, redfish (red drum), whiting, flounder, sharks, pompano—the list is almost endless.

GEAR

The choice of terminal gear can strongly influence an angler's success. One technique is to have a single hook and leader attached directly to the line with a sliding sinker above the connecting swivel so that whenever a fish picks up a bait it doesn't feel any resistance.

Rather than use a homemade rig, you can buy what's called a Nylon Sinker Slide, which places the sinker directly on the leader instead of above it. The nylon capsule that encircles the leader has a metal sinker holder which slides to just above the hook. That arrangement would seem to place the clump of bait and the sinker too closely for an easy pickup, from the success of the slider rigs today, that problem never seems to occur.

Whatever the sliding system, a stout leader is essential for bluefish and some other species. Big blues will easily slash through 30-lb test mono, so 50-lb and higher is advisable on a long shank hook. Short shanks, which better hide the bait, offer too much leader-severing opportunity. Flexible wire leader, certainly the most secure approach, also works successfully. Whatever the method, your leader should run about two feet, easily measured by holding line/wire along the length of your arm.

Try to avoid the ready-made hook and sinker rig that consists of a 12- to 16-inch piece of heavy leader with two small metal "arms" protruding from the side. A prerigged leader and hook are snapped to each arm and a sinker is added at the end. These rigs conjure up enticing images of a double hookup, a real possibility in a blues feeding frenzy, but the rest of the time all that hardware seems to turn off fish. They may consider all the paraphernalia as appealing as kissing someone with braces. I've had good luck bottom fishing this way, but never surf fishing.

You may find it helpful to spray the swivels and any other shiny terminal hardware with black paint. In their feeding frenzy some fish may be drawn to the flashing metal instead of the bait dangling a few inches away. Having a fish hanging on the line is one thing, but having it on the hook is even better.

Sinker selection is limited to pyramid shapes, which don't roll along the bottom as round sinkers will. In flat water, a one-ounce is sufficient, but when the surf runs high, I use either a four- or five-ouncer to keep the bait from migrating shoreward.

Several days spent casting into the surf with a long, heavy rod can build up muscles a stevedore would be proud of. Surf rods vary anywhere from seven to ten-and-a-half feet long, and some people even use sticks that extend out thirteen to fifteen feet. The bigger rods are used for throwing out heavy bait fish or large lures. In Florida, a ten-and-a-half-foot rod will handle most heavy duty work, unless you're after sharks.

When it comes to the big rods, it takes two hands to handle these whoppers. To cast, your right hand holds the butt just under the reel and the left hand grabs the butt at the base. With either a spinning rod or revolving reel, the cast begins by

A fish can be returned unharmed if it has only been lip-hooked

extending the rod behind you but in line with the target area. Then you swing the rod up and forward.

As the rod nears vertical, release the line but follow through on the swing, as in golf. With a revolving spool reel, be sure to keep a slight thumb pressure on the spool after the line is released. Then clamp down as soon as the line hits the water to prevent that old nemesis, backlash. Regardless of reel type, use 20 to 30-lb test line.

Small spinning outfits properly rigged also provide considerable sport. The only problem is keeping sharp-toothed fish from fraying or breaking the line: that's where the 30-lb test monofilament leader is essential.

Probably the biggest mistake a surf fisherman can make is to randomly select a spot on the beach and start fishing. If you do this, you're simply counting on the law of averages to eventually work in your favor, that a fish some day, at some time, will wander by and take a bite. You might also win $50,000,000 in the Florida lottery.

There are better ways of approaching the surf. When visiting unfamiliar coastline, scan the water with binoculars to see if you can spot birds feeding off the water or any sign of bait-fish activity on the surface.

If you see either, that's the place to head. Of course, such nice "Fish Here!" markers aren't always evident, which means a little preplanning is in order.

For surf fishing, you need to know the lay of the land as well as a bass fisherman knows the bottom structure of his lake. This means a visit to the beach at low tide to study the terrain, because it's what's out front that counts.

And what you want out front are channels and sloughs that run parallel just offshore. At low tide, you should be able to spot the surf breaking over these sandbars, or the sandbar may be entirely exposed.

After breaking over the sandbars, the water rolls into deeper, darker colored water between the bar and the beach. That dark water is the place to cast since game fish will be in these troughs feeding on the bait fish washed over or trapped by the sandbar.

Also worth fishing are the channels or sloughs that cut through the bars and lead out to the ocean. You can identify these by the receding waves curving and moving seaward through them. Game fish are likely to congregate here, too, at high water.

One of the attractive features of fishing the New Smyrna area is the relatively steep incline of the beach, which automatically creates a trough at high water. And there's a sandbar (covered but obvious at low water) paralleling the shore.

I have yet to check out the other parking lots, but fishing quality can vary considerably along the beach. At No. 3, as we pull in sporadic bluefish, anglers to the south of us find only catfish. It still amazes me how much the fishing can vary along a relatively short stretch of beach. But what in the world can be calling in all the saltwater catfish? I'd like to switch it off.

LANDING, BY HOOK OR CROOK

A successful landing is important not only to airline passengers. It's also a vital part of the fishing process that must be mastered for any angler wishing to be totally successful. An angler who doesn't know what to do once a fish is ready to be retrieved is likely to lose it.

Landing problems are more common than they might seem. Ever been on a fishing pier, bridge or high bank and seen someone who hadn't mastered landing latch onto a big fish? That can be high comedy. Landing a fish from a bridge or pier twenty feet above the water takes a certain amount of forethought and advance preparation.

Following are the most common situations an angler is likely to encounter, and what he can do to make sure he gets his catch home. On the other hand, if you are fishing strictly catch and release and want to set free the fish unharmed, cut the line where it's tied to the hook. Man-handling a fish while trying to yank the hook out of its mouth is likely to cause considerable harm to the fish. As long as you're not using stainless steel, the hook will soon rust away.

Piers and Bridges. Piers and bridges present several landing problems, none very difficult if you are prepared ahead of time. First and most obvious is to use heavy rods and lines so a fish can be cranked up through the air. You'll need a good stiff boat rod and about a 50-lb test line to be on the safe side.

But what to do when the fish is simply too big to horse up? One way to land a fish is to walk it to shore and drag it up on the beach. Unfortunately, this works well only as long as the pier or bridge is empty of other people; on a crowded walkway, it's a poor way to win friends.

In crowded situations, long-handled gaffs and nets prove indispensable. However, they won't work from towering heights of fifteen to twenty feet or more, in which case homemade ingenuity is called for.

This involves taking a large weighted treble hook (10/0 size or larger) and attaching it to a nylon rope about the diameter of a water ski towline. Then, once a fish is worn out and on top of the water, you lower the treble hook, snag it into the fish's jaw, and pull it up. Since there's always the chance the hook will pull loose, keep enough slack in the fishing line so that it won't snap if it suddenly has to carry all the weight. Obviously, this is a technique to use only if you plan to consume your catch, not release it.

Gaffing. A gaff is often necessary for any fish too large to net or whose sharp dentures and gill plates make direct handling inadvisable. Gaffs come in a variety of sizes, from small hand gaffs all the way up to six- and eight-footers for boats with high transoms.

The hand gaff, small enough to be stored in most tackle boxes, works well in many situations. The handle is just big enough to grip and is attached to a hook with a two-inch bite (the distance from the point of the hook to the shaft). In landing a fish, the gaff point is simply stuck through the fish's lip, and then the fish is hauled in.

Big gaffs, however, require a certain expertise. It even helps to know karate because of the chopping action required to set a large gaff. When a fish is ready, the gaff is chopped down in the water in front of the fish as hard as possible and then pulled upward, lifting the fish. That's all there is to it, but it's easier said than done. It can take time to learn to set a gaff smoothly. Again, slack line should be made ready in case of a miss so the fish won't break off.

Chopping a fish in the side, of course, presumes an angler has no intention of releasing it. On the other hand, a small hand gaff will allow an angler to return a fish unharmed if it's only been lip-hooked.

Beaching. Beaching is the favorite method of surf fishermen. As soon as a fish is on, an angler should start slowly backing up toward shore and keep going until he's several feet up the bank. Once the fish has tired, slide it slowly up onto the sand. With an exceptionally big fish, keep cranking slowly until the fish's head is clear of the water, then quickly grab the leader and haul it onto the dry sand.

Anyone who stays in the surf while trying to land a fish is likely to run into trouble. Working against both wave and fish movements with a short line can be tricky. It's not only a good way to break the line, there's a good chance of slipping and falling.

Caring for Your Catch. The proper handling of fish is probably as badly misunderstood as the latest tax forms. Preparing fish for the table needs to begin as soon as you've taken it out of the water.

Ironically, many anglers who take care to chill their drinks leave their fish on the beach or throw them into a pail of water. Either method is guaranteed to spoil the fish and possibly the angler's digestion.

There's no telling what and when a fish last ate. Therefore, a good rule of thumb is to gut the fish sometime within an hour of being taken out of the water, even if it's going to be put on ice. Otherwise the meat could become tainted because of partially digested cut bait or minnows, which can contaminate the meat around the rib cage.

Probably the best way to keep saltwater fish fresh is to put them right back where they came from—in salt water. But it should be salt water that's been poured in an ice chest with a big block of ice or several containers of blue ice.

The salt helps the water to cool more quickly and keeps it cold longer. Because there's a lot more conductivity between ice and water than ice and air, fish thrown in a chest containing only ice will never stay as cold as fish chilled in salt water.

But when using the chilled salt water method, don't gut the fish first. Even though it may spend its entire life in the stuff, a fish's flesh will soon become mushy and unappetizing if it's left in prolonged contact with water. The outcome can be almost as bad as if the fish had been left to ripen on the beach or pier.

Who

You'll find guides for every other possible type of fishing imaginable, but not surf/pier fishing. You are completely on your own in deciding where to fish and how to fish. Maybe that's why surf/pier fishing is so popular. However, you can obtain helpful hints on which locations, baits, and terminal tackle are currently proving successful from the bait and tackle shops lining the Florida coasts. The bait will cost you, but the advice—often invaluable—is always free. And don't be surprised at how friendly and helpful other surf/pier anglers tend to be. There are few secret techniques or closely guarded spots in this type of angling.

What

For latest information on fishing conditions, call 800/ASK-FISH, which covers salt- and freshwater fishing forecasts as well as the current regulations.

Where

SURF FISHING

With over 6,000 miles of coastline, the opportunities for fishing from shore are tremendous. Following are some of the better locations:

Gulf Coast:
- Gulf Islands National Seashore near Pensacola
- Beaches surrounding Panama City, Destin, St. Joe Peninsula
- St. George's Island
- St. Petersburg, Bradenton, Sarasota beaches
- Sanibel-Captiva
- Barrier Islands of Pine Island Sound
- Naples
- Marco Island

Atlantic Coast:
- Amelia Island
- Any of the Talbot Islands GEOpark
- Anastasia Island near St. Augustine
- Flagler Beach
- Canaveral National Seashore (Apollo & Playalinda Beaches)

Inlets: (from Jacksonville, south)
- St. Mary's, St. Johns, St. Augustine, Matanzas
- Ponce de Leon, Sebastian, Ft. Pierce, St. Lucie
- Jupiter Lake, Worth, Boca Raton, Hillsboro
- Port, Everglades, Bakers, Haulover,

Government Cut
- Lower Biscayne, Bay Marathon, Big Pine Key
- Whitewater Bay (Everglades National Park)
- Chokoloskee (Naples), Cape Coral , Tampa Bay
- Piers and Bridges

PIER FISHING

Some of the more productive piers and bridges are located in:

- The Keys—sections of old U.S. 1 bridges have been turned into fishing piers throughout the Keys. They are among the longest fishing piers in the world.
- Naples
- Ft. Myers
- Venice
- Skyway State Fishing Pier, Palmetto
- Tampa, St. Petersburg
- Pensacola
- Jacksonville
- St. Augustine
- Daytona Beach
- Cocoa Beach
- Sebastian Inlet
- St. Lucie Inlet
- Miami area causeways

9

The Mermaids
of Crystal River

Snorkeling in the cool spring waters of Florida's Crystal River, I can see a pair of mermaids straight ahead, resting on the bottom. One of them, needing a breath of air, glides silently upwards. Her huge nostrils break the surface and, sounding just like a dolphin, she inhales deeply. Then she sinks a few feet below the waterline, gives a slow flip of her broad tail, and returns to rest on the bottom.

Real mermaids? In this day and age? No, but these odd-looking creatures, actually West Indian manatees, apparently were the basis for the mermaid legend.

Although manatees hardly resemble the voluptuous sirens shown on ancient maps, Columbus immediately labeled them mermaids when he encountered manatees in the Caribbean . . . although he noted they were not as handsome as artists traditionally depicted them.

What an understatement. The adult female just a few yards in front of me is of awesome dimensions—well over 2,000 pounds and almost twelve feet in length. Her face, adorned with spiked-hair jowels, is more akin to that of a walrus, than some sexy seductress. The rest of her body isn't much more alluring, either. She looks like the result of some bizarre genetic experiment. Her walruslike head is tacked onto a fat, sausagelike torso, and a broad beaver's tail is attached on the other end. A pair of front flippers serves as her hands. Truly a strange conglomeration of parts. Yet this is a very streamline shape: a single flip of a manatee's powerful tail usually leaves the fastest human swimmer far behind.

From a distance, I can understand how a manatee could be mistaken for a creature half-human, half-fish. Manatees are vegetarians, and when one chomps down its dinner, it sometimes bobs with its head and hands above the waterline, just as a person would. If startled or frightened, a manatee will dive underwater so that the tail is often the last part of the creature you see. Mermaid mystery solved.

How the manatee got its name is uncertain. The term evidently has its roots in the language of the Carib Indians. Their word *manati* translated as "woman's breast." An unlikely term to apply to a marine animal, but the manatee is a mammal and its mammae do resemble those of humans. Manatee flippers also have what look like vestigial fingernails, a link to their closest living relative, the elephant.

Despite their huge size, manatees are quite harmless and docile. I find them perfect snorkeling subjects since they spend most of their time dozing on the ocean bottom. Manatees don't lie flat but balance their weight on their head and tail only, bending in the middle like a bow—an awkward pose that would seem to require considerable effort, but apparently not.

Despite the manatee's peculiar appearance, there is something majestic, almost regal, in the way these animals act. Normally, they move slowly, never appearing to be in a hurry. True, they may have a face that only a mother could love, but sometimes it's easy to imagine their faces appearing very sad, tired . . . almost as if they can foresee the fate that may await their species.

It is always an eerie feeling to realize I may be watching a living fossil, a species in danger of joining the dinosaur and the mastodon as part of earth's past. Manatees once ranged from the Carolinas to Texas, but Florida now has the only resident population remaining in the United States. Scientists are not sure how many of the creatures still survive; a count in the mid-1990s reported just over 2,600 animals. A truly accurate census is difficult because manatees are normally shy, reclusive animals.

The only time they gather in numbers is during winter when they are forced to congregate in warm water areas. Despite their blubbery appearance, these warm-blooded mammals have only a partial layer of fat to insulate them. In winter, they are forced to seek out natural springs or warm water discharge areas since, prolonged exposure to water temperatures below 60 degrees may cause pneumonia and death. Yet, no matter how cold the air, the freshwater springs that feed Crystal River maintain a constant 72 degrees.

Manatees are endangered because of the loss of their traditional breeding and grazing grounds. Decades ago, many of Florida's bays and estuaries were rich in aquatic growth, but they were dredged and filled to build new homes and shopping centers. In addition, increased boat traffic on Florida waterways generated more manatee deaths. Boats are responsible for about a quarter of the annual fatalities. The problem is that manatees apparently are unable to distinguish sound direction under water, so they sometimes surface directly in front of a watercraft. Scars are so prevalent that scientists identify individual manatees by their scar pattern: I have yet to see a manatee that doesn't bear the white marks caused by a boat prop.

To help the manatee survive, Florida has designated certain waterways as manatee refuges, closing them to boat traffic or severely limiting speeds during winter when the manatees are most concentrated. As one of the state's most important refuges, Crystal River has banned snorkelers from certain parts so that those animals who are afraid of people can enjoy a serene sanctuary.

Yet snorkelers and manatees are obviously coexisting quite well. In the 1960s, the data showed that few, if any, manatees wintered in Crystal River. Today, the average number of animals reported each season is slightly over 300, including adults and calves. If manatees in general found snorkelers a nuisance, the number of animals would never have increased so greatly. They simply would have stayed away.

After snorkeling with manatees for two decades, I've discovered that if you want to see a manatee up close, the key element is to let the animal make the first move and voluntarily approach you—not for you to see how close you can get to the animal before it moves away.

This technique not only is more respectful of the animal, but also if it appears a snorkeler is harassing a manatee, the snorkeler may be slapped with a fine by authorities who patrol Crystal River, which is a designated national wildlife refuge. Some preservationists would like to keep snorkelers completely away from the Crystal River manatees, so watching the creatures is really a privilege none of us can afford to abuse.

The two manatees I am watching have been oblivious to my presence. They have been doing what manatees do best, which is periodically rise to the surface to breathe . . . then rest . . . breathe . . . then rest. Manatee watching is never a very strenuous activity.

The manatees seem to be surfacing and sinking automatically while still asleep, and they may well be since I am here soon after daybreak to view them when few other snorkelers are present. I have an underwater camera and strobe with me, so I am often rising and descending with them.

The water bordering the main spring, known as King's Spring, is as shallow as three to four feet, but my manatees are in water closer to eight to ten feet deep. Still, dropping to the bottom with them is certainly no difficulty.

Eventually, one of the manatees awakes and recognizes that a guest is present. Its response is more than I can hope for. It does indeed seem that some manatees have almost a playful sense of humor, and this is one of them. The manatee swims to me from my left, then turns on its side so its stomach is exposed when it passes directly in front of me.

This one is a real clown and as playful as a puppy. Now it comes back and stops directly in front of me. It stands upside down on its head, then keeps moving closer and closer. It obviously wants me to scratch it or pet it. This is one of the animals that really likes interacting with people.

Snorkeler with camera swims with manatee. Note the second manatee in the distance.

Other manatees seem to be waking up. Not far away, a mother and calf swim leisurely. The calf matches its mother's speed and stays just above her. The mother stops, and the calf begins to suckle the teat located just behind her right front flipper. Manatee-rearing is a long, involved process that lasts about two years. That means a female has a calf only about every three or four years, a factor that prevents the population from ever increasing rapidly. Once this calf finishes breakfast, it and the mother move away.

The clown manatee has now taken up residence on the surface right beside me. It floats placidly on the surface, occasionally bumping and rubbing against me. Its body may look like a spongy bowl of jelly, but the animal feels as solid as an automobile. Well, at twelve feet long and almost 2,000 pounds, it is almost as big as some compact cars. I'm glad it is a strict vegetarian—the only marine mammal that is.

I am manatee-watching on a very cold, weekday morning, the best time to view the creatures. Manatees don't mind a few snorkelers, but when a horde of flippered folk show up, the animals move away from the most accessible viewing areas. Weekends often see crowds of divers.

Although the 72-degree water of Crystal River feels bathtub warm compared to the air temperature—a very chilly 45 degrees—I am wearing a full wet suit, including booties and a hood. I've always considered a wet suit vital for prolonged manatee watching, because 72 degrees is cool enough to sap body heat and energy from anyone . . . except maybe a member of the Polar Bear Club, those crazies who break through ice in the Great Lakes to go swimming in mid-winter. I find that snorkeling becomes very unpleasant, very quickly without a protective outer covering of neoprene. Probably you will, too.

Who

For complete information on facilities at Crystal River, write or call:
Crystal River Chamber of Commerce,
1801 Northwest Hwy. 19, Suite 541
Crystal River, FL 34429
904/795-3149

The following dive shops can supply you with up-to-date information about where the manatees are. Besides conducting tours, Crystal Lodge and Port Paradise also have small boats for rent if you wish to dive on your own. They can also supply you with a map of the waterway, which is sheltered and flat calm most of the time.

American Pro Dive
715 SE Hwy. 19
Crystal River, FL 34429
800/291-DIVE, 904/563-0041
Fax: 904/795-4119

Birds Underwater
8585 N. Pine Needle Trail
Crystal River, FL 34428
904/563-2763

Crystal Lodge Dive Center
525 NW Seventh Ave.
Crystal River, FL 34428
904/795-6798

Plantation Inn Marina
9301 W. Fort Island Trail
Crystal River, FL 34429
Mailing Address: PO Box 1093
Crystal River, FL 34429
904/795-5797
Fax: 904/795-1368

**Port Paradise Scuba Center
& Marina**
1610 SE Paradise Circle
Crystal River, FL 34423
904/795-7234

What

The Crystal River wintertime manatee population these days is estimated at around 300, which would make this the single greatest concentration in Florida. Ironically, in the 1960s when few divers were present, no large herd of manatees was recorded.

Manatees are big business for the local dive shops who know precisely where the manatees are most likely to be found at any given moment. Dive shops also rent small john boats with engines of 10 hp and under, well suited for Crystal River. When waves in the nearby Gulf of Mexico look like Alpine peaks, Crystal River has only small ripples on its surface.

Crystal River also is a giant holding pen for both fresh- and saltwater fish. In winter, huge schools of saltwater species enter from the Gulf: rays, sharks, grouper, jacks, and snook have all been sighted. Spearing is strictly prohibited.

For an in-depth view of the manatee's life history, look for *Manatees, Our Vanishing Mermaids* (by O'Keefe, Larsen's Outdoor Publishing, Lakeland) which is available at most of the area dive shops.

When

From December to mid-February, Florida's Crystal River is perhaps the only place in the world where snorkelers may swim with West Indian manatee in relatively clear water. As many as 300 animals, including adults and newborn calves, spend the winter there.

Where

Crystal River and the town of the same name are located about 80 miles north of Tampa at the junction of US 44 and US 19.

10

Camp Town Races:
Camping at the Daytona 500

From around the world race fans come by the thousands to watch the fast cars and their famous drivers lap the track at speeds approaching 200 miles an hour in the annual Daytona 500. Although the Super Bowl and the World Series receive far more media attention than this or any other auto race, the annual receipts collected at the nation's speedways are the richest of any spectator sport in the world, something few people outside of racing realize.

The Daytona 500 is not only the richest stock car racing event in the country, but also is probably the most unforgettable. It has the costume variety of Mardi Gras, the wetness of a New Year's Eve, and the action of a Kentucky Derby rolled into one.

For many of us attending, the ideal vantage point is not from the bleachers. Instead, we prefer to witness the noisy, flashing spectacle from atop our recreational vehicles parked right in the middle of the speedway.

The big race doesn't start until just after noon on a Sunday, but many of us have been crowded into the infield since before dawn on Saturday morning—Well before dawn. My RV didn't get set up in the infield until after 3 AM, and that was after waiting in line for a dozen hours.

Waiting half a day for a parking space may seem crazy, but for dedicated race fans, this is like getting a weekend pass to stand at the gates of heaven and watch the anointed pass through. Saturday is also an exciting racing day, offering two electrifying warm-ups to Sunday's big event. Saturday features both the annual Goody's 300 NASCAR series for the grand national divisions, and the final NASCAR Winston Cup series practice for the Daytona 500.

Like myself, many campers have rented their RV only for the weekend. Regulars who attend every 500 will reserve another RV for next year when they return their unit on Monday.

Since about 160,000 people attend each Daytona 500, the hotels and motels for fifty miles north and south of Daytona on I-95 are sold out. As regular motorists are lined up for miles competing for parking spaces and restaurant seats, we RVers are sitting high and pretty, already enjoying some of the best seats in the house.

Well before the race starts at noon, lounge chairs, blankets, and well-stocked coolers decorate most RV rooftops. Determined not to miss any facet of the race, we also have a TV up top and a few people in our group are wearing headphones that allow them to overhear the conversations between the drivers and their pit crews. You can't do that at the Super Bowl.

Although other racetracks around the country may attract the same top-notch drivers, Daytona is considered special. This is where racing started, and why one of the most popular attractions for these fans is the Birthplace of Speed Museum (160 E. Granada Blvd., between Halifax Drive and Seton Trail; 904/676-3346).

America's first automobile race was held on Daytona Beach in 1902, where the top speed for even the fastest car was under 30 mph. Daytona racing began when Ransom Olds, founder of Oldsmobile, challenged his friend Henry Flagler, the railroad tycoon, to race on Daytona's beach.

This site was chosen because the sands of Daytona Beach are unusually hard-packed—so hard-packed it's possible for anyone to drive on the beach using normal tires and not get stuck. As we await the start of the race, the string of cars rolling along on Daytona Beach at this very moment is probably stretching almost to the horizon, as it does on most weekends. The speed limit there is 10 mph and it's strictly enforced.

To take part in that very first race, Olds transported his Stanley Steamer auto by ship since there were no roads. Gasoline was still a relatively new invention and not something that many ship captains understood very well. According to legend, the captain of Olds' ship knew that gasoline was explosive, so he ordered Olds to drain all the gasoline from his car, even though there would be no additional supply once the ship docked at Daytona. Olds agreed, but drained his radiator instead. The captain, far more familiar with the workings of his ship than an automobile, never knew the difference.

Sanctioned racing began at Daytona in 1903, just a year later. It may not have been the most convenient place to come, but no roads anywhere in the United States were as straight and smooth or as wide (as much as 500 feet) as Daytona's remarkable beach.

Even though the races took place on the beach, they were anything but sandbox league. In 1935, a rocket-powered car established a 276-mph land speed record. Amazingly, sanctioned racing on the beach lasted for over a half century, until 1959, when the 3.5-mile track opened at the Daytona International Speedway in whose infield we now sit.

Although little is heard about the raceway itself in between the highly publicized races, tire companies, auto manufacturers, and racing teams frequently rent the track. Even competing go-carts have lapped it.

Anyone who's never attended an auto race like the Daytona 500 may find it hard to understand the fanaticism of race fans. Why do so many make this an annual pilgrimage, some coming from as far away as Germany?

It's not an easy thing to explain. This is certainly a festive blast, the holiday mood kept alive by the nonstop consumption of beer at bring-your-own prices. On the morning of the race, breakfast beers may rival bacon and eggs for the day's first nourishment.

Race fans are as avid as those who follow football or basketball like a religion. Many individuals wear brightly colored T-shirts reflecting the names and gaudy colors of their favorite cars and drivers. In fact, many in this crowd know far more intimate detail about the lives of their favorite race car drivers than they do about their back-home neighbors.

The Daytona 500 attracts nothing but the best competitors. Every person has to qualify to enter, regardless of their past track record. At Daytona, every 500 is a fresh start.

So when the final field of forty drivers takes to the track, it's far more than just two teams competing in the Super Bowl or for the NBA championship. These are the forty fastest drivers in all of racing vying in a free-for-all with the best man taking the winner's purse. Where many NFL teams may have individual standouts, at the Daytona 500, every driver is a superstar. It's better than putting the Dolphins, Cowboys, Forty-Niners, or any other champion NFL team on the same playing field at the same time to battle it out.

Few other spectator sports offer as many champions on the same playing field at one time. You never hear fans complaining about a boring Daytona 500, whereas an exciting Super Bowl has been rare over the last decade. And if these drivers have a truly bad day, they face far more severe consequences than bruised ribs or a sprained finger. In a serious crash, a driver may become dead meat, and everyone here knows it.

But there's more to it than the partying or the anticipation of disaster—something no fan, regardless of how partisan, would wish on any driver. No, you must be close to the sidelines to understand fully what really attracts all of us here. Tyrants, dictators—and race fans—all savor it: the exhibition of sheer, raw power.

At the start of the race, the sleek vehicles look much like any other group of brightly colored cars on a crowded highway. But as they speed up, the air suddenly snaps with a tremendous force, howling and almost alive. It's as electrifying as if a jet engine had fired up only yards away.

When the cars scream by, just a scant few feet away, only a concrete lip and a wire fence separate spectators from the vehicles. Whenever I stand this close to the action, my legs tremble and my belly flutters. The energy that flows into me from the screaming cars is exhilarating.

Somehow, in a primitive way I cannot begin to comprehend, part of the awesome power in those car engines transfuses into my own nervous system. The adrenalin jolt is always a shock. My instinct is to run.

It's like coming out of a sound sleep to find a prowler pointing a flashlight in your eyes and a gun at your head.

Or discovering on a rain-slick road—as you carom out of control toward a crowded intersection with the red light against you—that your brakes have just failed.

It's fear, excitement, and unbelievable tension, something that embraces each spectator every time the cars thunder by.

The ability to experience this kind of power is rare. The only other times I've felt the air as charged and electric was when the ground trembled under my feet at Cape Canaveral, when we used to fire men at the moon. Those old Apollo rockets transformed every launch into a Fourth of July as they detonated the atmosphere with a fury that reverberated like an endless stream of huge firecrackers. These days, the Daytona Speedway is the next best thing to a lunar launch.

At the Daytona 500, the cars roar on for almost five hours. They continually bank and circle like a squadron of jet fighters whose line becomes progressively ragged until only the best are left. As long as there are men gutsy enough to pilot these awesome, addictive machines, the crowds will always come.

For as long as the race lasts, we are connected to it, linked to all that enormous energy that no other spectator sport can provide. To a devout fan, the end of a race is a let down, a period of withdrawal—and a prelude to the next racing high.

At the 500, our infield camping area looks like a shopping mall parking lot during a holiday sale. The RVs are packed so close together it's almost possible to walk from one rooftop to the next. With so many strangers clustered in such close quarters, it's understandable if the occasional temper flares or if rival factions wage name-calling contests.

If this crowd was here to see the Florida Gators vs the FSU Seminoles in a college football game, rescue squad workers would have a tremendous backlog of bloody noses and black eyes to repair, and the police would be present in triple shifts to maintain order.

Amazingly, at the 500, strangers are pleasant to each other in ways they'd never be in real life. It's almost as if one huge extended family is holding a huge reunion, which is really what this race is all about. The Daytona 500 not only is the biggest purse of all, it also marks the start of the stock car racing year. It's like starting off the baseball season with the World Series.

Lots of visits are made back and forth especially among relative newcomers who like to check out the different RV units people have fashioned together. Besides the price of admission, the only rule for being allowed to camp in the infield is that your vehicle must be self-contained. Most importantly, that means having your own bathroom since there are no facilities anywhere in the middle of the track. We are, after all, only in a big parking lot. (Cooking grills, however, are permitted.)

One group of a dozen people who show up in a large rental moving van are made to depart since they are outfitted only with ice chests and sleeping bags. They have nowhere to dispose of all that liquid they planned to consume.

Not so for the NASCAR Good Time Gang whose bright red moving van has their name boldly lettered in white on the side. The van looks like it should be in the pits unloading vehicles and spare parts. It's loaded with plenty of spares, for certain, all in the 12-ounce aluminum can variety to keep the Good Time Gang in good spirits.

Buck Taylor of Valdosta, GA, is the man responsible for detailing this thirty-five-foot former furniture hauler. "I got this rig about three years ago," he says proudly. "Anywhere from five to fourteen of us take it to the races regularly. How many of us there are depends on how everybody's money is running.

"We've used everything from pickup trucks to motor homes, but this van is the best," Buck continues. "We've built in a stove, a sink, bunks, a bathroom—everything."

Despite the vehicle's impressive size, Taylor says he's had to invest very little in converting it to a mobile sports bar. "There's only about a thousand dollars invested in it," he admits happily. "Most everything in it was a gift from someone. I'm a real good sponge," he grins.

The decor definitely is eclectic—or early flea market. The trailer has a variety of cots, mattresses, and lounge chairs. Few colors match except for the sheets. A large Budweiser curtain separates the sleeping quarters from the living area.

"I keep this thing stored in the yard when I'm not hauling it around to races," Buck says. "During hunting season, I put it out in the woods. It also makes a real good hunt camp."

Weather for the February 500 can be hot or cold. That's the advantage of having a generator for our RV to make our own climate. When it's hot, the combined hum of all the generators in the infield sounds like an assembly plant of window air conditioners. Yet no matter how hot it ever is, when the cars scream into their first lap in the middle of the day, the rooftop of every RV is filled with its occupants. It may be bad for us, but we know it's worse for our heroes. Temperatures inside a race car can climb to a hellish 160 degrees, and drivers literally have had skin stick to their vehicles. For this reason, there's talk of some drivers testing the use of discarded insulation scraps from the space shuttle to cool down the race-car cockpits.

Regardless of who wins today, every driver is considered a king. We are present to pay homage to them all.

Who

The Daytona 500 has a weekend admission charge for each person plus a fee for the vehicle itself. The price is amazingly low, only $30 per person for the weekend. Although tickets for the stands may be sold a year ahead of time, tickets for the infield go on sale just a few days before the races and must be purchased in person. Grandstand tickets can be ordered well in advance by calling 904/253-7223 between 9AM to 5PM Monday through Friday.

What

Once your RV is positioned in the infield campground for the 500, it's there for the duration. Do not expect to motor in and out. You may want to bring a second vehicle, which you can park outside the camping area, so you can move around Daytona before or after the races. If you become too restless, you can always walk out of the infield to visit the shopping/restaurant areas across from the Speedway. The walk takes at least a half hour each way, depending on traffic.

When

The Daytona 500 weekend is the culmination of Speedweeks, a two-week-long extravaganza at Daytona International Speedway that begins the first weekend in February; camping in the speedway infield is available at most of these events. Almost two dozen races and qualifying events take place before the 500. Speedweeks usually begins with a 24-hour endurance contest that attracts as many as 300 drivers. The Daytona 500, besides being the year's biggest spectacle, is the season opening race of the Winston Cup Series. It is also the richest purse in stock car racing. Driver Sterling Marlin compares the Daytona 500 to being "like the first day of school. Daytona means things are off and running again, and it's the start of a new year."

In addition to February's Speedweeks, there is also the action-packed Fourth of July weekend when campers also crowd the infield at the Daytona International Speedway for the Pepsi 400. It can get blistering hot then (90 degrees is the mean temperature for the month). An air-conditioned RV is critical.

You'll want to show up Friday afternoon to get into the RV staging area. Follow the signs, which may seem to take you well away from where you want to be.

According to the Go Camping American Committee, an estimated 25 million Americans use RVs, which include something as simple as a pop-up camper. However, RVs with basic living facilities (that means indoor plumbing in all aspects) qualify as second homes under the current tax code. Any interest payments are therefore tax deductible.

Renting, however, is the preferred option of only occasional RV users. To rent an RV, look in the yellow pages of your telephone directory. If you would prefer to rent an RV somewhere in the Daytona area (RVs are notorious for their poor fuel mileage), the following sources can provide the names of RV renters:

Recreational Vehicle Association (RVIA): 3930 University Dr., Fairfax, VA 22030; 703/591-7130 or 800/336-0355. They provides a directory with 250 listings of RV dealers in the United States and Canada, categorized by state, rental site, and vehicle size. Free with a $7.50 order for *Rental Ventures*, a guide to renting RVs.

The following are national rental chains, the RV equivalent to Budget or Hertz. El Monte, the smallest, is where I rented my vehicle from in Orlando. It couldn't have been in better shape. Although it had 48,000 miles on it, except for the edges of the upholstery in a few places, the interior looked and functioned like brand new.

Cruise America RV Depot
11 West Hampton Ave.
Mesa, AZ 85210
602/262-9611

El Monte RV Center
3702 Rio Vista Ave.
Orlando, FL 32855
800/367-2120
Vehicle comes with an eighteen-page instruction manual, which sounds more intimidating than it actually is.

Go Vacations, Inc.
777 West 190th St.
Gardena, CA 90248
310/329-8999

11

Hiking the Tosohatchee:
Sections of the Florida Trail

True Grit. John Wayne had it. So does barbecued chicken dropped in the sand. But the real question: just how much of it did we trekkers have? Would we let the weekend rain interrupt our plans? Or would we show True Grit and tough it out?

For weeks three of us had planned on camping in the Tosohatchee State Preserve, 28,000 sprawling acres of almost pristine Florida that borders nineteen miles of the St. Johns River in east Orange County near Titusville. But at the Tosohatchee, you don't just drive up to a campground and set up your tent.

For all of its acreage, Tosohatchee has just two camp sites, both of which can be reached only by backpacking. The Tiger Branch camp is about a four-mile walk, while the one we'd reserved—Whetrock—was an 8.5-mile walk.

Did we want to walk all that way in the rain, set up a tent in the rain, sleep and cook in the rain, and then walk back in the rain? Was our level of True Grit such that we could endure such a waterlogged weekend and still think it fun? And not kill the person who had proposed the outing?

The latter point was of keen interest to me since for over two years I had told everyone of my incredible trek through the Andes of Ecuador. I'd convinced them that trekking was a great way to see the countryside anywhere, including Florida (where extensive hiking trails are more common than most people realize—see Appendix A).

The Tosohatchee would be a perfect introduction. Its natural features are outstanding: a virgin pine flatwoods (one of only several remaining in the entire United States) and a huge 900-acre virgin cypress swamp, one of Florida's last. Not only has the Florida panther reportedly been sighted here, but bald eagles regularly nest in the refuge.

The flat terrain would assure an easy stroll through the park, I guaranteed my fellow trekkers, even if the stroll lasted eight miles each way.

"We'll get mugged by the rain," one fair-weather trekker commented. "If we walk eight miles in a downpour, you'll never hear the end of it," she promised.

Recalling that even for all his grit John Wayne hadn't been able to cope with unreasonable females, I agreed to postpone the trip. As I dialed Tosohatchee to cancel our reservations, I mistook my companions' huge sighs of relief for an increase in storm intensity. I was told the next opening would not be for another month, which, when I repeated this aloud, prompted more "whooshing" noise. This was a strange storm.

The next three weekends were mostly blue skies, but as the fourth approached, the forecast sounded like a bad joke: gale-force winds that would be tossing the seas as high as eight to twelve feet ("but the breeze will keep the mosquitoes down," I laughed) and between two to four inches of rain. Even I couldn't come up with an answer for that.

The evening before our soggy departure I borrowed a few pieces of spare equipment from my friend Jeff who (since he was staying home) made light of the impending adventure. "You're going to be putting up a mighty wet tent," he said. "And then it might blow away!"

No, this time my hearty group would go forth, I scoffed. We had all pledged to go camping, come Hell or High Water. True, we'd never anticipated both could occur the same weekend. "But this time we have the closer camp," I pointed out. "We won't have to walk nearly as far."

On Saturday morning, I awoke early to pack the last few items, including a compact waterproof camera to record the weekend's events. My son Pat, who prefers to sleep until noon whenever possible, came into the living room only a few short minutes later. "Excited to get going?" I asked.

"Can't sleep for all the rain washing through the gutters," he responded sleepily.

Pat came suddenly awake as he saw all the gear. "You mean we're still going?" he asked in a tone strangely shrill for someone who had gone through puberty years earlier. He remained highly agitated even after I presented him with a brand new rainsuit. Well, some kids never appreciate how much you look out for them.

A phone call to the only other member of our party found her still asleep, somehow under the mistaken impression the trip would again be postponed. "Nonsense," I countered. "We're tough. We can take it. Besides, this weekend is my birthday and I get to be as ornery as I like." She assured me I was off to a fine start.

As we left Orlando, the sun came out briefly, then disappeared behind ominous black clouds. The sun was a good omen, I predicted. It had even stopped raining. Didn't the forecast say the rain would be tapering off? (Later that night after the downpour in Orlando, Jeff would think of us with trepidation and worry if we might not truly drown in our sleeping bags.)

Arriving at Tosohatchee, the ranger, eyeing my Bronco's fresh coat of mud acquired on the dirt road leading to the preserve gate, was surprised to see us. "I hope you plan on getting your feet wet," he said. "We've had an inch and a half of rain in the last 24 hours."

In looking over the check-in sheet, I noted that the campers at the more remote Whetrock were still there (stranded, perhaps?) and a group of nine who'd checked in at the youth camping area the night before were still present. I was about to comment, "We won't be the only fools in the woods," but somehow that didn't sound quite right.

We followed the winding road to the parking area located at the Hoot Owl Hilton. As we unloaded our packs, I studied the map the ranger had given us. Its trail of dotted lines was supposed to lead us to Tiger Branch, our designated campsite. The black lines showed up extremely well against the green folder—the sun was out! And the sky was an amazing blue, with hardly a cloud anywhere! The miraculous, unforecast appearance of the bright sun and clear sky was akin to a religious experience; we felt as elated as Noah after the flood.

But this sudden bequest of good weather presented an unexpected problem: where to store the rainsuits? Our packs were so stuffed there was no room for them anywhere, so they were tied on top.

With map in hand, we set out, coming first upon a small crossing, then an intersection where all the signs had been smashed. Previously, one marker had pointed to the youth camp, the other to the two primitive camp sites. Apparently the youth

A sunny spot on a Florida trail.

camp members considered it great fun to use the signs for firewood; replacement signs would be better off hung from high trees where teenaged primates couldn't reach them.

Fortunately, the main hiking trail was blazed, with silver stripes painted on the trees just above eye level. It was an easy trail to follow. Farther on—evidently beyond the roaming pattern of camping delinquents—we located other directional signs that also indicated the distances to the primitive sites.

In spite of all the recent rain, the trail was surprisingly dry except for a few isolated spots. We walked for three miles before our feet ever got truly wet. In some places it didn't look like it had even rained at all.

Besides the obvious reasons, I was quite thankful the sun was out. Tosohatchee should never be seen under drab clouds, only in bright sunlight where its remarkable beauty can truly be showcased. The tall pines (some as much as 250 years old) are so unlike much of Florida you feel you could be hiking many hundreds of miles farther north. Gradually, the pine forest gave way to a lower swampy area where we were serenaded by frogs.

As we approached the lowlands, the humidity noticeably increased. Jean remarked, "Now this really feels and smells like Florida."

It certainly did. Gone were any lingering impressions of a cooler location; this was the real Florida, good old muggy swampland.

Finally we came to the marker pointing to Tiger Branch. My pack, which became pregnant during the march and tripled its load, was no longer the thirty to forty pounds it had initially weighed. I was not unhappy to see the end of the trail.

However, I wish I could have felt just as kindly toward our campsite. It was truly amazing that after all the high, dry woodlands we'd encountered that a section of swamp was set aside for a primitive campground.

We squished through the tall grass, finally locating a small space of dry ground where we could pitch our two tents. This undoubtedly was the spot: at the edge of the area was the essential wooden outhouse.

Looking at the ankle-to-knee-deep water surrounding the structure, Pat observed: "It looks like they forgot to leave us a boat so we could get to it."

Later, Jean came back to report the place was inhabited by tsetse flies, scorpions, spiders, and other unwelcome creatures. So much for the modern conveniences.

Just as we got the tents up, a small squadron of dark clouds appeared above the treeline. We decided on an early supper, just in case. The last campers had been kind enough to leave some dead pine branches for firewood, along with several sharpened tree branches for cooking hot dogs or marshmallows. In spite of the damp conditions, we got a fire going.

Following the hot dog hors d'oeuvres, I served thick slices of lasagna for everyone. Rather than pack dehydrated foods that would have required us to carry more water, I opted for fully prepared and cooked foods protected in aluminum foil. The foil packets needed only to be placed in boiling water for about five minutes, opened and served. The foil, of course, wouldn't burn so we packed it out.

Just as we completed our meal, the rain began; our reprieve was over. We fled into one tent, where Jean suddenly presented something she had been carrying all day: a slightly dented and very juicy blueberry pie—my favorite kind. Better than any birthday cake.

Despite the close quarters of three of us in a two-person tent, Jean insisted on lighting birthday candles, which soon had the tent filled with smoke. To make matters worse, these were trick candles and after my third attempt to blow them out we tossed them outside. Even the rain wouldn't extinguish them. I had to bury them in a small mound of wet dirt.

Fortunately, the rain proved to be a mild one that lasted only about an hour. We later learned that other nearby places were deluged. As we sat in the smoky tent dining on birthday blueberry pie, I was just thankful the rain had held off as long as it had. This would truly have been a miserable experience to undergo entirely in the rain. Our tents probably would have been wet both inside and out if it had been pouring when we arrived.

As it turned out, it was a pretty good way to spend a birthday after all.

Who

For complete information, write the Reserve manager at 3365 Taylor Creek Rd., Christmas, FL 32709; or call 407/568-5893.

What

The William Beardall Tosohatchee State Reserve was purchased in 1977 under Florida's Environmentally Endangered Lands Program in order to protect this unique habitat, vital to so many endangered species. The nineteen-mile-long stretch extends along the St. Johns west bank from SR 50 to the north, through the Bee Line Expressway and SR 520 to Lake Poinsett.

The Tosohatchee landscape is a showcase of how plant communities are shaped by alternating cycles of flood and fire, creating a patchwork of swamps, marshes, hammocks, and pine flatwoods. Animals include numerous wading and shore birds, deer, snakes, armadillos, bobcat, turkey, hawks, gray fox, hawks, owls, and even endangered species such as black bear and bald eagles. The fall wildflowers are spectacular.

As protection of the habitat is the primary concern, activities are limited to hiking, primitive backpack camping, nature study, horseback riding, fishing, and limited quota hunting. Pets are permitted in the Reserve, but not on the hiking trails, which were developed and maintained by the Florida Trail Association.

The hike, while an enjoyable one, is not in a total wilderness environment. A set of power lines and numerous dirt roads cross the trails at various points. At night, traffic on the Bee Line Expressway is clearly audible, making it seem like you're really camping in an urban environment. But, that's typical for almost anywhere in Central Florida.

See Appendix A, which has a list of all state parks with good hiking and backpacking trails. In addition, there is excellent hiking in the three national forests: Apalachicola, Osceola and Ocala. Everglades National Park is riddled with good hiking trails. For additional hiking descriptions, see *The Hiker's Guide to Florida* (O'Keefe, Falcon Press).

References: *The Hiker's Guide to Florida* by M. Timothy O'Keefe, Falcon Press, 1993; also contact The Florida Trail Association for its trail guide (See Appendix J).

When

Hiking and camping in summer is not very popular in Florida due to high temperatures, regular afternoon showers, and the accompanying high humidity. Early morning in the summer can be quite pleasant, but within two hours of sunrise, the heat and humidity are often stifling. Generally, the best hiking months are from October to early May. The driest months tend to be January to April, though some wet weather usually precedes winter cold fronts.

Where

The Reserve is located on Taylor Creek Rd., which is located four miles south of SR 50 at the town of Christmas, between Orlando and Titusville.

12

Houseboating
the St. Johns River

The St. Johns River is unique. It is one of the few northward flowing rivers in the Western Hemisphere. It runs approximately 300 miles, then empties into the Atlantic Ocean just north of Jacksonville.

The largest stream of water entirely within the state of Florida, it is one of the South's most scenic rivers. Palm trees, bald cypress, and live oaks festooned with beards of Spanish moss line the river banks, which are largely undeveloped in many sections. The river holds a mix of both freshwater and saltwater species, including largemouth bass, bream, catfish, eels, blue crabs, and mullet. Endangered manatees are also common. One of the state's most important sites used by manatees during winter is just off the St. Johns, at Blue Spring State Park near Orange City.

The best way to come to know the beauty of this river is by houseboat, essentially nothing but a floating recreational vehicle (RV). Like RVs, houseboats are rented by the weekend or for a week. Houseboats come fitted with all the comforts of home—hot showers, bedding, refrigerator, stove, plates, and cutlery—plus a few extras: cane rods for fishing and a ladder for swimming. All you need to bring is yourself and your groceries and you're underway.

You don't need to be a skilled sailor to pilot a houseboat on the St. Johns. The channel is clearly marked and no problem to follow, even without a map. However, only half the length of the river, the section between Sanford (near Orlando) and Jacksonville, is navigable by a boat this size. Still, that's a distance of about 150 miles.

As for piloting a houseboat, it's not any more difficult than an RV. Anyone renting a houseboat is usually taken on a quick shakedown cruise to learn how the boat maneuvers and shown how to maintain the engines and appliances. There's also an instruction book for backup.

As I discovered, you become qualified very quickly to cast off on your own for a long weekend or a week. Before leaving the dock, I asked if there was one particular mistake most first-time houseboaters make. The dockmaster responded immediately: "They don't adequately use their crew. Some people compare this to driving a car, but on a boat everyone can help. It's not all the driver's responsibility." In the interest of group harmony, I had him repeat this to my crew.

Before heading north in the general direction of Jacksonville, we made a short detour southward to Hontoon Island State Park. Hontoon Island is a place that appeals to the Tom Sawyer and Huckleberry Finn in all of us since it can be reached only by boat. A ferry operated by the park staff shuttles continually back and forth during daylight hours, bringing in mostly picnickers and a few campers.

My reason for docking was the eighty-five-foot high observation tower, which provides an excellent panoramic view of the river. From here you can see the St. Johns winding southward as well as several small bays that form a short distance from the tower. You also get an eagle's-eye perspective of the boat traffic and the area's extensive marina complex.

After descending from the tower, we spent several hours exploring Hontoon Island. The 1,050-acre park has been left mostly in its natural state. A mile-and-a-half nature walk through the dense shrubbery will lead you to a thirty-five-foot-high Timucuan Indian shell mound, one of the largest on the St. Johns. The mound is said to be one huge garbage heap that the now extinct Timucuan Indians created over generations as they survived off the river's bounty. It's hard to believe they ate the whole thing.

Incidentally, if you've never encountered it before, you'll probably be surprised at the helpfulness and consideration of your fellow boaters; houseboating really is just like RVing. When it came time for me to tie up and cast off at the Hontoon dock, two other people were there assisting with the lines without having to be asked. When you're piloting a thirty-nine-foot-long, ten-foot-wide vehicle for the first time, you do appreciate all the help you can get.

One very important thing to keep in mind when houseboationg: any part of the river near a marina should be considered a go-slow, no-wake zone. On weekends in particular, authorities patrol to enforce this restriction. A fine for a serious violation could run into the hundreds of dollars, and you would also be responsible for any damage your wake caused to other boats.

Heading northward, we passed by the Lake Woodruff National Wildlife Refuge (established in 1863), which borders most of our eastern bank. The refuge is a premier place for bird life in particular but also prime habitat for raccoons, otters, black bears, and alligators, to name only a few. The area is quiet and undeveloped, perfect for exploring by boat. The most sensible means is to anchor and use a dinghy to paddle close to shore, or simply anchor for the night in one of the small cuts and view the wildlife through binoculars at sunrise and sunset.

With little to do but pilot up the river until our first stop, I had the opportunity to refresh myself on the history of the St. Johns. Its recorded history is almost as old as that of North America. In 1513 when Ponce de Leon sighted the coast of Florida in his quest for the fountain of youth, he apparently landed near the mouth of the St. Johns at Jacksonville. The Spaniards who settled just a few years later named her Rio de San Matheo, the San Mateo River. This was later changed to Rio de San Juan, the St. John's. Eventually the apostrophe was dropped by the English chroniclers to the modern day spelling, St. Johns.

Regardless of what these explorers-come-latelies did, it was the Timucuan Indians who named the river first, the Welaka, "river of many lakes," a perfect description of the river's main characteristic. The town of Welaka on the St. Johns above Palatka comemmorates the river's original name.

Although the last Timucuans were killed off before 1800, their legacy is still present. There are at least fourty-eight shell mounds located along the river banks, many situated where the river joins with a lagoon or creek. Most of the still remaining mounds are in the form of long ridges parallel to the shore. The mounds were used for cooking and camping. Objects found in them include pottery, tools, and human bones in such a condition to indicate the Indians at one time probably practiced cannibalism.

As twilight approached, I decided to look for an anchorage well away from the channel. I picked a large lagoon just south of Lake Dexter. The sky was a mixture of purple, grey, and pink, a tapestry to give any photographer an itchy shutter finger. I threw out the anchor and estimated the amount of rope (five times the water depth) that would hold us and allow the boat to swing 360 degrees without holding up on the shoreline. Then it was over the side into the dinghy for some sunset shots.

When it came time to turn in, we were suddenly serenaded by a pair of screech owls. If you've never heard owls in the Florida wilderness before, it's easy to mistake them for wolves. They sound nothing like "who, who, who" but have a more plaintive quality.

Joining the wolf-like howls were all sorts of sudden strange creakings and scuffling sounds from all sections of the boat. Anyone with an overactive imagination would likely conjure up visions of piratical boarding parties making ready their assault. As writers often have this sort of imagination, it took me several trips to check both the bow and stern to convince me our craft wasn't about to be invaded. It does take some time to adjust to the new sounds of St. Johns houseboating.

Sunrise on the St. Johns is something not to be missed. There is always a feeling of peace during this period, of a pause before living begins anew. All is quiet except for the faint lapping of the river against the bank and the sound of your own breathing. Then from the distance comes the gentle, haunting cry of the killdeer penetrating the fog—mysterious yet reassuring. The bird is a reminder you are not totally alone.

I would loved to have lived when many other sounds were common on early St. Johns mornings. Imagine being awakened by the crowing of wild turkeys greeting the sunrise from their roosts in high trees. Or the continuous roar of alligators during the breeding season. Once their sound was so pervasive and loud, it was likened to distant thunder and said to make even the ground tremble. And to sit by a fire at night, to hear the chilling cry of a wolf. Two hundred years ago it was this way.

We continued northward the second day and before long reached the borders of the 366,000-acre Ocala National Forest on the St. Johns' west bank. Ocala was the first national forest east of the Mississippi. Its name—the meaning now lost forever—was taken from the Timucuan term for this region, Ocali. You'll notice many tributaries leading into the forest, which are seldom explored. For a stretch, at least, most are open to something as wide as a houseboat, but turing around can be a problem once a waterway starts to narrow.

Astor was the first settlement of any size we encountered after leaving the boat docks at DeLand. Astor makes an interesting stop since it has dockside fuel pumps, restaurants specializing in hush puppies and catfish, and several places you can stock up on blue crabs during the annual run. That's another of the things about the St. Johns I like, the way it contains a mixture of both freshwater and saltwater species.

It's just a short hop from Astor to Lake George, one of the many lakes formed by the river along its main channel. Lake George is Florida's second largest body of freshwater (Lake Okeechobee is first), and crossing it can be treacherous under high winds, which cause the shallow lake to whip up quickly. Waves of six to eight feet have been recorded during such blows, and this is not a place to be in a houseboat under such conditions. Steer clear when there's fog as well, since it's all too easy to stray from the channel and run into trouble on the ten-mile-long lake.

However, Lake George provides the access to one of the most pleasant stops on any St. Johns voyage: Silver Glen Springs. The captain's manual gives detailed instructions on how to find and navigate the spring run where the vodka-clear water is 72 degrees all year round.

Although people visit here regularly, the river and the land have given up little of themselves. They retain much of the bounty that attracted the Timucuan Indians to settle in the same spot 4,000 years ago. The clear spring run remains filled with large numbers of bass, bream, and tremendous schools of mullet that migrate in from the Atlantic. The land animals are also amazingly abundant.

On arriving the first night, we spotted several deer feeding in a nearby field. They displayed no fear or even curiosity at seeing our boat anchor so close to their territory. Osprey—we must have seen as many as fifteen-twenty—ignored us as they fished from the rich waters. In addition, we spotted limpkins, otter, owls, vultures, and several sorts of herons.

At twilight, we were greeted by a most unfriendly visitor. I brought out my copy of *Travels of William Bartram*. A pioneer naturalist, Bartram explored the St. Johns River in the mid-1700s. I looked up the heading "Thunder storm." Bartram had this to say: "The late thunder storm had purified the air by disuniting and dissipating the noxious vapors. The falling of heavy showers, with thunder and brisk winds, from the cool regions of the N.W., contributes greatly towards restoring the salubrity of the air and purity of the waters . . . ."

Well, obviously Bartram never saw a fast-moving front on the river like the one approaching now from the west. His description of a thunderstorm was too calm.

The clouds moved over us with incredible speed, the way old low- budget science fiction movies always depicted the beginning (and end) of the world. A continual barrage of lightning struck all around us. The thunder rolled so loudly it was almost impossible to speak.

This would have been a wonderful spectacle to enjoy from the safe haven of a well-grounded front porch, but I wasn't sure a houseboat anchored on a deserted island was the best place to be. When a lightning bolt struck on the other side of our island, I knew there was only one thing to do. If death was imminent, I would meet it on my own terms. I went to bed, pulled the sheet over my head, and fell asleep.

When I awoke just past midnight, the sky was clear, the stars bright and crisp. The "noxious vapors" were gone and the St. Johns once more was its usual tranquil self.

No, tranquil wasn't the correct term: frogs, crickets, and other critters created a constant racket that seemed far above the decibel level of most city traffic. But it was a soothing, relaxing sound that, once acknowledged, became a natural Muzak that quickly lulled me back to sleep. I couldn't have been happier. These were parts of the sounds and sights of the unspoiled St. Johns I'd hoped to find.

Above Lake George the river widens and in some sections seems almost as broad as Lake George. At this point you're entering what's advertised as "The Bass Capital of the World." If you're a serious angler, you can tow a bass boat behind your houseboat so you can maneuver it around weedbeds, pilings, and other fishy habitat.

Big bass have been recorded here since the mid-1700s. Naturalist William Bartram described the impressive appetites of largemouth bass back then: "The head of the fish makes about one third of his length, and consequently the mouth is very large: birds, fish, frogs, and even serpents are frequently found in its stomach . . . This fish is remarkably ravenous; nothing living, that he can seize upon, escapes his jaws; at the moment he rises to the surface to seize his prey, discovering his bright red gills, through the transparent waters, give him a terrible appearance indeed."

After many days of exploration, Bartram was moved to write: "The natural features of the St. Johns make it one of the most beautiful and remarkable of American rivers."

I found it still is.

Who

Despite the length of the St. Johns, the number of marinas renting houseboats is limited. This is because south of Sanford the river is shallow and the channel difficult to follow. In the Jacksonville region, the shoreline tends to be very developed. The best houseboating is where the river flows through the Ocala National Forest.

Hontoon Landing Resort & Marina
2317 River Ridge Rd.
DeLand, FL 32720
800/248-2474

What

Since all the bedding and cooking utensils are supplied, the most serious consideration is the menu. Everything needs to be purchased ahead of time and then stored in the houseboat's refrigerator or freezer. Since most modern rentals even have microwaves, many people like to prepare meals like spaghetti or stews ahead of time and then warm them up. Grills are often provided, too, so burgers, hot dogs, and steaks are good choices, too.

For clothing, be sure to take a swimsuit (and beach towels). Jeans, walking shorts, tennis shoes for hiking, both short and long sleeve shirts, sunblock, insect repellent, hat, and sunglasses are all good items to bring. Jackets and windbreakers may be needed during the winter months. Bring binoculars for bird-watching and keeping track of the channel markers in case of early-morning fog. Serious anglers may want to tow a fishing boat behind; these can be rented at the marinas in Sanford and DeLand.

Anytime of year is good for houseboating on the St. Johns since most rental units come with air conditioning. Anyone interested in the St. Johns' excellent bass fishing will want to visit in March, April, or May. Afternoon showers are frequent from June through September. The best all-around months for weather and scenery are spring and fall.

13

How to Catch
a Million Dollar Bass

There is a largemouth bass probably swimming somewhere in Florida waters right now that is worth well over a million dollars to the angler lucky enough to snag it.

It may seem hard to believe that kind of value could be placed on a single fish, but since the 1980s the largemouth bass has had anglers around the country in a fishing frenzy. That's when the Bass Anglers Sportsmen's Society (B.A.S.S.) of Alabama turned bass fishing into a competitive sport worth big bucks. Some professional anglers such as Roland Martin made millions from product endorsements, TV appearances, and more. The ultimate goal of all this activity was—and always will be—to catch the world's biggest bass.

It's estimated that whoever catches the next record will become an instant millionaire thanks to their own product endorsements, public appearances and the like. The current record of twenty pounds, four ounces, was set back in the 1920s, in Montgomery Lake, GA. Anglers figure that a new heavyweight title is long overdue.

Big-money tournaments held around the nation have established what everyone has known for a long time: Florida has the nation's biggest and best largemouth bass fishing. And, if a new world record is ever set, it will probably come from the Sunshine State. The Florida bass, which is considered a subspecies, grows much faster because of its more favorable environment. Capable of growing well over twenty pounds, its greater size and different scale count are the only distinguishing features of the Florida subspecies. The record pulled from a Georgia lake over three-quarters of a century ago may have been a cross of the Florida subspecies and the northern largemouth bass since South Georgia and North Florida do intergrade. The largest certified state record is 17.27 pounds, caught in 1986. There is an uncertified record of 20.13 pounds that goes back to 1923.

In the meantime, tackle manufacturers drool at the chance to associate their products with the world's most sought-after fish. With new high-tech equipment never dreamed of in the 1920s (such as a single device that reads the water temperature, PH level, and bottom depth in a split second), many anglers thought it would only be a matter of time before a new record was set.

It's still only a matter of time. Despite the hundreds of thousand of hours spent bass fishing annually, no one can catch a largemouth bigger than twenty-two pounds, four ounces. Of course, there have been stories not only about the ones that got away, but also about the ones that were mistakenly eaten before weighing, or devoured by the family cat, or . . . every excuse imaginable, it's been used.

The big-game hunt continues, particularly in the spring when the huge females are bedding. That's the time anglers converge from all over the country. More than a few hope to set the new record. Others are content to catch a trophy bass of eight- or ten-pounds or more, a size not close to attainable in colder waters back home.

However, anglers totally unfamiliar with the ways of Florida bass fishing don't stand much of a chance of taking a big fish unless they use a professional guide. Florida bass fishing is unlike almost anywhere else in the country. There are few deep reservoirs or deep lakes. Instead, Florida's best bass waters tend to be shallow and, increasingly, weed-choked.

Still, anyone who comes prepared with the right lures and general know-how has a good chance for an eight- to ten-pound trophy. And if you happen to catch the world record, just remember who offered all this sage advice . . . 10 percent of the take would be just fine, thank you.

First, the lures you'll need. As an old friend once advised me, the condition of your tackle box often reflects your approach to fishing: either jumbled and confused, crowded and unfocused, or simple and neat.

I learned that simpler is better many years ago while fishing with an older friend named Clint, one of the best anglers I've ever known. As I kept fumbling through my jumbled, crowded tackle box, trying to figure out which lure to try next, Clint spent his time catching and releasing bass, lots of them. He never changed lures; he didn't need to.

Finally tired of watching me search for the Holy Grail of bass lures, Clint took my tackle box and dumped the entire contents on the boat deck. "What a mess of junk," he said. "Most of these lures were made to catch fishermen, not fish." With that, Clint selected three different lures from his own small collection of bass baits. He handed the box back to me. "Learn how to use just these three basic types, and you'll catch all the bass you want in Florida anytime, anywhere."

Time and experience have proven Clint's simple approach to be the correct one. Years later, I still rely heavily on the three lure designs he singled out.

BASIC LURES

Following are the basic types of bass lures. My favorites are surface lures, worms, and crank baits because they best suit Florida largemouth bass fishing, but spoons and jigs also have their place in certain conditions.

Surface Lures: These are popular with most anglers since there's nothing more exciting than watching a bass actually take the lure. Quiet surface plugs, best used when the water is calm, include minnow-shaped baits and darters. Both are worked by allowing the lure to remain still on the surface for a few seconds, then twitching it several times before starting a slow retrieve.

Minnow-shaped baits like Rapalas and Rebels swim straight under the surface during the retrieve, while the darters wander all over the place. Strikes can come at anytime, even right at the boat.

Popping plugs that have a hollowed, almost cup-faced head are good for night fishing since bass seem to be able to home in better on the loud noise. Normally a soft pop works best, with periods of silence between pops. If fish don't pay attention, or there's a surface chop, try a series of loud pops to get bass motivated.

Plastic Worms: Some bass anglers fish with almost nothing else, so great is their faith in worms to produce well year-round in every type of weather. Worms come in all colors and sizes, with so many different types to choose from you could fill several tackle boxes with nothing but the plastic critters.

Some important points to keep your worm selection to a manageable size: use darker colors for murky water and night fishing, lighter colors in clear water or sunny conditions. While many anglers prefer worms that are six- or seven-and-a-half inches in length, try to find a pack of four-inchers for the days bass just won't take the larger ones.

Worms are usually fished along the bottom, allowed to sink and then slowly jigged back up with pauses in between. A worm lead is often needed to get the bait to the bottom quickly. These cone-shaped sinkers (from a fourth to a half ounce) are preferable to the egg-shaped variety since they don't catch on snags or weeds. Use the smallest lead possible to maintain constant "feel" with the worm.

Worms can also be used just like surface lures, retrieving them steadily at different speeds to see which speed produces best.

Crank Baits: Technically, these are any plug that runs below the surface; since many of them will not float, they must be worked continually to create the proper action. By varying the retrieve, you can make most crank baits run anywhere from just below the surface to almost ten feet. Some large-lipped, heavy crank baits are made to run twenty feet or deeper.

Generally, you need just a couple of the shallow or deep runners, depending on your water conditions. Shad-like and bass-like crank baits are good consistent producers.

The next two lure types are usually called upon for very specific conditions:

Spoons: These heavy, fast-sinking lures are tailored for deep water situations when fish are bunched up on "structure" or suspended in deep water. Silver is good for clear water, gold or black for dark days or nights. The Johnson weedless is a surface spoon intended to attract fish holed up in vegetation or just below the surface. Add a pork rind or plastic worm trailer to supply even more animation.

Jigs: Especially good for deep water and in thick patches of weed where most other lures would hang up. Yellow and white have been standard choices for years, but jig weight is the most important consideration. Some jigs come with flattened heads which allow the jig to wobble or glide as it sinks for added action.

Regardless of the kinds of lures you end up using, remember what's most important is not how many you have but how well they match local angling conditions and how well you fish them. That's why most anglers find the more they fish, the less they need.

WEEDING OUT BASS

Now that you've got the proper tackle, where are some of the best places to look?

You wouldn't expect something as big and powerful as a largemouth bass to be such a reclusive figure, preferring to hide in shadows like some fugitive. Yet bass definitely like to stay under cover, and what they favor depends on the time of year. When the weather warms up, nothing tops shallow weeds and grasses for finding fish early and late.

Different types of plants demand different kinds of approaches and baits. And, unfortunately, what worked last year may not work today or tomorrow since exotic vegetation is steadily moving into more lakes around the state.

Thick mats of weed are now an unavoidable fact of fishing life. Groaning and complaining won't change the situation or produce fish. However, staying current with the latest weed-fishing tactics will.

Lily Pads: The classic method for fishing lily pads is a weedless silver spoon with a plastic or pork trailer. The key is to keep the lure moving across the surface, all the time anticipating an explosion of white spray and red gills as you retrieve the flashy outfit.

If that isn't successful, you'll need to go deeper and work a lure beneath the green canopy. Use either a plastic frog or a weightless plastic worm, moving it up and down through the pads. You'll need to pay close attention to your line and the feel of the lure since latching onto a bass isn't likely to be as cataclysmic an event as slaloming a silver spoon.

After casting the frog or worm and letting it settle, twitch the rod to make it jiggle, then let it settle again. Do this several times before really moving the lure anywhere. All the time you'll be waiting for the worm to start feeling heavy, your indication that a bass may have picked it up. That's when you set the hook.

If nothing happens, you may want to make a complete retrieve and cast to a different opening. Yet some anglers prefer to crank the worm to the next clear water opening, continually repeating the performance until they reach the edge before retrieving.

If all else has failed to this point, fall back on a buzz bait to motivate bass to action. Since fish will often follow these for a time before striking, maintain the same steady retrieve almost to your boat. No sense in snatching your bait from the jaws of success.

Blades of Grass: Grass blades are my favorite type of vegetation to fish, perhaps because the places that hold bass are fairly obvious. Make sure there's decent water depth, between one and two feet, or you may end up fishing barren shallows.

The first thing I look for is where the grass bed forms a point, no matter how small. It's a break from the normal pattern, which seems to attract fish.

The most productive lure usually is either topwater or a topwater/diver. Pinpoint casting is necessary, too, since you need to throw as close to the grass as possible.

When the lure lands, let it settle for a moment, watching the small swirl made by the splash turn into an ever-widening circle. Sometimes you never get a chance to see the plug land: the fish seems to see the lure coming and noisily greets it right at the surface.

But if nothing happens, wait a few seconds, then twitch the rod tip so your floater will create a few additional swirls. Next, snap your rod sharply to force the lure under the water for just a couple of feet. When the plug resurfaces, let it rest for a moment, create a few swirls, then snap the rod again. Too many anglers retrieve their baits after their initial toss and never really spend time working them. The result: the bait spends more time sailing through the air than actually being worked in the water.

Another place to try for fish—but these never seem to hold as many fish as the points—are small openings back in the grass. A weightless plastic worm works well in this situation, since you can retrieve it through the grass once you've worked it through the clearing.

If you take a fish in one of these open spots, you're going to need considerable cranking power to get your fish through the weeds. That means between seventeen- to twenty- pound test mono and a good baitcasting outfit. Spinning rigs work well on the grassy points but not for true dredge work.

Hydrilla: From a sportsman's point of view, hydrilla has nothing going for it. It mats the surface in summer and becomes almost unfishable; it clogs boat props; and once it takes root in a lake, it's impossible to stop without some sort of drastic countermeasure.

Water depth doesn't deter hydrilla: it can grow in three feet or twenty feet of water. Spring is often the most fishable period since rising water levels and winter cold may temporarily leave the weed tops a foot or so below the surface. In this kind of condition, it's actually possible to catch bass over the hydrilla with a crank bait or plastic worm.

You can either plunk a worm directly over the opening or cast it slightly beyond the pocket, then bring the worm to it. Either way, let the worm fall to generate its own action. A bass will often take the worm while it's still in free-fall, so be prepared.

The reason some anglers like to cast beyond the pocket is that they believe a retrieve to the opening is a much more natural approach (as opposed to things falling out of the sky) and is less likely to spook a fish.

Fortunately, even thick patches of hydrilla sometimes have clear water openings. Jigging these clear openings—assuming you can maneuver your boat close to one—is often fruitful.

If you confront nothing but a solid surface mat of weed, your only option is to

Search out isolated grass beds away from shore. They have several different sides to fish.

fish the surface edges of the weed bed. The problem is that the bottom may be quite deep, ten feet or more, so you'll have to pay unusually close attention to water depth.

When fishing areas with hydrilla, it's essential that none of the weed gets dragged out on your boat trailer. Unwitting anglers have transplanted hydrilla from lake to lake in just this way, and the results have been devastating.

Regardless of whatever type of vegetation you fish, don't make the mistake of believing that if you take a bass from one particular spot, there's no sense in casting there again, that you've fished it out. Quite often a large point or pocket will hold two or three fish. You won't know unless you find out.

And just because you caught fish in one place during the morning, don't ignore it later in the day. I'd swear that small bass must hang around the most favored spots, waiting to become the replacement tenant for the one you just evicted. A spot that holds fish one day will frequently hold them every day. Whatever natural fish attractor is present is at work all the time, until the bottom or weed structure changes somehow.

After all, you don't really think you were the very first angler ever to find fish in a particular spot, do you? You're probably just the latest in a long line of Christopher Columbuses.

Finally, don't work just the grassy areas contiguous with the shoreline. Search out isolated grass beds away from shore. They have several different sides to fish, not just one long shoreline. More importantly, they are sometimes removed from the heaviest fishing traffic.

The majority of anglers stay close to shore, figuring that anything removed from direct contact with land will be too deep.

Not necessarily. These solitary grass beds may grow on a hummock so the depth may be much less than you'd expect.

In summer, added depth is often attractive to bass as the weather gets hotter. Areas that are productive in the morning may warm up too much by the afternoon, causing the fish to move deeper.

Who/Where

The largest bass tend to come from the central part of the state: the Ocala area, the Kissimmee Chain of Lakes, and Lake Okeechobee. Yet there are always exceptions, including the world record caught in Georgia. For the latest information on fishing conditions around the state, using a Touch-Tone phone only, call 800/ASK-FISH.

Who earns their living as a full-time bass guide tends to change with some regularity, but the chambers of commerce in the good fishing areas always have the latest and most complete list. Quite often, too, they know who tends to produce the most fish:

Putnam County
Chamber of Commerce
P.O. Box 550
Palatka, FL 32178-0550
904/328-1503
Fax: 904/328-7076
Covers the St. Johns River.

Ocala-Marion County
Chamber of Commerce
110 E. Silver Springs Blvd.
Ocala, FL 34478
904/629-8051
Fax: 904/629-7651
Good information on the many lakes in the Ocala National Forest.

DeLand Area
Chamber of Commerce
336 N. Woodland Blvd.
DeLand, FL 32721
800/749-4350, 904/734-4331
Fax: 904/734-4333
Covers a more southerly part of the St. Johns.

Kissimmee/St.Cloud Convention
& Visitors Bureau
P.O. Box 422007
Kissimmee, FL 34742-2007
800/327-9159, 407/847-5000
Fax 407/847-0878
Lake Kissimmee underwent a drawdown the first half of 1996 to better stabilize the vegetation. Fishing here should boom until at least 2001.

Okeechobee County
Chamber of Commerce
55 S. Parrot Ave.
Okeechobee, FL 34972
941/763-6464
Lake Okeechobee is Florida's largest freshwater lake and the second largest in the continental United States.

Clewiston
Chamber of Commerce
P.O. Box 275
Clewiston, FL 33440
941/983-7979
Clewiston (and Moore haven below) are two of the main gateways for fishing Lake Okeechobee.

Glades County
Chamber of Commerce
P.O. Box 490
Moore Haven, FL 33471
813/946-0440

Because of intense fishing pressure, Florida has severely limited the number and size of largemouth (black) bass that may be kept. The daily limit is five fish, of which only one may be twenty-two inches or longer in total length.

In addition, in recent years, high levels of mercury have been detected in fish from a number of freshwater locations around the state. Information is available from the HRS State Health Office at 904/488-3385.

At press time, the following areas were considered safe for unrestricted consumption of all species of freshwater fish:

Lakes and Ponds	County
Blue Cypress	Indian River
Bryant	Marion
Cherry	Lake
Crescent	Flagler, Putnam
Farm-13 Reservoir	Indian River

St. Johns River Water Management District	County
Ida	Palm Beach
Jackson	Leon
Kingsley	Clay
Lochloosa	Alachua
Minneola	Lake
Lake Okeechobee	Palm Beach, Marin, Hendry, Glades, Okeechobee
Ocklawaha Chain (Orange, Yale, Griffin, Alachua/Apopka, Harris, Eustis, Marion/ Lake/Dora, Beauclair, Carlton)	Orange
Orange	Alachua
Panasofkee	Sumter
Parker	Polk
Rodman Reservoir	Putnam
Rousseau	Levy
Sampson	Bradford
Seminole	Jackson
Shipp	Polk

Trafford	Collier
Tsala Apopka	Citrus
Weir	Marion
Wildcat	Lake

Fish Management Areas	County
Ivanhoe	Orange
Santiago	Orange
Richmond	Orange
Lorna Doone	Orange
Delevoe Park	Broward

National Wildlife Refuges	County
Crystal River	Citrus
Florida Panther	Collier
Lake Woodruff	Brevard, Volusia
St. Marks	Wakulla
St. Vincent	Franklin

Rivers	County
Alafia	Hillsborough
Apalachicola	Gadsden, Liberty, Franklin
Aucilla	Jefferson, Madison, Taylor
Kissimmee	Highlands, Osceola
Little Manatee	Hillsborough
Myakka	Sarasota, Manatee
Rainbow	Hernando
Lower St. Johns (SR 415 Bridge near Sanford downstream through Lakes Monroe and George to the Buckman Bridge in Jacksonville)	Clay, Duval, St. Johns, Putnam, Flagler, Volusia, Lake, Seminole
Vortex Blue Spring	Holmes

Canals	County
C-11	Broward
C-17	Palm Beach
C-51 (West Palm Beach Canal)	Palm Beach

14

Incredible Bass Fishing
at Disney World

You're not going to believe where some of Florida's best largemouth bass fishing is . . . for real!

It flies in the face of the old adage that every fisherman knows well: the more remote the location, the better the fishing. So it came to me as a surprise to discover that one of the nation's best lakes for huge largemouth bass is right in the middle of Walt Disney World in Orlando, the world's number one tourist destination.

This little-known attraction of Disney World was a very pleasant surprise to one recent Minnesota angler who caught fish after fish on one March morning. At the end of his two-hour trip, he'd pulled in almost ten bass, including one over six pounds.

Beaming happily, he told his guide, "I just did an entire year's fishing this morning. This is more than I'll catch all year back home!"

Largemouth bass fishing at Disney World's Bay Lake is so good it was chosen as the site for one of the B.A.S.S. Classics, the Super Bowl of tournament fishing. However, conflicts between Disney and B.A.S.S. officials over which brands of boats and motors would be used in the event forced the tournament to be held elsewhere. And although the big money pros never got the chance to fish Bay Lake, you can.

Although much of Disney World has been fabricated, Bay Lake is a large natural spring-fed lake, almost oblong in shape. One side is bordered by the Fort Wilderness marina and swimming beach, just opposite the Contemporary Hotel. Much of the shoreline is still bordered by tall cypress and grass beds. In the middle of the lake is another attraction, the nature sanctuary known as Discovery

Island. Except for the Contemporary Hotel, there is little to distinguish Bay Lake from any other Central Florida lake.

The spectacular bass fishing is not something that was natural to Bay Lake, or something that occurred overnight. Before Disney World opened in 1971, Bay Lake, connected to the manmade Seven Seas Lagoon by a long canal, was drained and cleaned out. When it was refilled with water, the lake was stocked with 70,000 large-mouth fingerlings. Then, for more than ten years, Bay Lake went virtually unfished.

It was left undisturbed to establish itself and to allow the fingerlings to grow. Ironically, when the lake was stabilized and the bass were a respectable size, fishing was ignored for many more years. Disney officials believed that—considering all the other activities on the property—visitors wouldn't be interested in fishing. They eventually discovered how wrong they were after hosting several private bass tournaments.

So regularly scheduled fishing trips were begun, but fishing is still done on a limited basis to keep the lake from being overfished. Only two boats fish Bay Lake, each making two-hour trips early in the morning and late in the afternoon. (Anglers do have the option of traveling to the Seven Seas Lagoon, but most stay in Bay Lake where the fishing is usually much better.)

A two-hour outing isn't very long, but typically it's all anglers need. Between three to five fish are caught on a typical trip; sometimes as many as fifteen to twenty. The fishing is so consistent that Disney, jokingly, has been accused of supplying audio-animatronic bass for the anglers to reel in. In fact, catching bass is such a sure thing, some major tackle manufacturers have visited Bay Lake to test out new products.

It's not just the sheer numbers of bass that makes Bay Lake so impressive—it's also the size of the fish. They average between two and four pounds. Six-pounders are not uncommon. Bass well over ten pounds have also have been taken. The deep holes that pock-mark the lake's bottom provide the best angling most of the year. It's not necessary for you to figure out the proper fishing patterns in only a short two-hour period: every boat has its own Disney guide.

You might want to keep in mind that the Disney-provided fishing tackle is fairly lightweight. These rigs work well in open water but not around heavy weed beds. If you wish, you can bring your own tackle. Other supplies provided are a net, a dozen shiners for bait, towels, coffee or soft drinks, and juice. Extra shiners are available for purchase.

If you prefer to fish in greater privacy, bass fishing is also available in the several miles of canals that crisscross the Fort Wilderness Campground. Canal fishing is normally done by canoe, and anglers are strictly on their own, without a guide. The Disney people say the biggest bass reside in these canals. At the same time, the canals don't hold as many fish as Bay Lake.

Who

You do not need to be staying at either the Fort Wilderness Campground or any of the Disney hotels to fish Bay Lake. But you must have advance reservations, since this is a very popular outing. For reservations and complete information, call 407/824-2621 between 8 AM and 4 PM daily.

What

Cost of the two-hour guided fishing trip is $132 per boat. A boat is capable of carrying up to five people plus the guide. It's possible to fish more than two hours at the cost of $50 per hour per boatload. Plan on releasing all your fish unless you come up with a real trophy; even then you can measure the fish and release it, since few bass mounts these days use any of the real fish. A Florida fishing license is not required to fish Bay Lake in a canoe unless you do it on your own.

Where

Follow the signs to the Fort Wilderness Campground and park in the campground's specially designated parking lot. Take the bus or tram that inevitably leads to Pioneer Hall and disembark. Walk past Pioneer Hall to the marina, which is just a short distance. At present, the only fee is for the fishing charter; there is no admission fee or parking fee.

15

Sport Shrimping
the Indian River Lagoon

Most outdoors people would consider Ralph Stokes a mighty lucky man. Not many wives ever consider exchanging a Mother's Day present for a shrimp net. Yet as Annette Stokes herself explained, "I certainly didn't need a new black dress, but we sure did need a shrimp net!"

That fateful gift exchange occurred shortly after Ralph and Annette moved to Florida from Indiana. They were visiting New Smyrna Beach on Mother's Day when both noticed a couple on a pier dipping the water with long-handled nets. Intrigued, Annette decided she and Ralph should rent a net and try their hand at shrimping.

They deposited their considerable catch in an old cardboard box. Annette was so impressed with their good luck that the next week she swapped her new dress for a shrimp net. That was several decades ago.

Soon, Ralph was shrimping regularly off the pier at a fish camp near the town of Oak Hill. By accident, Ralph had found one of the best places in the entire state to shrimp on his very first outing. "For most people, Oak Hill is just another stop in the road. To a sport shrimper, it's about as close to heaven as you can get," Ralph told me.

And so for years thereafter, Ralph spent almost every weekend from the end of March through the month of June shrimping at Oak Hill. He was sometimes there on a Friday night, sometimes on a Saturday evening, often both. For four consecutive months, the rhythm of Oak Hill's outgoing tides—and the delectable shrimp that accompany them—controlled Ralph Stokes' weekends.

All of which makes Ralph Stokes quite a knowledgeable shrimpologist. Furthermore, he also developed several neat contraptions that should aid shrimpers anywhere in scooping up the sometimes maddeningly elusive critters.

According to Ralph, shrimping anywhere in Florida can be boiled down to three essentials: water temperature, moon phase, and tide conditions.

"From what I've seen, there definitely are fewer shrimp—but they're also a lot larger than they have been, which helps balance things out. Still, even on the best nights, not everyone is going to get their limit, and no one is going to do it every time."

When the shrimp start their annual run varies from year to year. Shrimp may run early or late, depending on how cold the winter. Ralph claimed water temperature is what determines the season. "Shrimp stay buried in the sand in cold water. It takes warmer temperatures to get the runs started. The best shrimping begins when the water temperature hits 66 degrees."

Stokes believed it's never too hot for shrimping, even though his catch usually dropped off markedly in July. He still wasn't sure what slowed the shrimp runs then, although he admitted that on rare occasions he had scooped the legal limit of five gallons as late as August.

With the water at 66 degrees, Ralph concentrated his efforts in the five-day period around the full moon, from two days before to two days after. That's the time he was most likely to scoop his limit on each and every night.

"On a really good run, the shrimp would sometimes cover the whole water like someone opened the gates to let them out," Ralph said with excitement. "Then it's dip, dip, dip all night. You can never catch them all," he sighed, "but it's fun to try."

Just as important as water temperature and moon phase is the state of the tides. Ralph learned it's vital to coordinate all shrimping efforts with the outgoing tides. He said the good shrimping may occur during the first hour of the ebb, but that typically it took an hour or two for sizable numbers of the critters to get moving.

Ralph advised that, "Overall, you have about six good hours for shrimping, though it may not be consistent. It may be good for an hour, then you have to wait another two hours for it to get going again. Also, you need to be on the lookout for the 'shrimp boil' at the point the tide changes, when the shrimp just come up and float by."

Wind direction was sometimes another variable Ralph had to consider. He said the most favorable wind for Oak Hill was one out of the south. "That moves the tide a lot better. If the wind is from the north, you may not even see the tide move. That's when the shrimp run deeper and you can't see them as well. They seem to hug the bottom then and go with the current."

Stokes said he was once told that shrimp tend to travel in almost funnel fashion, that they take one clearly defined path through the river. Overall, that did appear to be true, which means that at any given time they could be bunched up on the dropoff, out in the middle of the channel or moving in the shallows. If

Stokes didn't find the shrimp running along the channel, edge after the first two hours, he went looking for them.

Figuring where to shrimp at Oak Hill during the height of the run is not difficult even for first-timers. The boats sometimes are so thick you can almost walk across them.

Most boats anchor at the edge of the channel, in line with the markers. Stokes suggested, "Try to get right on the dropoff. I move along the edge until it starts dropping—that's where I like to anchor. That will put you in about five to six feet of water. As you'll see, all the boats line up on the east side of the channel."

To find the dropoff, Stokes used only his shrimp pole to chart the water level. A depth finder, of course, would work even better.

Shrimping from a boat requires two anchors in order to position the boat perpendicular to the current. Stokes recommended looking for a sandbar and anchoring behind that, since the shallow bottom requires the shrimp to come closer to the surface for easier pickings.

Being an especially serious shrimper—Ralph bought a boat expressly so he could shrimp on the water instead of being confined to a pier—Stokes spent considerable time experimenting with homemade lighting devices for attracting shrimp.

For surface light, he'd run two 50-watt bulbs screwed into regular electrical cords that floated in small styrofoam bases. The electrical cords were not waterproofed or shielded in any way. Either a battery or generator supplied his power. Stokes tried larger bulbs but felt the 50-watt is the size shrimp prefer; 100-watt bulbs definitely are too bright.

Stokes said you can keep reusing the same cords (and bulbs) as long as you put the bulb in the water before turning on the power. That way the bulb won't explode when it comes in contact with the cooler water. The bulb doesn't even need to be sealed if it's rinsed with fresh water right after shrimping. Otherwise, he suggested using silicone sealant to keep water from reaching the socket.

Ralph believed that, besides floating lights on top of the water to attract shrimp, it helped to put another light on the bottom because that sends to the surface the deeper-running shrimp that otherwise would be lost. To draw shrimp up from the bottom, Stokes anchored a regular lightbulb on a 125-foot cord.

It's a strange-looking device, like something that would hang from the ceiling of some derelict's shack. But I saw first-hand shrimping with Ralph that it worked.

To fire up his lights, Stokes used a generator, which he pointed out was "easy to transport and not as heavy as a battery. A generator is definitely an expensive purchase, but in the long run it may be a lot better."

As far as the generator noise, it's hardly a distraction, especially when the shrimp are running well. On a full tank, a generator can last for six hours, roughly the full length of a run, but Stokes always took a little extra gas just to be safe.

"I started with Coleman lanterns," Stokes recalled. "Salt water is rough on lanterns. Plus, even if you put shields on them, they throw back an awful lot of glare off the water. Floating lightbulbs are a lot easier on the eyes. It's more like looking at a fluorescent light."

Ralph admitted that perhaps the worst drawback about shrimping was that it's often an all-night activity. After staying awake all night and possibly consuming a few brews, driving home was not the healthiest thing to do. Stokes avoided this on his five-day, full moon expeditions by having another family member bring over a pop-up camper.

"You can be awfully tired when you get done," Stokes said. "It's nice not to go far to lie down. We can spend the next day fishing or at the beach, and then get ready for the next night."

On those nights when, despite all the favorable conditions, the shrimping still is slow, Stokes sometimes threw out a line for trout. He's caught as many as nine trout between shrimp dips. "Trout do seem to be attracted to the lights," Stokes observed.

Beginning shrimpers, Stokes said, should talk extensively to their local fish camp operators for advice. "They usually give straight answers. They'll pretty well tell you whether the shrimp are running or not and how many people are catching." But Stokes also had a word of advice for beginning shrimpers, especially at Oak Hill: "It seems everyone gets the fever when they first start shrimping. Eating such fresh shrimp—that's what attracts everyone."

With his boat and generator, Stokes had quite a lot invested in his hobby. Did he ever expect to come out ahead? "Of course not. I'd do better if I simply went to the store to buy them, but I wouldn't have the pleasure of catching my own. After all, this is a sport."

Who

It's always bad to lose track of people, and I haven't been able to track down Ralph or Annette for the past few years. I'm not certain they're in Orlando, or still with us. It makes no difference. Ralph's knowledge, like life itself, is as timeless as the tides.

To find out how the shrimp are running at Oak Hill (located 15 miles north of Titusville on US 1 in East Central Florida), call Kelly's Bait and Stuff at 904/345-0990, 123 N. US 1, Oak Hill. They have the knowledge and the shrimp nets, and directions on where to launch.

Sport shrimping is popular all along the East Coast of Florida during the spring months after the water warms into the upper 60s. To find where people are shrimping, inquire at any coastal tackle shop. If shrimp are running anywhere in the vicinity, you can be sure the store will have all the fixin's for netting them. Live shrimp, after all, are one of the best baits for most inshore saltwater species, and many anglers prefer to catch their own.

Quite a few of the bridges spanning the Intracoastal Waterway bordering the Atlantic Coast have catwalks that were intended for anglers, but sport shrimpers claim them as their own at night during the shrimping season. The fishing pier at Titusville that juts out into the Indian River off State Road 402 is more the domain of sport shrimpers than anglers during the annual spring/summer nighttime run. The bridge walkways at Sebastian Inlet State Park at Melbourne Beach on A1A can also be quite good.

16

Cave Diving:
the Lure of the Dark

The current raging out the cave's narrow mouth is too strong to swim against. Millions of gallons of water gush from the entrance daily, so we use hands, feet, elbows—every means available—to crawl against the powerful flood.

Finally we push our way inside the limestone cave system that will be our home for the next forty-five minutes. In the big cavern the current slacks off so much it almost seems peaceful and still, like we've closed the door on a windstorm.

This is only the start of our dive but already I am wondering about the problems of getting out. We'd probably have to wedge our bodies against the walls and gradually inch upward to keep from being catapulted out of the cave mouth. It might seem silly to be anticipating the end of our dive at the very beginning, but preplanning is critical in every phase of cave diving. Divers who don't, die.

The cave is darker than any night. Each of us carries three flashlights, one that is on and two for emergency backups. We each carry a spare regulator mouthpiece in case the other runs into trouble. All our life-support equipment is duplicated so malfunctions won't turn into deadly situations. Such redundancy not only provides an extra safety margin but also inspires confidence to face this totally alien environment.

Conquering a realm as hostile as anything faced by space astronauts is one thing that lures us into these caves. That, and knowing we're going where few people have ever gone before, or are ever likely to go, is a powerful motivation. Cave divers are among the last of the world's true explorers, and since it is genuine exploration, it is also dangerous. That, too, is a seductive part of cave diving.

Looking around the chamber, I notice it is several stories tall. However, we are not confined to narrow walkways or limited in any manner as people are in air-filled caves. Rather, we can swim to any level and stay as long as we like while examining the tombstone-gray walls. But it is not our purpose to remain in just this one spot. This underground cave system is an extensive one, mapped as far back as 3,400 feet. We grip the temporary safety line left by divers who have been before us and swim farther underground.

I feel wonderfully alive and my every sense is especially alert, almost magnified, as we see how far we can penetrate the system. The cave may lack fish life or spectacular stalagmites or stalactites that can form only in the air, yet every underwater formation is special to us. We are among the handful of humans ever to see them since the beginning of time.

We continually monitor our equipment, particularly our air supply. The golden rule of cave diving is the rule of thirds: consume only one-third of your tank going in, use another one-third on the way out, and keep one-third in reserve in case something goes wrong. Divers who abuse this dictate are the ones usually taken out in body bags. I'm mindful this supposedly has happened more than once here, in this place called the Devil's Ear.

Just as important as monitoring our air consumption is keeping tight emotional control. If my light goes out, or my regulator stops working, or somehow my buddy runs out of air, I must act calmly and quickly and banish any sense of panic. Panic is a cave diver's worst enemy, his most deadly. When a diver panics, he makes mistakes. Caves are unforgiving of sloppy error.

Our lights penetrating the gloom leave an obvious trail, like searchlights cutting

We approach a narrowing in the walls where the floor and ceiling almost touch.

through the sky. The wide beams splash on the walls to reveal stones that are anything but uniform in this passageway. It looks like we are swimming through the middle of a huge pile of giant boulders. Of course, this limestone rock is a solid mass and not made up of individual stones, a common characteristic of water-filled tunnels throughout the state. That's why underwater cave-ins are rare.

It's funny how to some divers caves seem to have split personalities, according to how you're viewing them—either on the way in or coming out. Swimming in, they are about as unfriendly a place as can be imagined. They are a gaping hole in the earth's floor filled with a blackness darker than any cloudy night. The lights illuminate only small patches of the interior. The time of day is irrelevant; diving in a cave is always a night dive.

On the other hand, when you're swimming back into the friendly sunlight and the relaxing blue water in the outside basin——then a cave's disposition is totally different. Gone are the imagined threats or any sense of impending danger. Although at this point you may be shivering inside your wet suit, coming out is often a warm sense of celebration, especially among those who've never dived underground before. I've heard some divers compare leaving a cave to going home for Thanksgiving.

As we move forward, I flash pictures in many places, and it is always a challenge to keep my subject in the viewfinder whenever we encounter even the mildest current. It's difficult to keep a spotter beam on my buddy when he poses near a rock formation. I have to wrap my leg around the guide rope to stay stationary. It's easier and safer than performing a highwire balancing act; fall off, and I'll go flying backwards instead of straight down.

We approach a narrowing in the walls where the floor and ceiling almost touch. The disappearing safety line shows that other divers have gone beyond this point. To proceed, we must remove our tanks and push them ahead of us through the restriction. I look at my buddy, who shakes his head and signals he wishes to go no farther. This is his limit and I must respect his wishes. To go ahead, alone, would be courting suicide. We turn back.

If our movement forward has been a struggle, our return alternates between floating in a gentle breeze and being shoved rudely by the wind. The amount of push varies according to the narrowness of the passage. The guide rope keeps us from getting tossed forward by the current whenever the cave walls are closer together.

Many caves are devoid of life, but not too far from the entrance, I spot an eel swimming near the bottom. Close to the bottom and hugging the wall, it moves effortlessly in whatever direction it desires. Larger, clumsier, and less streamlined, I cannot keep up with it but do manage to fire off at least one shot before the eel disappears into the darkness.

The ascent from the cave will be a rapid one because of the strong current. My particular problem is to exit without demolishing my camera equipment against the stone wall. I hold the camera and strobe just above my head, start exhaling, and ride the current out of the cave. We're spit out of the ground and into a clear stream formed by the several nearby springs.

Back on the surface, I shiver as we talk animatedly of the sights we've seen. The fast-flowing 72-degree water that has sapped my strength in spite of my thick wet suit. But I shiver also from the excitement of once again swimming on the razor edge and coming out on top. As much as I am lured to them, caves scare the hell out of me.

So why do I keep going back? The same reason some people ride roller coasters or jump out of airplanes. It's for the adrenalin spike.

Except for the daily commute to work and the chance of getting mugged, the possibility of encountering real danger is almost absent from our lives. So some people, like cave divers, create artificially dangerous situations in order to experience that fantastic adrenaline rush that comes only from putting your life on the line and walking away a winner. Sky diving and auto racing are other popular examples of technologically-generated thrills that have no other purpose except to test the limits of a person and his equipment.

Unless you challenge a grizzly with a knife or venture into the Everglades without bug repellent, there aren't many real risks left in the outdoors—except cave diving.

What

Anyone who has basic certification and feels comfortable under water should earn cavern certification before coming on a dive vacation to Florida. Cavern certification qualifies a diver to penetrate inside a cavern or tunnel just short of the point where they lose sight of daylight.

Only cave diving certification qualifies a person to safely penetrate the inside of a cave. Cave diving is taught at two levels, basic and advanced. Many casual cave divers do not go beyond the first course. In Florida, it's not difficult to take cavern and basic cave in three or four days. It's even possible to obtain cavern, basic, and advanced cave dive training during a single week of intensive instruction.

The following agencies offer cavern and full cave training. Contact them for course specifics.

**American Nitrox
Divers International (ANDI)**
74 Woodcleft Ave.
Freeport, NY 11520
800/229-ANDI
516/546-2626
Developing a new cave/wreck penetration course.

**International Association
of Nitrox and Technical Divers
(IANTD)**
9628 NE Second Ave., Suite D
Miami Shores, FL 33138-2767
305/751-48731; fax: 305/751-3958
Overhead Environment course taught in cavern or wreck environment following cavern guidelines.

**National Association
for Cave Diving (NACD)**
P.O. Box 14492
Gainesville, FL 32604
904/877-43851; fax 904/656-1355.
Cavern through Full Cave.

**National Association
of Underwater Instructors**
P.O. Box 14650
Montclair, CA 91763
714/621-5801; fax: 714/621-6405
Will issue cavern certification if NAUI instructor is cross-certified as NSS-CDS or NACD instructor.

**National Speleological
Association-Cave Diving Section**
P.O. Box 950
Branford, FL 32008-09501
813/528-4202
Cavern through Full Cave.

PADI
1251 E. Dyer Rd., #100
Santa Ana, CA 92705
714/540-7234; fax: 714/540-2609
Offers a cavern specialty course; directs cave students to NACD or NSS-CDS.

Scuba Schools International
2619 Canton Court
Ft. Collins, CO 8525-44981
303/482-6157; fax: 303/482-0883;
Will issue cavern certification if SSI instructor is cross-certified as NSS-CDS or NACD instructor.

YMCA National Scuba Program
6083A Oakbrook Pkwy.
Norcross, GA 30093
404/662-5172; fax: 404/242-9059.

**Technical Divers International
(TDI)**
207/442-8391
European branch offers cavern and cave certification overseas only; in United States, recognizes NACD /NSS-CDS certification.

Anytime of year. However, during the rainy season some springs are flooded by nearby rivers, and although the caves will always be clear, the entrance to them could be obscured by dark water. That's more of an aesthetic matter than a training problem.

Where

Following are some of the most popular cave dives in Florida. The entrance to all of them is regulated to ensure that only certified cave divers have entry.

Blue Spring State Park: Near Orange City in Central Florida. This spring has claimed quite a few lives because divers insist on going past the first major restriction, where the strong current pins them against the ceiling, making escape impossible. Not a place to be messed with. Camping available. State operated: 904/775-3663.

Ginnie Springs Resort: Located near the town of High Springs, this site has several excellent caves and caverns with some of the clearest water in the state. Camping available. Commercially operated: 800/874-8571; 904/454-2202.

Madison Blue Springs: Located near the town of Madison, this has a maze of stone passageways. The spring run feeds into the Withlacoochee River. Commercially run: 904/971-2880.

Hal Watts' 40 Fathom Grotto: This is one of the deepest springs, reaching 240 feet (40 fathoms). Located near Ocala, this spring is used for advanced technical dive instruction. Commercially operated: 904/368-7974.

Little River Springs: Located near Branford, an excellent cave dive. No one on site. For information, direction, and air fills, call the Steamboat Dive Inn (904/935-2283) or the Branford Dive Center (904/935-1141).

Morrison Springs: Near the town of Ponce de Leon in the extreme western Panhandle, offering good cavern and cave diving. Commercially operated: 904/836-4223.

Paradise Springs: Near Ocala, this is a limited but very interesting cave dive because of all the fossils, including the vertebrae of a whale. Commercially operated: 904/368-5746.

Peacock Springs State Recreation Area: Located north of Mayo, this is serious cave diving territory with more than 28,000 feet of connecting passageways. State operated: 904/497-2511.

Vortex Blue Spring: Near the town of Ponce de Leon in the western part of the Panhandle off I-10. Both cave and cavern diving. Camping and a diver's lodge. Commercially operated: 800/342-0640; 904/836-4979.

17

Canoeing
the Everglades

The temperature this night is in the low 30s, something that rarely happens as far south as the Everglades. My sleeping bag is better suited for summer, but I am more than toasty warm. For emergencies, I'd packed an aluminum space blanket which I've stuffed inside the bag. The space blanket certainly works well, but at what a price!

Every time I turn, it crinkles. I sound like logs crackling on a fire. After a half hour, I am sweating like it is the hottest day of summer. My sleeping bag-turned-sauna makes me so rank I begin to smell myself. Well, the morning's smokey fire should help cover up the odor.

Shortly after midnight, as I continue to snap, crackle, and pop every time I adjust my sleeping position, I hear dragging/slithering sounds next to my tent. I don't dare venture out for a look since there's only one thing this can be: an alligator.

Canoeing the ninety-eight-mile-long stretch of Florida Everglades known as the Wilderness Waterway, my paddlemate and I knew we would be sharing the creeks and bays with sharks and alligators, but actually having a gator crawl between our two tents . . . well, that is more than even we bargained for.

The things I think about at such times! Such as, how keen is the smelling apparatus of alligators? And don't gators store their food under water for several days to age it before dining? Thanks to the space blanket, I must smell like I've been dead for several days. My scent of Eau de Corpse could be like cat nip to it.

I keep my knife handy just in case I have to exit through the side of my tent. Of course, I will escape successfully only if the gator is very clumsy and very slow at clawing through my tent's thin fabric. I suspect strongly it can move faster than I ever will.

Breathing is a luxury I deny myself as I listen intently for more gator sounds. The animal is soon even with my head, which puts it precisely between my companion's tent and mine. I have an uncharitable thought about which direction the gator should go. Fortunately for both of us, the gator keeps sliding forward. Finally I hear it slip into the water. I breathe again, easily.

I'm curious, but I don't bother to unzip my tent to note the size of the gator's tracks until shortly after dawn: the mosquitoes keep me prisoner inside my tent from twilight to sunrise.

Happily, that's the last gator we see until our final evening's paddle when at twilight our canoe suddenly hits the back of one resting just below the water. This causes quite a lot of activity under the surface—and a bit of a commotion inside our canoe, too.

One thing about this adventure, we can never predict what will happen next. That, of course, is the beauty and challenge of our week-long canoe trip.

The Wilderness Waterway skirts the western edge of the 1.4-million-acre Everglades National Park. We launched outside the Park at Turner River so we could explore a narrow, eight-mile stretch not open to larger boats. It's our intent to deviate from the Waterway at many points to penetrate into less visited creeks and rivers, since the official route was designed for powerboats to pass through. We will wander south for almost a hundred miles until we reach the old fishing town of Flamingo at the southern end of the Everglades. There, we'll be picked up and brought back to my vehicle waiting outside the park.

It will take us eight or nine days to travel the length of the waterway; anyone in a powerboat can do it in only eight or nine hours.

The people at The Everglades Outpost in Everglades City prove to be invaluable in helping plot our off-trail side trips through the Turner River and the particularly awesome stretch known as the Nightmare. They also advise us to pay careful attention to the scenery: "Ninety percent of the people who go down the Wilderness Waterway find it repetitive because they don't notice the differences in habitat. There are many subtle changes, almost inch by inch. It's not like the Grand Canyon when you know you're suddenly there."

It is a cloudy January morning when paddlemate Bill Belleville and I launch our canoe onto the Turner River. Rain seems almost certain, so foul weather gear is at hand.

The canoe is so packed it looks like a supply barge, which in a sense it is. As a precaution against a delay, we carry enough provisions for nine days even though we plan to be on the water only eight. But the real problem is the amount of fresh water we must pack aboard. We follow the recommendation that we carry at least a gallon of water per person per day, but each gallon weighs a hefty eight pounds. Our twenty gallons of water equal the weight of a third passenger, which makes our canoe sit low in the water.

We have our food, clothing, cameras, and other dry goods packed in five-gallon white plastic paint cans. They all look alike so we labeled the lids with Magic Marker.

I sit in the bow with my camera can sandwiched between my legs, a location it will retain throughout the journey so the cameras will always be within easy reach. Should we swamp, these cans theoretically will stay afloat. The canoe should too, for that matter.

Although we will not face true rapids, we will encounter Florida's version of whitewater: tall whitecapped waves in the wide shallow bays we must cross. It is the wind, more than anything, that determines how we will fare, whether we will be able to keep to schedule, become delayed, or get swamped. Regardless of where we wander during the day, we must rejoin the Wilderness trail each night so we will have a dry place to land. Because the Everglades is made up primarily of water and almost no land, we must reach a specific, preplanned campsite at the day's end or spend the night sleeping in our canoe—not a pleasant prospect with our craft loaded with water jugs, tents, sleeping bags, and other gear.

Waterway campsites are scarce (only thirty-two in all), so every canoe party must register in advance with the Ranger Station and file an itinerary to ensure the campsites don't become overcrowded.

Most of the land campsites tend to be small, located atop old shell mounds created by Indian tribes long extinct. The land camps are supplemented by chickees, wooden platforms built over the water with the added convenience of a roof. Chickees are named after the dwellings used by the Seminoles, the Indians who currently live in the Glades.

Park personnel do not patrol the campsites to make sure everyone is on schedule. They start searching only when someone is overdue. If severe winds prevent canoes from crossing any of the wide shallow bays, campsites sometimes get heavily overpopulated as canoes backlog. Before setting out we heard several stories about stranded canoeists who had to sleep on the roofs of crowded chickees. However, there is no way people can stack themselves on top of one another on the land sites. Overcrowding at such locations definitely means sleeping in the canoe, unless we happen to have claimed the place first.

Now, as we paddle to our first site, we continually scrutinize the maps and compass readings to avoid a wrong turn. It's one thing to run up and down the Waterway with a powerboat and miss the proper channel, quite another when you're in a canoe. We need to be right every time.

The Turner River at first is nothing but a narrow stream bordered by tall grass. I dub one section Vulture Valley because of the large number of the carrion eaters that accompany us for a short way. They fly ahead, wait for us to catch up, then move in front of us again. If I believed in omens, this ugly escort would have me paddling back to the highway and abandoning ship. Instead, it's almost morbidly fascinating to get this close glimpse of vulture culture.

We leave the vultures behind where the river begins to tunnel through a winding canopy of big mangroves. Mangroves and mosquitoes often go together, but fortunately not today. From the Turner, we go into Chokoloskee Bay, where we pick up our first official channel marker.

Nearing a place called Cross Bay, we hear what at first sounds like an approaching sheet of rain. It is overcast, but the clouds seem too high for a downpour. As we draw level with the mouth of Cross Bay, I see one of the strangest sights I've ever witnessed in the outdoors. Scores of ducks—perhaps a hundred or more but difficult to tell because they are so far away—are flapping their wings on the water, apparently corralling a school of baitfish. As the circle tightens, the birds begin to feed in a frenzy.

The slap of duck wings on the water sounds like a cascade of distant shotgun shells. Then the ducks explode off the water, circle over the bay, and disappear south. I am speechless. I knew dolphin and white pelicans performed such intelligent maneuvers, but ducks?

We paddle leisurely until we near our campsite on the Lopez River. The tide is against us, and it's all we can do to shove the canoe forward with our paddles. For forty-five minutes we dig fast and deep, exhausting ourselves by the time we reach camp. We're going to hurt tomorrow.

A couple from Michigan is already at the site. They, too, saw the ducks herding the fish, so the phenomenon wasn't something we imagined.

At twilight, the sky overhead faintly begins to buzz like a bee swarm. The mosquitoes who have been so kind to us during the day are now announcing their presence. A night under the stars in the Glades, out in the open, is reputed to be one of the most hellish things a person can experience. It's been compared to being mauled by swarm after swarm of miniature vampire bats. The mosquitoes are what keep savvy canoeists off the Waterway except for the coolest, driest months of winter. It's why we've chosen January to make this journey.

The mosquitoes send Bill and me to our separate tents, where we'll stay prisoners until dawn. In January, it's dark for almost twelve hours; the amazing thing is I sleep through most of that first night.

The second day is foggy with a strong wind against us from the south. We'd brought a makeshift sail to power the boat if the wind ever cooperated, but it doesn't this day or any other day. Perhaps that's just as well since we're still not certain how well we can steer a loaded canoe with only a paddle. Most sailing craft have a centerboard to help guide and control it.

Later that morning, we see dolphin in two widely separated places. I keep hoping they will race beside our bow as they do with powerboats, but they do not. We must be too slow to offer any challenge.

Our second camp is at a place called Watson's, a forty-acre shell mound where a small sugar plantation existed in the early 1900s. The site is named after Ed Watson, one of the Everglade's most notorious residents. Watson reputedly shot outlaw Belle Starr in the back while in Texas. After he moved to Florida, he quickly gained a fearsome reputation for killing anyone who crossed him. Residents of the town of Chokoloskee on the edge of the Glades were so afraid of him that one day, when Watson came to town, practically almost all the townspeople assembled to shoot him full of bullet holes. It wasn't until Peter Matthiessen's best-selling novel *Killing Mr. Watson* came out in the 1980s that Ed Watson became world famous.

Watson's old plantation site, very spacious and high and dry, is excellent for camping. Concrete pillars mark the location of the old buildings. An old syrup kettle and steam boiler remain in relatively fair condition. The river bottom at Watson's slopes off gently, which makes it possible to bathe in the cold river water. I do not know it, but this is my first and last bath of the trip.

As we set up camp, a kayak and a canoe pull into the Watson site. These are the first people we've seen all day. The threesome are from the Midwest, and they have come to the Glades to observe birds.

There may be plenty of camping space, but Bill and I strongly resent their presence because they turn out to be a bunch of know-it-alls, though it's quite obvious they have no idea what they're doing. The best example of their stupidity occurs when Bill and I make a smoky campfire. They become upset with us, claiming that the smoke will attract mosquitoes. Any moron who's camped before should know that smoke is a time-honored deterrent against insects. Furthermore, it's apparent they know nothing about Florida, since the first white inhabitants in the Glades used to fire up smudge pots almost every night for protection against mosquitoes.

The trio's dinner turns out to be several ladyfish, a hard-fighting species that is regarded as an inedible trash fish. In provisioning, they assumed they would be able to eat fresh fish at the end of every day, so their dinner is ladyfish or nothing. As Bill and I eat beef stroganoff near our smokepot fire, we make no comment when they later start complaining about the "disgusting taste" of ladyfish. They end up discarding most of their meal. Well, what can you say to people who have provisioned themselves with plastic jugs prominently labeled "Buffalo Bob's Camp Water?" Perhaps Bill and I are starved for amusement, or maybe it's Watson's ghost working on us, but we dub the bird-watching trio "The Tweeters" and do our best to politely avoid them. Unfortunately, it turns out we will be crossing paths constantly the next few days.

As they tried to swallow their ladyfish, Bill and I thoroughly enjoyed our rehydrated meal. All of our dinners will consist mainly of dehydrated foods. A typical day's menu starts with a breakfast of hot chocolate, oatmeal, and peanut butter and jelly. Lunch while underway in the canoe comes from a can, something like a mixed fruit or pudding—anything wet and loaded with sugar and carbohydrates to keep us moving. Dinner is our most elaborate meal, consisting of soup and a pouch of something like lasagna, beef stew or spaghetti. Even with all the starches, we will lose weight thanks to the nonstop activity. On this second night, following a day when the temperatures have been in the 80s, I fantasize about the thing I miss most: ice.

The third day finds us on Alligator Creek, a narrow corridor almost as striking as the mangrove tunnel on the Turner River. As we paddle to the end of the creek, we meet three incoming dolphin. They roll playfully on the surface until they notice us. Then they rocket past us, generating a canoe-rocking wake.

Our third camp site is called Lostman's Five. Appropriately, we've been warned to precisely follow the marked channel here and not take any shortcuts to avoid becoming the Lostman's Two. We've been advised that canoeists who've left the trail here have been disoriented for days in the maze of mangroves. Good advice, and we should have remembered it better the following day.

We have the Lostman's camp to ourselves. The Tweeters are camped on a chickee several miles back. A good thing since this is a very small place. The soft, mucky ground is also the most unstable place I've ever camped: the globe of the lantern atop the wooden picnic table rattles when I stomp next to a table leg.

At 12:20 AM, I am awakened by a noise near our canoe tied to the Lostman's dock. It is a strange sound: a huge splash followed by a loud gulp, just the thing that would make sailors believe in sea monsters large enough to swallow whole ships.

Bill hears the noise, too, and we both venture out to check the canoe in case the rising tide has trapped it under the dock. The canoe is where it should be, tied alongside the tiny pier. The moon is bright and full, yet we see nothing that might have made the noise. Bill decides to fish but the mosquitoes soon drive him inside his tent. I puzzle over the noise . . . what could it have been? . . . then I fall back to sleep.

Day four starts with pink-tinted clouds on the horizon, looking like an instant replay of last night's beautiful twilight. I should have remembered the old sailor's warning: "Red sky at night, sailor's delight; red sky in morning, sailor take warning."

As soon as we shove off, the wind picks up. It blows from behind us with such strength that retreating back to Lostman's Camp is not an option. What's worse, today it is mandatory we cross one of those wide, shallow bays that can become so dangerous in just the kind of high winds we're experiencing. As we approach Lostman's Bay, we see that the surface resembles a mini-mountain range: white caps and rollers between three and four feet high will make this a perilous crossing because of our low canoe. On the Wilderness Waterway, it's in the bays in exactly these conditions that canoes are most likely to capsize.

The gusts are so strong and the waves so high we are committed once we enter the bay. To try and turn the canoe broadside in order to retreat definitely would swamp us.

Ironically, for the first time the wind and waves are at our back, but I would rather plow into them. Propelled from behind, it's much more difficult to keep the canoe on track, pointed where we need to go.

A particularly big wave crashes into us, pouring several gallons of water into the boat. This one wave could spoil the trip for us. Assuming that some things float—the sleeping bags and food stored in the plastic buckets should, but the heavy tents and water jugs certainly will not—the wind and waves will scatter our belongings beyond recovery. We've already discussed what to do if our canoe rolls over or swamps: stay with the boat, keeping a firm grip on the frame as well as our paddles. There's no walking out of this place.

As it turns out, we experience one of those lucky days when we should have played the lottery. Although waves threaten to swamp us many, many more times, they do not. We make it across Lostman's Bay right side up.

After Lostman's, we're confronted with another bay where the waves appear even worse. We decide not to press lady luck but to skirt the trough of rough water. We sneakily paddle behind several mangrove islands, intending to use them as buffers against the waves.

Well, we were warned not to stray from the course here, and we should have listened. Our shortcut soon has us completely lost. The mangroves, instead of fringing the bay as we thought they would, lead us far away from it. And, wouldn't you know it, we end up in yet another bay. Our compass says we should cut directly across, which will put us broadside to the wind and waves and greatly increase our chance of getting swamped.

Rather than take the risk, we let the wind push us the wrong way, intending to reach the far end of this strange bay and then hug the shoreline on the lee side where conditions are slightly calmer. We have absolutely no idea where we are, much less the name of this new bay. We know we should travel southeast in the direction of our next site, called Willy Willy. Fitting name; these high winds are giving me a good case of the willies.

For the next hour, we carefully inch forward against the four-foot waves topped with white caps and streamers of foam. To be certain that we are following the proper route, we each consult our compass continually, never taking a pause as we paddle through the chop and spray. We head directly southeast, since it's the only way we know to go.

To our incredibly good fortune, we see a Waterway marker in the distance,

Marker No. 47, which puts us back on track. The last marker we saw was No. 57, so we were off course (lost is a more accurate term) for quite a few miles.

Marker 47 takes us to a canal that deposits us on yet another wind-whipped bay. Fortunately, we have an alternate route, up a small side creek that should take us to the campsite by a back route. To find the creek, we have to cut diagonally across one corner section of this bay where the wind will come from the right. Definitely not the best approach for keeping water out of the boat, but what the hell. It's the only way open to us, and we're close to exhaustion.

We remain exceedingly lucky: we cross the bay upright and find a creek—which we decide to call Life Saving Creek—directly in front of us. Of course, we're not precisely sure this is the creek that will take us to Willy Willy, but finally we're out of the wind. At least we can sleep in the canoe here if we have to.

Life Saving Creek puts us at Willy Willy at 3 PM We should have been here hours before since the paddle was a short one, only eight and a half miles. But who's complaining? We're just happy to be here at all.

Heavy rains come at 3:45 PM. The tents are up by then. The Super Bowl starts at 4. My radio picks up mostly static. The Tweeters, who took the long way around, arrive around 5, after spending more than an hour in the chilling rain.

The temperature begins dropping quickly: the single radio station I can pick up warns that it will drop into the low 30s in the Glades before morning. It is this night that the gator crawls between our tents.

In the morning, after examining the sizable tracks of the departed gator, we joke about how the night was one long nightmare. As if last night's visitor wasn't enough, today we must confront a real Nightmare, the name of the channel off the main Waterway that clearly deserves its fearsome name. Everyone has warned us about the perils of the Nightmare. In this channel, the mangrove trees are supposed to be unusually tall and are said to form a thick canopy over the narrow creek. The trees are said to form a gigantic system of twisted roots that are reminiscent of nightmarish horror movies. After all the wind-whipped bays, I consider this a nice change in scenery.

However, the creek is notorious for leaving people stranded high and dry at low tide when the water flows completely out. The mud bottom is too deep for anyone to walk a canoe through; we were told we'd sink up to our waists. Once stranded, the only thing to do is sit in the boat and wait for the tide to reappear. And, as in Transylvania, hope to get out before nightfall when the blood suckers show up.

To avoid experiencing a full-blown Nightmare, we've plotted the tide beforehand. We should arrive at the entrance on a rising tide. We do, and the paddle through the forest of mangroves is uneventful. Not even one of the dreaded stinging caterpillars falls on our head. Somehow, we don't mind the lack of excitement.

Eventually, we leave the Nightmare behind us and rejoin the main Waterway. At last, we can truly relax and enjoy the subtle beauty of the Glades. We paddle through familiar-looking natural regions where orchidlike bromeliads hang from the trees, porpoises flash under our canoe, and fish hawks fly above us so closely their wings "whoosh" like helicopter rotors.

People may regularly visit the Everglades, but parts of it obviously remain as wild as they've always been.

Bill trails a fishing line as we paddle. Angling opportunities throughout the trip are a real mixed bag. We first encountered stretches of freshwater creeks and then moved into salt water. Big largemouth bass are rumored to exist in several places we visit, but the cold front virtually kills all fishing activity. Saltwater fishing for trout and redfish is also dead. Embarrassing to admit, our only fish of the entire trip is a mullet that jumps into the canoe after it collides with my paddle. Bill later smokes the mullet on a grill, and it makes a wonderful snack.

As we proceed steadily to the south, it turns out that neither alligators or mosquitoes are our most serious wildlife problem. Rather, it is the comic-looking raccoon. Like us, raccoons require fresh water to survive, but fresh water is extremely scarce once the Waterway turns salty.

Raccoons visit our camp after dark in several campsites, hoping to raid our precious water supply. Bill and I either sleep with the water jugs in our tents or hang them from trees to keep the coons from reaching them. There is no opportunity for reprovisioning anywhere, not even from a jug of "Buffalo Bob's Camp Water."

Our final contact with the Everglades wilderness turns out to be quite memorable, thanks to yet another alligator. It happens just a few miles from the old fishing town of Flamingo, our final destination. The approach is via a long canal—more of a ditch really—and we reach it at twilight. We hug the right bank since powerboats charge by us without regard for their wake or our safety. The wakes first broadside us, then hit us again as they roll off the narrow canal sides. It's like being back in one of the treacherous bays.

We never see the gator. Instead, we paddle right onto the animal's back as it floats just below the surface. The noise of the collision is pronounced. The surprised gator flips its powerful tail, shaking our canoe from side to side. Then it dives.

We realize instantly what's happened. We sit still in case the gator resurfaces. It's hardly necessary, but we keep our paddles poised in case it tries to imitate the crocodile in Peter Pan and board us. But we see no more of it.

This second gator encounter adds incredible strength to our strokes. The canoe fairly zips over the surface.

When we arrive at Flamingo, we have the option of pitching our tent or taking a motel room. The choice is not difficult. I have needed a shower so badly and for so long that I have to seal my paddling clothes in an airtight garbage bag for the drive home.

Who

See Appendix C for canoe liveries and outfitters who serve this region. If you have your own canoe or sea kayak, as we did, you can make arrangements to be picked up at Flamingo.

What

Information on the Waterway and the backcountry campsites is available from:
Everglades National Park
P.O. Box 279
Homestead, FL 33030
305/242-7700

The visitors center carries "A Guide to the Wilderness Waterway," a sixty-four-page description of the trail by William Truesdell, which contains invaluable information. Study it thoroughly before undertaking this trip.

For shorter excursions, ask about the five designated canoe trails (three to twelve miles each) that are not part of the Wilderness Waterway but are still within Park boundaries. (There's also more about these in the following chapter.)

Although the Wilderness Waterway is marked, maps and compass are absolute necessities. NOAA charts needed include Lostman's River to Wiggins Pass (11430); Shark River to Lostman's River (11432); Everglades National Park: Whitewater Bay (11433).

Overnight camping along the Waterway is free, but sites can be reserved only 24 hours ahead of your departure (at the Homestead or Everglades City Ranger Station). That helps park officials have an accurate count of who is on the Waterway so that the limited sites don't end up with more people than they can hold.

Because winter cold fronts frequently plow as far south as the Everglades, it helps to have a radio to pick up the latest weather forecasts.

When

The cooler drier period from late October to early March is best; afternoon thunderstorms and ravenous saltwater mosquitoes make an extended canoe trip unbearable the rest of the year. Even in the cooler months, mosquito repellent is mandatory, and plan on spending the night inside your tent between twilight and sunrise. Otherwise, you could become one big welt.

18

Other Outings
in the Everglades

Everglades National Park is one of the nation's largest national parks, second only to Yellowstone. Although the Wilderness Waterway is the most challenging of all the Everglades' outdoor activities, you'll find plenty of other paddling on shorter canoe trails, hiking, biking, nature watching, and houseboating.

All of the following activities take place along the park's main road that leads to Flamingo, or leave from Flamingo itself. You could easily spend a week and still not do everything the park has to offer.

HIKING

Most trails are fairly short, and you could walk all of them over the course of a few days. Walking, perhaps even more than canoeing, is the best way to view the diverse ecosystem that makes up the Everglades. The hikes are listed in the order that you would encounter them after leaving the visitors center.

Incidentally, it's possible to hike the forty-mile paved road from the park entrance to Flamingo, but do it in cool weather. Summer, in the open sun with virtually no shade, would be a killer.

Anhinga Trail: Less than a half mile, it will take you about thirty minutes for a round trip. This trail winds through a saw-grass marsh with alligators, turtles, anhingas, herons, and egrets. This is a terrific place to go gator spotlighting at night (see Chapter 23).

Gumbo-Limbo Trail: Another short half-mile walk that also requires thirty minutes for a round-trip. Before Hurricane Andrew in 1992, this trail meandered through a thick, shaded hammock of royal palms, gumbo-limbo trees, lush ferns, and orchids. Much of the vegetation was destroyed but new growth is appearing.

Pineland Trail: Less than a half mile, this takes thirty minutes round-trip. As the name implies, the trail enters an area full of pine trees, many of which still show the devastating effects of 1992's Hurricane Andrew. Evidence of the storm's impact will probably remain for decades. The pitted limestone bedrock under all of southern Florida is quite obvious on this trail.

Pahayokee Overlook Trail: Less than a quarter mile, a round-trip on this boardwalk trail takes from fifteen to thirty minutes. The boardwalk ends at an observation tower that provides a sweeping view of the "river of grass," called Pahayokee by the Indians. Red-shouldered hawks, red-winged blackbirds, and vultures are frequently sighted here.

Mahogany Hammock Trail: Less than a half mile, it winds through a dense hardwood hammock where the largest living mahogany tree in the United States grows. The bright and colorful liguus tree snails live here as do golden orb weaver spiders. Round trip takes thirty minutes.

West Lake Trail: Also less than a half mile, with a thirty-minute round-trip. The trail wanders through a forest of red, white, and black mangroves as well as buttonwood, often incorrectly classified as a mangrove. The trail leads to a brackish lake. Mangroves are a vital nursery for many marine animals including shrimp, spiny lobsters, stone crabs, snapper, and mullet.

Long Pine Key: This is the first serious walk: seven miles that take four to five hours to complete round-trip. The connecting trails go through unusually diverse pinelands, including approximately 200 types of plants, 30 of which are found nowhere else in the world. White-tailed deer, opossums, raccoons, and even rare Florida panthers live in these pinelands.

TRAILS OF THE FLAMINGO AREA

Many of these start out in shade but proceed to open coastal prairies where the wildlife viewing can be quite good.

Christian Point Trail: Another good walk of one and eight-tenths miles each way. Plan on three hours for a round-trip. This is a good place to look for birds of prey. The trail begins by going through a section shaded by buttonwoods, then opens onto a coastal prairie.

Snake Bight Trail: About 1.6 miles each way, requiring two to three hours for a round-trip. The trail first passes through a hardwood forest, then ends at a boardwalk. Another good place for bird-watching.

Rowdy Bend Trail: This is 2.6 miles each way and eventually joins the Snake Bight Trail. It takes about three to four hours round-trip. The walk starts under the cover of buttonwoods, then moves through open coastal prairie.

Coastal Prairie Trail: This is seven and a half miles each way, the second longest walk in the park. It begins in the Flamingo Campground at the back of

Loop C. This is a full-day walk and some people like to camp overnight, but you need a permit. Salt-tolerant plants such as cactus and yucca grow in the prairies. The trail was once used by commercial fishermen and cotton pickers.

Bayshore Loop: A two-mile walk along Florida Bay. This starts at the same place as the Coastal Prairie Trail in the Flamingo Campground at the back of Loop C. The bay shore trail veers to the left. The hike will take you to the remains of an old fishing village.

Guy Bradley Trail: Starting at the Flamingo visitor center, this is actually a one-mile shortcut to the campground's amphitheater. It's also a good walk for seeing both birds and butterflies. The trail is named after a warden killed by plume hunters.

Eco Pond Trail: Located on the right just past the Flamingo visitor center, this is one place you are certain to spot wildlife. The half-mile loop trail is loaded with birds, particularly ibis and egrets that nest in the large mangrove trees. Wading birds and alligators are other regulars. A viewing platform near the start of the trail is ideal for nature photography, but you'll get closer to the nesting birds by bearing right and taking the loop trail.

Shark Valley: This is Everglades National Park's northern entrance, located off US 41, which is also called the Tamiami Trail. A fifteen-mile paved loop road used by hikers, cyclists, and trams takes you past alligators, snakes, and turtles. An observation tower at the end provides a great view of the Glades. The trail loops to return by a different route. There are also a couple of short side trails worth exploring.

CANOEING

More than one-third of the park consists of marine areas and estuaries. Canoeing is a great way to see the water birds, sea turtles, and endangered manatees that live in the park's waterways. You can rent canoes at West Lake at the canoe rental outlet. The concessioner will shuttle you to the following trailheads and pick you up at a set time afterward. Or take your time and call for a pickup with your cellular phone when you get back. All of the following canoe trails begin near Flamingo.

Noble Hammock Trail: A two-mile loop that takes one to two hours to paddle.

Hell's Bay Trail: This has a number of segments, and you can even camp overnight if you obtain a camping permit in advance. It's three miles and two hours to Lard Can. Another three and a half miles and three to four hours to Pearl Bay. From Pearl Bay, it's five and a half miles and five to six hours of paddling to the Hell's Bay Chickee.

Nine Mile Pond Trail: This trip is only 5.2 miles and requires three to four hours on the water.

West Lake Trail: A nice trip of eight miles that takes five to six hours.

Bear Lake Trail: It's 1.6 miles to Bear Lake taking 1.5 hours and 11.5 miles to Cape Sable, a combined distance that takes a full day.

BICYCLING

Because of the straight, flat road leading to Flamingo, a bike is a great way to explore the main road and to stop at the ponds on the side of the road to see which birds are present. Bring your own bike or rent one at the Flamingo Marina store or the Shark Valley visitor area.

CAMPING

Offered year-round. During winter, the sites usually fill every night. Arrive as early as possible since camping is offered on a first-come, first-served basis. The campgrounds at Long Pine Key and Flamingo both have drinking water, picnic tables, grills, tent and trailer pads, and rest rooms. Cold showers are available at Flamingo. RVs are welcome at all sites, but there are no hookups.

Campground stays are limited to fourteen days during the peak season. Checkout time is 10 AM. The Everglades backcountry is accessible by boat, foot, or bicycle. A free backcountry camping permit is required. Available in person at the ranger station, it will be issued no more than 24 hours prior to your trip. Backcountry campsites include beach sites and ground sites.

You need to come prepared since there is no place to buy provisions inside the park. The nearest store is at Homestead, about a twenty-minute drive from the park entrance.

FISHING

Available year-round in the inland and coastal waters of the Everglades for both salt water and freshwater fish, including snapper, sea trout, redfish, bass, and bluegill. Saltwater fishing areas dominate and include Florida Bay, Ten Thousand Islands, and other areas along the park's coastal zone. Freshwater and saltwater each require a separate fishing license. Due to mercury contamination in the environment, check the latest advisory about how safe it is to eat your fish.

WILDLIFE VIEWING/PHOTOGRAPHY

Not as outstanding as it once was because of man's disruption of the annual flow of water into the Everglades, this area still supplies some of the country's best bird-watching opportunities. Egrets, herons, wood storks, and other water birds nest and feed in numerous places that are easily accessible. Some animal species common here are rare and/or endangered in other parts of the world. The best birding usually is at Eco and Mrazek ponds near Flamingo in the dry winter months. The best times to see birds and animals are the early morning and late afternoon.

The Anhinga Trail is one of the most dependable areas for overall wildlife viewing, particularly alligators in the dry winter months. Rock Reef Pass, ten miles west of park headquarters, is particularly good for wildlife viewing from your car. Culverts normally hold alligators, while the area forested in cypress is good for other species.

In Shark Valley, look for an outstanding collection of animals which includes otters, snakes, turtles, and the ubiquitous alligator, all of which are common in winter.

Guided Ranger Tours: One of the park's most popular features. They are so popular in winter, the peak visitor season, you need to make reservations a day or two in advance. All guided tours are free and led by park rangers. These include hiking, canoeing, and nature talks. Tours are far more limited in the summer heat. Check at the visitor center for tour times and reservations.

Tram Tours: A two-hour naturalist-led tour departs from the Flamingo Visitor Center. It takes you along Snake Bight Trail, a lush, tropical hardwood hammock. The tour is not available from April to November because area roads are often under water. For the current schedule and departure times, call Flamingo Lodge at 305/253-2241 or 813/695-3101.

A tram tour is also available along the fifteen-mile loop road at Shark Valley. They generally start at 9 AM and depart hourly until 4 PM. Advance reservations are mandatory in winter. During periods of heavy rain when adjoining areas are under water, the tram is sometimes shut down so animals can take refuge on the only high ground around, the tram road. For reservations and the current schedule of the Shark Valley tram, call 305/221-8455.

BOATING

Cruises of Florida Bay and eco-tours of the area are available in Flamingo. For reservations and schedules, call the Flamingo Lodge at 305/253-2241.

Houseboat rentals are available for exploring the bays near Flamingo, with a two-night minimum rental. The boats accommodate up to eight people. Bring your own food. Reservations are required. Call the Flamingo Lodge at 800/600-3813.

The Flamingo Marina also has rental skiffs and canoes, charter fishing trips, tour boats with a naturalist aboard, and guided kayaking trips.

Who

The main number for Everglades National Park is 305/242-7700. The phone number for the Shark Valley office is 305/221-8776.

What

Everglades National Park encompasses one and a half million acres. Within its boundaries are 2,000 species of plants, 51 types of reptiles, 347 assorted birds, 40 different mammals, and 17 varieties of amphibians. Much of the park is comprised of saw grass that thrives in a layer of water about six inches deep.

When

The most comfortable time to visit is from late November through April when mosquitoes are fewest. This is also the driest part of the year, when the wildlife is most easily seen around the permanent ponds and other watering holes. Temperatures during this time range from the 40s at night to the 80s during the day. Summer tends to be humid, with temperatures in the 80s and 90s.

Where

The main park entrance is about an hour south of Miami near Homestead. The easiest route is to take the Florida Turnpike to Homestead, where a large brown sign on the right will point the way. There is no such sign visible when coming from the Keys. Shark Valley cannot be reached from inside the park via the Flamingo Road. Instead, you must leave the park and drive north to US 41, the Tamiami Trail. The fastest way to do this is on the Florida Turnpike, then take the US 41 exit west. The Shark Valley entrance is thirty miles west of Miami, across from the Miccosukee Indian Village. The Miccosukee restaurant is open from 8AM to 4 PM.

19

Seminole
Swamp Safari

The Mosquito Meter is an unusual device used in the Everglades, that's set according to how often you're likely to get bitten. The meter's five different levels are: "enjoyable," "bearable," "unpleasant," "horrible," and "hysterical."

I happen to be in the Everglades during one of the February "enjoyable" periods when a cold front has pushed temperatures down into the 30s. I can't believe that I'm once again present during another abnormally cold spell. Surely I can't have that kind of effect on Everglades weather.

Although I have no worry about mosquitoes, I am amazed that of all the weekends of the year I've chosen this one to sleep in a semi-open, grass-roofed hut. Still, it's much better than a tent.

This hut is actually a Seminole Indian chickee located at the Kissimmee Billie Swamp Safari on the Big Cypress Reservation in the remote heart of the Everglades. Chickees are the shelters the Seminoles were forced to adopt after they fled to the Everglades in the 1860s.

The chickee is nothing but a raised platform with a large overhanging thatched roof made from palmetto fronds. The roof, which projects far down the sides, does not fully enclose the platform but has plenty of open space near the bottom and under it to allow strong winds to pass through without destroying the structure. Other reasons the hut is on a raised platform are to deter snakes and to avoid flooding.

Speaking of strong winds, some are blowing outside right now. Cypress trees behind the chickee block the winds that regularly gust up to 30 mph and sometimes higher. The sturdy hut does not shake, which is more than I can say for my vehicle parked out front. The minivan rocks in the breeze, and my companion worries that a really strong gust might actually knock it over.

Tonight, few if any Seminoles will be in chickees. Instead, they're all sleeping comfortably in cinderblock houses and mobile homes while I spend the night outdoors in a shelter with no electricity and no plumbing. Clever revenge against the white man? No, not really.

The chickee's sides are partially enclosed by louvered windows, though the front door is made of screen. I'm quite comfortable under the covers, which consist of six Seminole-supplied thin wool blankets but absolutely no crinkly space blanket. Furthermore, the night passes uneventfully. The normal frog chorus is mute; probably all have sore throats.

In the morning, however, several hundred black birds known as grackles land in the cypress trees behind my chickee just before sunrise. Their noisy cackling is my alarm clock, so I get up. As I hurriedly slip on my clothes, which have hung on the wall all night, I'm impressed at how chilly ordinary cloth gets. But I'm warm again in minutes, anticipating another interesting day at the Kissimmee Billie Swamp Safari, one of the best ways any outsider can get to meet Florida's Seminole Indians, learn their history, and observe their customs. I'm especially looking forward to seeing Swamp Owl, the chief storyteller here. Not only are his tales always fascinating, but also he's always in some form of Seminole apparel. "Apparel" may seem like an awfully fancy word to describe traditional Seminole garb, but the tribe once dressed as elegantly as any of the Europeans, and for them it wasn't special occasion wear but everyday clothing.

This is something not widely known in or outside of Florida. The Seminoles have been called the nation's least-known Indians, and for good reason. After fighting three successful wars against the U.S. military, the Seminoles wanted nothing more to do with whites. By the end of that third conflict, all the Seminole chiefs had been killed or removed to Oklahoma. Only between 200 and 300 Seminoles remained in Florida, the true die-hards who refused to surrender under any conditions.

They disappeared into the swampy Everglades, the only place the tribe could isolate itself from the rest of the world. They barely existed on land that was so wet and mosquito-infested that no one else wanted it. Hiding among the mosquitoes, snakes, and alligators was the only way the Seminoles could remain a free people.

The land I'm standing on now was covered with water until well into the 20th century when parts of the Glades were drained for farmers and cattle ranchers. That the new drainage and ditching system might also give the Seminoles some dry territory was a fortunate by–product.

Yet, unlike a lot of persecuted minorities, today's Seminoles seem to hold little bitterness about their past treatment. As Swamp Owl has told me more than once, "All that happened a long time ago. It wasn't you that did it. What's important is how people treat one another today." Amen.

Swamp Owl stands out among the Seminoles at the swamp safari because he is the only one who dresses in the tribe's traditional clothing. This day, because of the cold, he is dressed in a long red coat. He explains why he is dressed so brightly. "We copied the dress of the British because we fought on their side. We dressed like them so they would know we were their allies and not shoot at us. We particularly liked to dress fancy like the Scots."

I ask Swamp Owl why so few other Seminoles dress as he does. After all, it is his costumes that help make the history of the place come alive. He shakes his head. "Others have said they would dress as I do, but those who did were made fun of by their family."

I'm puzzled. "Why would they make fun of the way they dressed? Because it's old fashioned and out of date?" I ask.

"Jealousy," Swamp Owl says, with some sadness. "Many Seminoles do not know much about our history, and that bothers them. It is especially embarrassing that some white people know more about our history than some of us do.

"But as I tell them, our people were warriors fighting for their survival. Many who knew our history were killed or moved to Oklahoma. There is nothing to be ashamed of."

Swamp Owl spends a couple of hours every evening describing the history and legends of his people around the campfire. It's at these night meetings that he usually wears his finest Seminole clothing, which is amazingly detailed and elaborate, especially in terms of the beadwork.

For Seminole men, it once was common to wear long-sleeve blouses with matching trousers and large stovepipe hats. Today, except for a few storytellers like Swamp Owl, it is worn only on special occasions. For everyday clothes, Seminole men now wear jeans and regular shirts and drive pickup trucks. They look more like cowboys than Indians.

Some elderly Seminole women who visit the swamp safari still dress in elaborate, billowing ankle-length skirts and long-sleeve blouses decorated with bright layers of geometric designs. These embroidered patterns, which differ with each woman, are a painstaking task. A single garment may take as long as a week to complete.

CAMPFIRE TALES

The night fire for storytelling is built inside a huge dirt floor chickee so that, rain or clear skies, Swamp Owl or another storyteller is always able to discuss tribal customs with visitors. To me, this is the most interesting and appealing part of the Kissimmee Billie Swamp Safari experience. I usually tape record it.

The way in which the nightly fire is built may be very revealing about the Seminoles' origins. The fire consists of four large logs with each facing a different direction: north, east, south, and west. The flames are built up or lowered by pushing the ends of the logs together or pulling them farther apart. When the logs are close together, their four ends make a very convenient cooking platform on which to place a kettle or frying pan.

This is the same type of cooking fire that's built in many parts of Africa today. A coincidence, perhaps, but the similarity has made some people speculate that this arrangement might have been adopted when runaway slaves sought refuge with and intermarried with the Seminoles, who are not a native Florida tribe.

The Seminoles are descendants of the Creek Indians of Georgia and Alabama who moved into Florida in the late 1700s. The Creeks had no difficulty finding land in North Florida on which to settle: all of the Indian tribes that were flourishing in the state when the Europeans landed in the 1500s were extinct by the late 1700s. Some Indians were killed in battle, but many died from European diseases against which they had no immunity.

After migrating into Florida, the Creeks built their customary log cabins and for a time continued to dress in the buckskins common to other East Coast Indians. They welcomed runaway slaves who appeared in their towns and camps, and the Indians refused to return any escapee even if an irate owner came to claim him.

The Indians were able to provide sanctuary to runaways and not fear reprisal because Florida was still Spanish territory. As time passed, the Creeks intermarried with other Indians as well as the black slaves and gradually became known as *Isti Seminoli*, a Creek term meaning "wild" or "free people."

It was the continued sheltering of slaves that caused the United States to attack the Seminoles, which resulted in the first Seminole War (1817–1818). General Andrew Jackson—called "Chicken-Snake" for all his lies and betrayals—invaded Florida to subdue the Seminoles even though they lived on Spanish land. Spain, unable to defend its territory, decided to turn Florida over to the United States in the 1820s. Once the land belonged to the United States, that was the beginning of the end for the Seminoles.

The seeds for the Second Seminole War were sown almost immediately after Florida became U.S. territory. The federal government made it known the Seminoles would have to vacate their land so white settlers could move in. The Seminoles were able to stall matters until 1835, when it became necessary to forcibly resist the attempt to move them to Oklahoma. The Second Seminole War lasted for seven years, ending in 1842. When it was over, most of the Seminoles and their Negro allies had given up and gone to Oklahoma.

The third and final conflict, which lasted from 1855–58, was caused by surveyors who harassed the Big Cypress Swamp camp of Seminole chief Billy Bowlegs. After this conflict, the few hundred Seminoles who hid in the Everglades were determined to stay free. Mostly, that meant absolutely no contact with the outside, with "non-Indians."

Florida's Seminoles might have lost the final battle, but they never lost their war. Of all the Indians in the United States, they were the only ones who never signed a peace treaty, who never officially surrendered. Comparatively, the Seminole Wars are considered among the most costly in U.S. history. Despite the use of blood hounds and every method of warfare, it cost the United States an estimated $10,000 and the life of a soldier or settler for every Seminole killed or moved to Oklahoma. Today, there are about 13,000 Seminoles scattered throughout Florida.

The Seminoles' hostility toward outsiders continued for almost a century after they disappeared into Everglades. They say it was considered fair sport in Florida to kill an Indian as late as the 1930s, and such things did happen. It's no wonder outsiders were unable to view their culture.

Eventually, the Seminoles realized they needed to enlarge their world if they were to accomplish more than bare survival. Finally, they were willing even to allow outsiders onto their lands. That's why the Kissimmee Billie Swamp Safari was built at Big Cypress, the largest and most remote of the Seminole reservations.

From what you see publicly at Billie Swamp Safari, it's easy to gain the impression that the men are in charge. For instance, it is the women who do the cooking, preparing such delicious items as pumpkin bread made in the shape of a turnover and the traditional sofkee, a ground corn mixture something like raisin-less rice pudding.

You probably would never guess that the Seminole society is actually a matriarchal one where the woman is head of the household. Not only are the women in charge, all matters of inheritance are calculated from the woman's side. When a man marries, he goes to live with his wife's family; however, the children take the husband's name, which confused and misled outsiders about the family arrangement for many years. That's why the evening meetings with Swamp Owl are always so riveting.

Seminoles and alligators are closely linked in the public mind, and Kissimmee Billie Swamp Safari has several alligator pens. One holds a huge monster of a gator they've named "Superman." No doubt that gator is strong, but to me a better nickname is "Jaws": when the animal opens its huge and well-armed mouth, half its body seems made of teeth.

Although the Seminoles are world-famous for alligator wrestling, it was white men who introduced them to it. Some years ago a champion Seminole alligator wrestler named Alan Jumper told me how the sport started. He said that at the turn of the century many, zoos were interested in purchasing live alligators for exhibit. Since no one knew more about the reptiles than the Seminoles, it was natural that the job of rounding them up should fall to them.

Jumper says the sport of alligator wrestling didn't emerge until the 1920s. The first person to do it was actually a non–Indian who thought the feat would attract more attention if a Seminole did it. The idea obviously caught on extremely well.

Visitors to Big Cypress at first could be intimidated or uneasy by how reserved or "stand-offish" some of the Seminoles appear to be. They may be talking and laughing with one another until you appear. Then they become silent. It is not unusual for an outsider to interpret this for unfriendliness. Seminoles say this is the outsider's misperception, that what is mistaken for aloofness is something very different.

As one tribe member explained to me, "It takes time for a Seminole to get to know you. We may be standing back to see what kind of person you are. Our life is based on right and respect, and it is with these principles that a Seminole greets another." Considering their treatment in the past, such caution in dealing with strangers is understandable. It also helps to place everything in better context by remembering that few cultures are as unreserved and informal as that of the United States, and Florida in particular.

Some of my best insights into the Seminole way of thinking have come from an afternoon I was fortunate enough to spend with James Billie, chairman of the

Traditional apparel helps make the history of the Seminoles come alive.

Seminole Tribe of Florida. I found him to be a very straightforward, blunt individual, a truly refreshing person. I did not feel like I was walking on eggshells, examining every word first to decide whether it was politically correct and therefore unlikely to cause him offense. For instance, despite what the politically correct say we should label him (and therefore how he should view himself), James Billie considers himself an Indian, and he calls himself an Indian. He does not use the term *Native American*; I got the impression he might not even like the name. A lot of Indians don't—a fact they will make public to anyone who bothers to consult them.

Although he calls himself an Indian, James Billie does not look or talk like Hollywood's stereotype of one. His closely cropped black hair, pale skin, and short but powerful frame clad in jeans and a solid black shirt seem more characteristic of an Irish dock worker.

"I'm a mixed-breed Indian," James explains as we talk and he takes a huge puff on a fat cigar and blows the smoke over his head. "My mother was a Seminole Indian of the Bird Clan. I'm not sure if I'm Irish, but I'm supposed to be part caucasian. However, I was born on a tourist attraction, a chimpanzee farm, so I'm not sure if I'm not half ape, gorilla—whatever," he jokes in a deep gravelly voice.

Tradition has it that James Billie was lucky to reach his first birthday. He was born in 1944, a time when Seminoles wanted little to do with whites.

"Seminoles didn't like half-breeds because they had already gone through the problem of being kicked around by what you call the white man," James says. "Then, somehow, this white person got a hold of my mother, either under protest or willingly, we don't know. I was created and I was born, and there was a lot of talk back then about getting rid of half-breeds. I've heard that my grandfather said 'Throw him in the creek or something.' I laugh about it. It makes a good story," James says.

Being born part Indian and part white—two South Florida worlds that were still tremendously hostile to each other during James Billie's childhood—undoubtedly helped forge the very tough but practical approach he has used to lead his people.

"When you find an Indian living in a swamp, it's not because he wanted to live there," James says sharply. "When he lived in the swamp, it was to stay out of harm's way. He was pursued by the military, and he was running and hiding out of fear for his life.

"It was only after 1936 that this fear sort of dwindled a little bit, where he could stick his head above the water, look around, and there would be no one shooting at him," James continues.

As a youngster, James lived in a traditional chickee hut made of palm thatch, was fluent in his native language, and also wrestled alligators. However, his boyhood heroes were all white: Tarzan, Superman, and even Hopalong Cassidy. The radio also introduced him to singers like Elvis, Harry Chapin, and The Eagles. James' link to both the Seminole and white man's worlds was probably the best thing that could have happened to the Seminole Tribe of Florida. James' ability—and more importantly, his willingness—to walk and work in both cultures changed forever the destiny of the Seminoles, if not all of Florida. He has been the perfect leader for his people in this time and this place.

James Billie brought the first real prosperity to the Seminoles, and in doing so turned Florida upside down, all with a child's game: B-I-N-G-O. In 1979, the Seminoles made bingo a high-stakes game that brought hundreds of millions of dollars into the Seminole government's coffers.

This cash windfall made it possible for Seminoles to improve their standard of living a hundredfold. Living conditions were so primitive that even after years of effort not all of the Indians yet have running water or proper sewage. That it should happen by the end of the century is an amazing accomplishment that just a few years ago no one would have dreamed feasible. Until the 1980s, and before James Billie, the Seminoles were about as poor as dirt.

It's likely James will shake up the state once again if his current plans go through. While other Floridians are arguing over whether to allow casino gambling, James Billie is ready to launch it.

"I am going to do casino gambling if I get the privilege and the opportunity, but it's got to be negotiated," James explained. "It's not like it used to be. They've got different laws. When I first got into bingo, I maybe should have challenged it then, and I'd be in casino gambling now. But I just sat back and let the dust settle a little bit, because as soon as I started bingo, every tribe in the United States started."

James believes the Seminoles will win casino gambling rights for the same reasons they won the right to play high-stakes bingo: both activities are already legal and regulated in other states. James points out that churches had played bingo for decades before the Seminoles got involved. All we did, he says, was change the rules and raise the stakes.

James gives credit for the bingo concept to the tribe's comptroller. When James read the comptroller's bingo proposal and found that the bottom line said the Seminole Tribe might make $3 million almost instantly, "The first words through my head were bull———! I didn't think there was that much money on this earth!," James says.

The comptroller pointed out that no other tribe in the United States yet had the courage to try it, that Indians had been sitting on the reservation for so long that they were afraid of the system, of Uncle Sam. So, the Seminoles borrowed a million dollars and opened their first bingo parlor back in 1979. James says they enjoyed such incredible success that six months later they were able to burn their loan note.

With the bingo funds, the Seminoles began buying up land to open reservations in other parts of Florida. The tribe did encounter some resistance but James says of the protests, "We figured out the term *lobbying* and how to operate in the political battlefield and wear the proper battle dress. That's called *a coat and tie.*"

Like most politicians, James Billie stands for re-election as tribal chairman every four years. He says he deliberately worked his way to the top from the ground level: by starting in maintenance, then as a stock boy, always climbing up to higher positions.

"That was the only way I could learn the tribal system, the in-house political gossip, and where all the skeletons lay within our own political system." He also enrolled in college courses, not to obtain any degree but to improve his speaking ability, which he considers one of his most important skills.

"I went to school because I was in charge of manpower development, and the people I had to deal with are what are called 'educated people.' They were sociologists, social workers, psychologists, and doctors. So, I thought to stay up with the language that they talk, I should take some basic classes so that when I hear the terms that they speak, I don't sit there and act like 'what you mean?'

"You can be ignorant, but after a while people start laughing at you. So, you go in there and listen to the man talk and pick up his habits. I shopped around for the type of teacher I wanted, men and women. I wanted a charismatic, no bull—— kind of person. I went into their class and looked at how they talked. If I wanted some sort of ethnic type lecturer, what we call Afro-Americans nowadays, I listened to him to see what his language was so that I didn't cross a certain barrier, of insulting without meaning to."

The other great benefit he received from college, he says, was gaining a deep appreciation for music. James admits he loves playing the guitar and composing songs based on old Seminole legends. "It's a good ventilation through my fingers instead of beating on somebody. Music is probably my first love in what they call hobbies or something."

James' first chance to seek the highest Seminole political office came in 1979, when the reigning chairman stepped down. The James Billie political platform was a modest one. He says he had no great promises to offer his people, that he just wanted to figure out how to make his tribe some money. He says that's still how he views his role.

James Billie expects to be enriching the Seminole coffers for many years to come. He is only in his fifties, and he never intends to give up the chairmanship voluntarily. "I believe in being defeated by someone only because . . .," he pauses, takes a puff on his cigar, then continues, "I look at the animals a lot. The reason an animal fights for a good position in the herd is because he has good genes, a good blood line. The weak one is defeated because he is old or something is wrong and the new strong one comes in. "I've got that same mentality. I want to be defeated by some good, mental, new modern-day somebody. That's the only way I'll step down, just to keep the good blood flowing in the leadership position.

"It was instilled in me that I will accomplish whatever it is I am going to do. I've been pretty lucky all my life. I'm like Jiminy Cricket—that if you wish for something you might get it. So I'm very careful what I wish for, because what I wish for, I've always gotten. So I don't try to wish too big, but not too small, either."

And what does he wish for his people in the future?

"Good health and sobriety. Money can't do jack—— for you, but your body can, while your brain still functions. Good health, that's probably the only thing I wish for. And passing on the legends in my songs!"

Kissimmee Billie Swamp Safari, like most places, has a gift shop. One of the items displayed is an album by "Jim Billie." The picture on the jacket is of the man beside me. It's a shrewd deceit to handle a problem the chairman has encountered.

"Too many people go around saying they're my friend, and now you'll know if they are. Anyone who claims to be a good friend of 'Jim Billie' is not a friend of mine," James Billie says, laughing.

I suspect Osceola, the great Seminole warrior chief who died in prison in 1838 after being taken prisoner in St. Augustine while under a flag of truce, and whose head was cut off by a doctor he regarded a friend, might be smiling at this moment, too.

Who

For reservations or complete information about the Kissimmee Billie Swamp Safari, call toll free 800/949-6101. Swamp Owl is present as a storyteller most weekends, but he does have two days a week off. Check to make certain he will be present during your visit. More than anything else, he is responsible for bringing Seminole history alive. If the person you're talking to is uncertain of Swamp Owl's schedule, ask for Leonard, who will probably know it. If you fly a small plane, ask about using the tribal airstrip just a few miles from the swamp safari.

What

There are plenty of things to keep you active for a weekend at the swamp safari. Swamp buggies will take you through the wet lowlands to the animal exhibits that feature Florida panthers and alligators. The panthers live in a totally natural environment almost a full acre in size. The one male and two females have produced three new panther kittens and more are expected in the future. Kissimmee Billie Swamp Safari probably has the most natural, animal-friendly panther habitat in the entire state.

The buggies also take you into areas with free-roaming bison (once native to Florida) and exotic species such as axis deer and antelope. But the best part is the stop at Swamp Owl's camp deep in the woods. Swamp Owl displays some of the traditional Seminole axes, guns, baskets, and other items and tells just enough about Seminole history to make people want to learn more at the nightly campfire near the main lodge. The nightly campfire stories usually begin around 8 PM, roughly the closing time of the safari's restaurant, called the Swamp Water Cafe.

In addition to the swamp buggies, you can ride airboats through several miles of Everglades canals. An elevated boardwalk through a cypress swamp near the chickees is a fine place for nature photography. In addition to photographing animals, you can also hunt wild hogs with your own rifle or shotgun anytime of year, but a three-day advance notice is required.

Just a few miles from the safari site, a museum of Seminole history is scheduled to open in August, 1996. The newly constructed building, the museum's first phase, is enormous.

The Swamp Water Cafe is a small restaurant with buffets for breakfast, lunch, and dinner. Most of the food is typical meat- and vegetable-fare, but try the Seminole pumpkin bread and fry bread whenever it's offered. You might also want to sample the Seminole hamburger, hot dog, or taco—particularly that huge Seminole taco that can easily fill two people.

Overnight accommodations are available in modified chickees with screens and shades—but no electricity (you have your own kerosene lamp but bring extra matches and a flashlight). There's no indoor plumbing, either, so note the location of the nearest stand-alone wooden outhouse. Of course, it's always possible to walk from your chickee to the 24-hour rest rooms that also contain several shower stalls for campers.

The chickees are quite dry even during heavy rains; the sound of rain on the thatch roof is a very soothing way to fall asleep. Bedding is provided but bring a towel and washcloth for the showers. Also bring insect repellent.

When

Winter, spring, and fall are most comfortable. The restaurant is air-conditioned. Expect afternoon showers and thunderstorms—some in the frog-strangler category—in summer, especially the afternoons. As damp and humid as the summer is, there is something to be said for watching dark clouds hanging over the Everglades saw grass as the golden sunshine of late afternoon causes the chickees to glow. It is a beautiful sight.

The Kissimmee Billie Swamp Safari is located on the Big Cypress Reservation, southwest of Clewiston, an hour's drive west of Ft. Lauderdale. Coming from the north, take Route 80 to State Road 833, then head south through a stretch known as the Devil's Garden. Bear to the left when the road splits. The reservation is clearly marked. Observe the posted speed rigorously. The Seminoles have their own tribal police who are very quick to give speeding tickets. The turnoff from State Road 833 to the swamp safari is on the right, marked by a prominent sign. This turnoff is also the location of the new Seminole museum and a tribally operated campground.

20

Getting High
Over Florida

The Wright Brothers may have flown the first plane at Kitty Hawk, North Carolina, but many other historic aviation firsts have occurred in Florida.

The first recognized commercial flight was made in the Tampa Bay region, just ten years after the Kitty Hawk flight. It happened in 1914, when pioneer aviator Tony Jannus began regularly ferrying passengers (one at a time) and cargo between Tampa and St. Petersburg in his "flying boat." A reproduction of the two-seater is displayed at the St. Petersburg Museum of History.

Just fourteen years later, in 1928, Pan American—once the world's greatest airline—initiated service from Key West to Cuba. This is generally regarded as the first commercial overseas passenger service. The original Key West terminal, now a restaurant, is marked by a sign.

Finally, the first men ever to walk on the moon were propelled skyward from the Sunshine State, just as Jules Verne predicted almost a century earlier.

As you can see, getting high over Florida has a long and honored history. Here are some of the most exciting ways to get an aerial view of Florida today.

HELICOPTER RIDES

I keep thinking of the old joke: an Irishman isn't drunk as long as he can hold onto a single blade of grass to keep from falling off the face of the earth.

At the moment, I am cold sober—crouched over and holding onto the ground with something of a death grip. Overhead, the helicopter rotors are turning ever faster and increasingly buffet me from side to side as I wait to climb aboard.

My relationship with helicopters is of the love-hate variety. I am always reluctant to ensure my safety to a machine that, theoretically, is as aerodynamically implausible as a bumblebee. Furthermore, a disabled chopper normally drops like a rock. I wish Leonardo da Vinci had considered more safety options when he made sketches of the first helicopter in the late 1400s or early 1500s. I still refuse to believe the reassurances I once received from an elderly chopper pilot who told me that helicopters have a certain amount of glide capability. Yeah, right. Helicopters can glide and cows can fly over the moon.

Finally, I'm signaled aboard. The circling blades drown out any attempts at normal conversation. I put on a set of headphones and listen to the pilot go through his checklist.

I remember another bit of advice from that old chopper pilot: "In a crash, fire is the greatest danger if the skids rupture the fuel tanks. Remain cool and collected and get away from the machine as fast as you can. You can shake afterwards!"

The blades cut into the air still faster. There is a slight hesitation as we begin to defy gravity and the chopper slowly lifts off, its nose tilted downward. The contest between gravity and machine seems to intensify as we pause once more—then we're definitely airborne, swooping above the trees and over the traffic. In the distance I see the skyline of Orlando to the east, the assorted towers of Sea World, Universal Studios, and Disney World to the west. Under a clear blue sky, this is an ideal mode for sightseeing.

Helicopters, because of their tremendous operating and maintenance costs, are usually out of the budgetary reach for us common folk. Normally, it's only wealthy corporate executives, rock stars and presidents who can afford to charter these craft. But around major tourist areas in many parts of Florida, helicopter rides are extremely affordable. In Orlando, for example, you can tour the amusement areas from the air for about the cost of a taxi ride. A very good deal, indeed.

Who

Helicopter tours are offered throughout the state. Look in the local telephone Yellow Pages under "Helicopters." In the Orlando-Kissimmee Area, contact Falcon Helicopter Services (407/352-1753) located off International Drive. Flights last about fifteen to twenty minutes, carry up to four passengers, and move you as fast as 120 mph.

HOT-AIR BALLOONING

So many things associated with ballooning read like they were taken from Ripley's Believe It or Not.

The goofiest ballooning stunt belongs to a Californian who, in 1982, tied forty-two weather balloons to his lawn chair and went sailing 16,000 feet over Los Angeles. He carried a BB gun for deflating balloons when he wanted to descend, which he did about ten miles from where he took off. Even though he struck several power lines when landing, the pilot still was able to fold up his lawn chair and walk away, definitely the sign of a successful landing. The grumpy Federal Aviation Administration fined him $4,000 for obstructing the airlanes.

Still, he fared far better than one of ballooning's pioneers, Frenchman Jean Francois Pilatre de Rozier, who took part in the first successful balloon flight, in 1783, over Paris. Just two years later, de Rozier died when his balloon exploded in flight, making him not only the first to fly but also the very first to die. Despite the rhyming, there doesn't seem to be any moral lesson here.

Florida, and Orlando in particular, has had a very strong tie to one of ballooning's real daredevils, Joseph W. Kittinger Jr., who for many years was in charge of the balloon flights at the Church Street Station entertainment complex. In 1960, as an Air Force captain, Kittinger jumped out of a perfectly good balloon at 102,800 feet in order to free-fall for sixteen miles, a world record; he fell as fast as 714 mph. In 1984, he was the first solo balloonist across the Atlantic—from Caribou, Maine,

Preparing a balloon for flight.

to Montenette, Italy, a trip that lasted 86 hours and covered 3,543 miles.

Ballooning is a lot like sailing in that you are totally wind-driven, and you go aloft not for the sake of traveling somewhere specific but for the experience. Considerably more than in sailing, the wind determines your direction and whether you will even go aloft.

Every hot-air balloon launch is akin to organized mayhem. First, the canopy has to be spread out, then filled with hot air. Once the balloon begins ascending from the ground, reminiscent of a punchy prize-fighter struggling to regain his feet, everyone scrambles to make certain the craft doesn't take off without all the proper people aboard.

Then it's several blasts from the propane tank and you're aloft. Your first flight will hold several surprises. You probably dreamed of standing in the basket and having the wind stream through your hair. It doesn't happen. Instead, if you close your eyes so you don't have ground references, it may not even feel like you're moving. A balloon usually travels at wind speed. When you're matching the breeze, there is no sensation of movement; you are cocooned within the wind itself. So, the ride probably will be a lot warmer than you expected.

Without wind noise, you can hear amazingly far. Conversations on the ground are incredibly clear even when you're a few hundred feet up. Also, you tend to creep up on people unless they've been looking skyward. A big blast of propane at low level can cause some awfully shocked looks—especially from those who've been sunbathing in the nude, believing themselves hidden from sight because of the privacy fence around their swimming pool.

Ballooning, like sailing, depends in large part on teamwork. The chase team not only helps assemble and take apart the balloon, but also they do just as their name implies: chase after the balloon, following roadways and trails, like the hound after the hare. Handheld radios are frequently employed so everyone can maintain contact. The more open spaces on the ground, the easier the job for the chase team.

When wind speeds are 6 mph or more, many balloonists will not launch. As they like to point out, there are three stages in ballooning when things can go wrong: at the launch, while you're in the air, and during landing. The latter, the landing, is always the most serious consideration, and, in strong winds, it's difficult to land without the balloon falling on its side and dragging the basket over the ground.

If someone loses their grip while the basket is being dragged, they could get hurt, and this kind of wear and tear doesn't do the equipment any good, either. Also, in strong winds, it can be very tricky to descend and avoid two of ballooning's greatest dangers, power lines and trees.

This dependency is why ballooning, time-wise, tends to be the most inconvenient of sports. In Florida, the majority of commercial balloon flights take off near sunrise. Although this practice does promote champagne breakfast balloon flights, it really is the best time of day for ballooning—before the winds awaken. Once the sun begins heating the ground, the breeze normally picks up significantly. Except during races or other special events, most balloons are back on the ground and packed away by 10 AM.

Who

In many parts of the country you have to wait for a race or some other special event for a balloon ride. In Florida's tourist areas, hot-air balloons are particularly common, so arranging a flight is no major problem. Once again, consult the telephone book Yellow Pages.

Expect to pay between $150 to $250 per person for a one- to one-and-a-half-hour ride, depending on the frills (such as champagne).

When

Anytime of year. Winter temps are sometimes too cold for enjoyable sky sailing, but nothing in Central or South Florida stays cold for long. Fronts usually vanish after a couple of days.

Where

Thanks to its thirty million annual visitors, the Orlando-Kissimmee area has one of the greatest concentrations of commercial balloon operations in all of Florida.

PARACHUTING

Parachuting is one thing I've always wanted to try, but I'm just plain too chicken to take the fall. It took me decades to get over just being afraid of heights. And I keep reading stories about parachutists, ranging from those making their first jump to grizzled veterans celebrating the 50th anniversary of World War II, who all encounter the same fatal problem—their chute doesn't open. I don't want to make a final impression on the world this way.

One of Florida's parachute hot spots is the small town of DeLand, which is close enough to Orlando that our local paper covers all the fatalities, and, admittedly, they are few and far between. I'm sure I'm at far more risk driving Interstate-4 through Orlando than I would be jumping out of a plane. It just doesn't strike me that way. I wish you luck, and a soft landing.

In DeLand, they can train you and jump you in a single day, though you go tandem. Call Skydive DeLand at 904/738-3539.

On the Southwest coast just above Punta Gorda, contact Air to Air Adventures at 813/494-0053 or 800/240-6111 toll free from within Florida.

Sky diving operations tend to be on the fringe of metropolitan areas. Always check the local Yellow Pages.

GLIDER RIDES

This is Florida's version of hang gliding. Since we lack high mountains to jump off, another airplane is required to tow these long-winged, engine-less planes from the ground and then release them thousands of feet in the air. The pilot's purpose is twofold: to remain aloft as long as he can by taking advantage of the air currents, and then to smoothly land at his home airport, often a grass strip out in the middle of nowhere.

I personally do not like gliding, though perhaps I should try it a second time. My heart definitely started beating faster when the tow plane set us free, but after a few minutes my biggest concern was not how long would we be up—but how soon could we get down. The cockpit was an airborne sauna!

There was almost no airflow in my front seat (the real pilot maneuvered our craft in the cockpit behind me). It was stifling. Definitely not something I should have tried on a hot summer afternoon. Starting early or waiting until a cool winter month would be much more pleasurable, I'm sure.

There is a lot to be said for gliding. It has to be the closest humans have ever gotten to imitating the flight of broad-winged birds who stay aloft for hours by riding the air currents and never once flapping their wings. This flight is a rare form of freedom, one we can only begin to appreciate with our artificial wings. We might not have been born with them, but we were smart enough to make them.

Incidentally, one of the first things you learn in Florida is how thermals differ over land and over water. Gliders do not always enjoy a totally serene ride: bumps exist even in the air.

In the Orlando area, contact Citrus Soaring on weekends at DeLand's airport: 904/736-6588. In the rest of Florida, look in the Yellow Pages under "gliders."

SEAPLANES

These were some of the first airplanes ever used in Florida, and for obvious reasons. With literally thousands of lakes and more than 6,000 miles of coastline—second only to Alaska—Florida has a lot of places for seaplanes to land.

At Key West, you can take a seaplane to the Dry Tortugas, another seventy miles south. Seaplanes either fly over the area or land at Fort Jefferson, where you spend the day exploring and snorkeling. Given a choice, stop and spend the day, by all means. Or, you can even camp overnight, as long as you pack in everything (including water). Relatively few people get this far south.

Fort Jefferson, called the Gibraltar of the Gulf and built in the mid-1800s, has walls eight feet thick and fifty feet high, with tiers designed for 450 guns. It is named after Thomas Jefferson, who intended for the fort to dominate the entrance to the Gulf of Mexico.

The largest of America's coastal citadels, Fort Jefferson never fired a shot. It wasn't built on very firm foundation, either, as the builders discovered after laying sixteen million bricks on the sand of the tiny sixteen-acre key. The supportive limestone base that was supposed to be at the surface turned out to be eighty feet down, so the fort began slowly sinking.

A prison after the Civil War, Fort Jefferson was the Alcatraz of its time, the place no one wanted to be sent. Guards supposedly disciplined prisoners by hanging them by their thumbs or having them carry around cannonballs all day.

The most famous inmate was Dr. Samuel Mudd, the Maryland physician who unwittingly set the broken leg of Lincoln's assassin, John Wilkes Booth. Mudd was sentenced to Fort Jefferson for life, but he was pardoned because of his diligent work during a devastating yellow fever epidemic that killed almost forty people. Mudd was freed in 1869.

There are no formal camping facilities on the island though y are permitted to pitch a tent outside the fort walls. You'll need to plan precisely, because you must bring all your own supplies, especially water and bug spray. In summer, camping here may be a hellish experience.

Who

In the Lower Keys, check with the Sugar Loaf Lodge about seaplane flights. Orlando, of course, has sight-seeing seaplanes that fly either from Lake Monroe at the small town of Sanford, just east of Orlando, or from Lake Eustis near Leesburg.

For the latest information on Key West seaplane tours, contact 800/LAST-KEY. In the Orlando area, contact Florida Seaplanes at 407/846-3878 or 800/FLY-7786. If you're in the Miami area and don't have a lot planned for the day, you can always take a seaplane to the Bahamas: contact Chalks International Airways at 305/359-0414.

VINTAGE AIRPLANE RIDES

Would you like a two-seater bi-plane or a DC-3 with stewardesses outfitted circa the 1940s and an intercom that plays big band music? We'd like to say the sky is the limit, but that's what the bank placed on your credit card.

Who/Where

In Ft. Myers, you can climb aboard a 1940 WACO open cockpit capable of carrying two passengers. There are some beautiful vistas in this part of Southwest Florida, which includes Ft. Myers Beach and Sanibel and Captiva Islands.

The vintage DC-3 flies between Kissimmee and Key West as an alternative to the cramped, tiny commuters that make the run from the rest of the state. DC-3s never needed much landing room, so these spacious aircraft are, in terms of comfort and roominess, the difference between a Rolls Royce and a two-seat Mazda Miata. Call 407/932-1400. The cost is over $200 per person.

FLY YOUR OWN PLANE

You can do this at just about any of the small airports around Florida. Just sign up for an introductory flight lesson. If you like, continue. Depending on your instructor, you might be able to take up the rest of the family, who can backseat drive while you're learning the controls. If their suggestions get too annoying, you can always point out that they have the option to leave at anytime.

21

The Scoop
on Scallops

The scallop's row of forty bright blue eyes stare back at me through my dive mask—eyes so blue they could belong to a Hollywood starlet. I'm startled. I have never seen a scallop underwater before. I'd no idea that their looks came anywhere near equaling their taste appeal.

It hasn't taken long to find a scallop bed as we snorkel a shallow bay in the Gulf of Mexico on Florida's west coast. The scallops are partially hidden in the seagrasses in four to six feet of water—easy grabbing distance.

So, with my first scallop now in plain sight, I do what I would do for any mollusk. I simply reach for it.

Armed with its array of sharp eyes, the scallop sees me coming right from the start. And it departs, rapidly, flying in a zig-zag pattern through the water like a stone skipping across the surface.

This sudden escape surprises me enough to make me stand flat-finned on the bottom and look around to make certain I'm not hallucinating. Everything above the surface, however, seems quite normal.

Yes, I've been told beforehand that scallops can move, but I didn't expect anything like this. The jet-propelled hop was more than ample to put the scallop out of my reach and allow it to disappear under thicker grass in deeper water. The pickings obviously aren't going to be as easy as I'd thought.

I'm about to go horizontal in the water again when my son Pat, age eight, announces triumphantly that he has secured his first scallop. "But it's trying to bite me," he adds uncertainly. "Here, you take it."

The scallop begins acting like an angry castanet as it hops around the palm of Pat's hand. The shell opens and snaps shut like chattering teeth as it attempts to propel itself away.

Not quite sure how to quell a cranky scallop, I take it from him and begin fumbling with the latch on my goodie bag, the mesh pouch for storing the scallops. Just as the bag flies open, so does the scallop—then it closes on the tip of my finger.

Surprised, I instinctively shake my hand to dislodge the tiny aggressor . . . realizing too late I've just given dinner its freedom.

Patrick has watched the whole encounter with wide eyes. He's gathered plenty of sedate, docile oysters before; but scallops—he didn't know they'd fight back.

"It's all in how you hold them," I advise him sagely. "Just pretend they're a set of plastic clacking teeth—only don't let them open their mouth!"

At that point Jeff Butler and his son, who have been snorkeling near us, start laughing. "Attacked by a vicious scallop, were you, O'Keefe?" Butler chortles. "I promise you won't hear the end of this one!"

Well, he is wrong. By putting my head back in the water I am able to muffle the rest of his words just fine. By now, all of the scallops near me have departed, but there are plenty more just a few yards away.

Since this is a weekday morning, we're sharing the flats with few other scallopers. On a weekend, many shallow bays from Steinhatchee to Port St. Joe on Florida's Gulf Coast hold many more scallopers.

To locate scallops, you almost always first have to find eelgrass. That is the most important factor to keep in mind when searching uncharted scalloping territory. If there's grass just below the low tide level, there's a good likelihood you'll find a scallop bed.

In any area, it's just a matter of snorkeling or wading until you locate the scallop beds. Compared to other sought-after mollusks—clams and oysters—I have to rank scallops as far more interesting, as well as the most tasty. Scallops just seem to have a lot more character. Or maybe I'm just a sucker for those Bette Davis eyes.

Undoubtedly the most fascinating feature of a scallop is its eyes. Each scallop has between thirty and forty of them just inside the edge of its shell.

Scientists say the eyes of scallops are relatively sophisticated. They are actually used for seeing and are not some decoration that create only the illusion of sight.

Each eye has a focusing lens, a receptive retina, and conducting nerve fibers. It's speculated that if scallops were sedentary, like oysters and clams, they might never have developed the capacity for vision. But movement and the ability to see usually go hand in hand, so the scallop apparently found it necessary to evolve eyesight.

Consider their design, too. Usually one side of the shell is more curved than the other. Naturally you would expect the scallop to rest on the flatter side, but it does just the opposite. The curved side serves as its resting platform, which keeps the opening off the bottom and enables the animal to take in cleaner water. It also allows a faster takeoff when it swims away.

Scallops propel themselves by flapping their shells together the way a bird does its wings. A scallop is the bat of underwater aviators. Its flight pattern is very erratic, a combination of forward movement and then free-fall between flaps, so that it seems almost to be staggering ahead.

In all its moving around, a scallop may develop an oversized adductor muscle, the same way weightlifters grow gargantuan biceps. This adductor muscle is the part of the scallop we eat.

Unfortunately, it takes a lot of those little muscles to put together a meal considering the small scallops that populate Florida's shallow bays. Scallops served in restaurants are a larger, deepwater variety.

Since the morsel from each scallop is somewhat Lilliputian, searching the shallow bottom for the creatures is more for fun than profit. The reward is in the meal, and for most of us that's more than enough.

As we continue to paddle through the water, each of us carries a small mesh bag so we don't have to make continued return trips to land to unload. We've decided not to haul a boat this particular day but to wade from shore and stockpile our hoard aboard a raft instead. Overall, this makes it much easier to maneuver in the shallows.

Despite the many scallops flitting over the bottom, it requires a surprising amount of time for the bags to start bulging. As the tide grows higher, there seem to be more of the creatures, but they also become more troublesome to catch. With a couple of young boys along, we are forced to retreat shoreward ever so gradually so they can stand up whenever they choose.

Considering all the eelgrass, I have a feeling after a while that we aren't making the most productive use of our time. We could have a fishing rod or two out for seatrout. Which wouldn't be a bad way for a family scalloping from a boat to divide the work: half the people fish part of the day while the rest scallop, then switch. Of course, a water rat like me would have a hard time passing on his snorkel.

Since we are snorkeling during the hottest part of the day, we all wear shirts. I'm sure many people who can develop dark tans wouldn't need the protection, but I recommend this precaution to any fair-skinned Celt like myself.

Once back on shore, we ice down the scallops immediately. Scallops don't seem to have anywhere near the out-of-water longevity of clams and oysters. Further, once they expire, their shells pop open. The meat can spoil quickly if not properly cared for.

Although some people apparently feel scallops are tough to pry open, the fact that they don't hold their shell together for very long makes them a snap to clean. Simply put them on ice and, by the time you get home, you should find most of the scallops open and ready for cleaning.

All the insides of a scallop are said to be edible. Like most people, I'm content to remove only the muscle and discard the rest.

Perhaps one day I will reconsider: if we complain about how many shells it takes to fill a goodie bag, we are always shocked to see how little scallop meat we actually end up with.

After a day of catching and cleaning, I'm usually ravenous, so I like to prepare scallops quickly. One of the fastest ways, as well as one of the tastiest, is simply to saute them in butter and garlic. As long as you don't use too much, the garlic is just the right complement to the scallop's delicate taste. A sprinkle of ground ginger is good, too.

As with most seafoods, scallops are also excellent when dressed up with a sauce. If you save the shells ahead of time you can serve them the following way: first, poach about two pounds of scallop meat in just enough white wine to cover them for about six minutes. Add salt and pepper to taste. Then drain and save the wine broth.

While the scallops are draining, saute a half-pound of chopped mushrooms and a chopped onion together in butter. Cook them until they become almost a paste. Spread the mushroom-onion-butter mixture in the bottom of the scallop shells.

Now it's time to saute another half-pound of mushrooms in butter for three minutes. Then add four tablespoons of flour and mix well. To this, pour in a half cup of tomato puree and the wine broth. Stir until the sauce is thick and well blended.

Finally, it's time for the scallops themselves to make another appearance. Put them in the shells, pour the wine-and-mushroom sauce over them, and sprinkle with bread crumbs. Heat quickly under a broiler.

This dish tastes so good there won't be any leftovers, which means there's only one thing left to do: go after more scallops.

Who

Local legal restrictions are always time-dated, so be sure to check with local tackle or dive shops or call the Florida Marine Patrol at 904/488-5600.

What

Mechanical, commercial harvesting is prohibited in water less than three feet deep, so snorkelers working the shallows should have the scallop beds all to themselves. Bay scalloping territory has become more limited in recent years because of overharvesting. Also, the day's limit has dropped from five gallons to two.

When

The season usually starts in early June and runs until early fall. How good a particular season is depends on how many scallops migrate into the shallows.

Where

Recreational scalloping is exclusively a Gulf Coast venture and takes place every summer between Port St. Joe and the town of Steinhatchee in the Big Bend area of the Panhandle. A boat is normally required since shore access is limited. Boat ramps are available at several places, including Steinhatchee, Keaton Beach, St. Marks National Wildlife Refuge, the Wakulla River, and in the many small fishing villages bordering US 98 from Newport to Port St. Joe.

22

Spotlighting Alligators
at Night

Some activities defy rational justification. Going out into the Everglades, alone, at night, to spotlight alligators is one of them.

Further more, this trip isn't turning out to be as simple as planned. I've spotlighted plenty of gators before, but always from a boat and always with fiberglass or metal separating me from the animals. In the Everglades, there are no barriers between man and beast. This is cause for some concern, since, in short bursts, alligators can move surprisingly fast, easily outrunning a person. The prescribed remedy if a gator chases you is to run zig-zag, since the animal can't make the same fast maneuver.

All well and good, except that I am on a pathway atop a sloping grassy bank only a few feet above the water. There is nothing to prevent a determined gator from joining me on the path, which is too narrow to perform the gator two-step. So, I shine my light not only in the water but also ahead of me to make sure a gator isn't already waiting on the trail.

It is rare to be in the wild with something as primal, as threatening in appearance, as an alligator. It is one of the few wild animals left in North America that can eat people for lunch whenever it wants. No other predator faces people so boldly, so routinely. Bears and panthers are cowards in comparison. Evidence of their presence is normally indirect, left only in their tracks. A gator, on the other hand, acts almost as if humans are irrelevant. It's hard to be dismissed by an animal, to be made to feel you don't count.

In some respects, gators *are* superior—one of nature's major success stories. They have adapted so well to their environment that they have not needed to evolve for millions of years. Comparatively, humans are late arrivals in the scheme of things.

However, not all alligator species have survived. Only two are left, here in the United States and in China. Everything else that even remotely resembles an alligator is classified as a crocodile or a caiman.

Although Florida has the largest gator population of anywhere, the American alligator ranges all along the Southeast from the Virginia/North Carolina border to central Texas. But only Florida and Louisiana have enough marshy terrain to allow the animals to live in every part of the state. In the rest of the Southeast, alligators are limited to the coastal flatlands. Here's a shocker, seventy million years ago, when the climate in Montana was considerably warmer, a small species of alligator once lived there.

Americans always like to think we grow things bigger, and when it comes to alligators, it's definitely true. Our American alligator makes the Chinese species look puny. Chinese alligators live in the freshwater marshes bordering the Chang Jiang River on the eastern coast are stockier, shorter, and rarely grow longer than five feet. The American gator averages between eight and ten feet, though some may even grow as long as nineteen feet. Those are the giants.

Despite the huge populationof gators, attacks on humans are rare in Florida, but that doesn't make it any less stressful for anglers who wade fish in the lakes throughout the state. Gators are notorious for making caves in the bottom of swamps and marshes called "gator holes." There's nothing like stepping into one that's over your head. You and God become friends for life, because that gator just might be at home; it's made my heart leap out of my throat. Gators like to stay in these warm holes in cold weather, and the rest of the time they often hide in them and use them as storehouses for their larger kills.

During droughts, gator holes become vital watering holes for animals who might otherwise perish. It's difficult to imagine this ancient eating machine as an important survival factor for other animal species, but it is.

Yes, it would be much more reasonable to be somewhere else, but I just have this urge to peer into a pair of gator eyes. I've chosen this location in the Everglades because of expert advice. Earlier, I asked an Everglades National Park ranger if he knew of any airboat rides that went out at night to spotlight gators. He'd told me to forget the airboat and do my spotlighting from shore at the Royal Palm visitor center just two miles inside Everglades National Park. The park gates never close, the ranger advised, so I could go at any hour and stay as long as I pleased. If I just walked the Anhinga Trail behind the Royal Palm center, I'd see all the gators I wanted. "The water level is a little high now, so there aren't as many as there were," he said at the end. "But how difficult can it be to find an alligator in the Everglades?"

I already was familiar with the popular Royal Palm site and the half-mile-long Anhinga Trail, one of the park's most popular stops. The trail borders a large pond located behind the rest room area, and I've always seen gators there. In fact, last time, a big gator was lazing on the grassy bank on the other side of a stone barrier, less than a dozen feet from me.

Somehow I'd forgotten that the stone barrier is a short one and does not extend all along the Anhinga Trail. This is why I'm recalling my childhood, thinking of Captain Hook and the fearsome crocodile, which, after sampling one of the captain's arms, was always in pursuit of other body parts. Of course, alligators are typically less aggressive than crocs, but at this particular moment such fine distinctions are unimportant. This walk in the dark is wreaking havoc on my psyche.

Logically, I know that any threat is more invented than real. What are the odds that a rogue alligator would be at the Royal Palm center this evening? Rationally speaking, I am more likely to win the lottery than be gator bait.

The problem is that the night noises are telling a different story. Once darkness is complete, all sorts of unidentified guttural grunts and croaks begin emanating from the swamp, gradually increasing in frequency and intensity. Occasionally, this chorus is interrupted by a loud splash, sometimes two, when everything becomes silent for a moment. In the darkness, the process of life and death turns into an eerie and disturbing soundtrack.

Surrounded by so much furtive activity, it doesn't seem unreasonable that something might crawl out of the swamp to greet me on the trail. Woosh-flap! Woosh-flap! The sudden noise is somewhere at the edge of the path ahead. I fling the beam of light in all directions, finally settling on a bird flapping its wings, trying to dry them. The black-plumed creature looks like a silhouette darting about against the backdrop of night . . . really strange.

It's an anhinga, the bird for which the trail was named. Am I glad to see it! So much so that I consider returning for a moment to the lighted rest rooms back at the parking lot—no, that particular emergency is behind me, so to speak.

The anhinga drying itself on the tree limb is also called a water turkey and a snake bird. It is one of Florida's most distinctive birds. It swims almost totally submerged, with only its snaky-looking long neck and head above water. It captures food by diving underwater and spearing a fish with its beak, then it surfaces and tosses the fish into the air, catching it, and swallowing it head first.

Definitely a neat trick, but that's not what makes the anhinga so remarkable. The anhinga is commonly seen sitting on branches, its wings extended like it is in a constant state of alarm, because it lacks the oil glands that other water birds have to keep their feathers dry. If the anhinga didn't dry itself regularly, it could get so waterlogged it would sink.

The anhinga must have been as spooked as I was. It takes to the air, flying with obvious difficulty, to find a roost well away from the path. Slapping a mosquito off my face, I apologize silently to the anhinga; I wanted his company.

I slap my forehead with the palm of one hand. The bug goop isn't working very well. I'm reluctant to look at my sleeves or chest, certain that I'll see a moving mass of wings and bodies. So with one hand, I spotlight the water. With the other, I swat mosquitoes.

Although alligators may seem to do little else but bask in the sun and play dead, their speed in short bursts allows them to enjoy a diverse diet of turtles, garfish, wading birds—and anything else that comes too close to the water's edge at dinnertime. I suspect that the occasional splashes are definitely from feeding gators, since few other animals here make much noise.

As more of South Florida has become populated, alligators have expanded their diet to include dogs (as in family pets). In gator country, a barking dog is a dinner bell, and the reptiles will go to a lot of effort to seize one.

I remember reading a recent story about a large gator living in a drainage canal behind a residential development. Dogs began disappearing. Finally, an alligator was spotted sneaking into the backyard to dine on a dog tied up in the yard. The gator was removed. Gators have even been known to break onto screen porches to grab a dog.

Earlier today, I once again witnessed the reluctance of tourists to accept that their pet is a delicacy. I stopped at the alligator farm near the Everglades Park entrance. The people on duty were working hard to convince an elderly couple not to take their leashed poodle with them while they toured the farm. The couple thought it was a joke.

"Your dog definitely will attract the gators," a gator farm employee told them. "We can't be responsible for you or your dog's safety."

If I was gator spotting near the coast, I'd also keep an eye out for saltwater crocodiles. I'd have to be extremely lucky to see one, since they are truly a vanishing species. Only an estimated 300 to 400 are said to remain, and these are believed to be the last remaining crocodiles anywhere in North America. It's easy to tell the difference between an alligator and a crocodile by the shape of their heads. Crocs have a narrow snout, while gators have a broad, blunt one.

So, if there are all these alligators around, why can't I find one when I need one? What's even more ironic is that so many people today complain Florida has too many alligators—a very different situation from the 1960s when alligator populations had plummeted so low the animals were classified as a threatened species. Gator numbers suffered a massive decline because of the water management policy practiced back then throughout much of South Florida.

Gators are smart enough to build their nests at the normal high-water level, but not much higher. When water management district floodgates released too much water, as they often did several decades ago, the gator nests were flooded and destroyed. When this management practice was altered, the gator populations came bounding back.

There are even enough gators now that hunting them (by special permit only) is legal again. Spotlighting gators at night is an old hunting technique, since the gators apparently are curious about the source of the light and draw near it. When they move close enough, they either get hit or shot in the head. A few hours later, they're made into food and clothing. Hmmmm. I wonder if word is getting around.

After the paved section of the Anhinga Trail, I follow the boardwalks that penetrate the marshland. I scan the sloughs from them but still can't locate any gator eyes, not even on the second boardwalk, which always seems to have gators during the day. The only thing to do is keep retracing my route. This should make the mosquitoes happy. Moving back and forth, I'll be an easy target, like one of those plastic sitting ducks in the shooting galleries at state fairs.

On my third circuit, I finally notice a pair of bumps protruding above the surface, near the middle of the pond. A gator? Finally? And it's right where I always thought it would be, in the pond closest to the rest rooms.

I place the spotlight beam level with my eyes and shine it at the gator. That's the best way to light up a gator's ruby red eyes. If the light is too high or too low, the gator's eyes are obvious, but are not the fiery, glowing coals that reside deep in those orbs. (Holding a flashlight at eye level is also a marvelous way to take children out at night in backyards and parks to spotlight spiders, whose presence is also given away by their bright red eyes.)

The gator seems drawn to the light. Soundlessly and without any obvious surface ripple, the eyes float ever closer. No other part of the gator's body, not even its nostrils, is visible. The disembodied eyes glare commandingly.

The alligator and I have an eyeball-to-eyeball standoff.

I can recall no movie alien that has ever seemed quite as menacing, as calculating . . . or so sure of itself.

I blink first.

On second thought, maybe we have too many alligators in Florida after all.

Who

Many airboat operators do run gator spotlighting tours. That's particularly true in Central Florida where the mosquitoes aren't near as bad as those in the Everglades region. Yet, it's not nearly as much fun with a group as it is by yourself or just with family members. On the other hand, you may prefer the greater security of being with a large group.

What

This is an excellent family activity, since children are usually thrilled by this light show. You need a strong flashlight or lantern to really make the colors of a gator's eyes explode. Insect repellent is essential. Long pants, long-sleeve shirts, and even a hat will also provide protection.

When

Other than after dark, I seem to see most of my gators at twilight and just before sunrise.

Although gators inhabit the marsh along the Anhinga Trail year-round, the best time to spot them is in winter, during the dry season from December to April, when as many as 200 gators may congregate in this deep pond. Once the rains begin in May, the alligators disperse for the summer and fall in the seasonally expanded marshland.

Where

The Everglades is an obvious choice, but it's been said that every body of water in Florida probably holds at least one alligator. It does seem true. Gators are often seen at the edges of lakes, in water hazards on golf courses, and in rivers. You name it, and it's probably got a gator or two living there.

23

Exploring
the Florida Keys

New York may be buried under several feet of snow and Chicago may be gripped by near-freezing temperatures, but the people in the Florida Keys will take little notice. In Florida's "Out Islands," the wrath of winter is a source of amusement, not concern.

There are far more important matters to consider, like the coming contest with a bonefish or perhaps snorkeling over the only living coral reef in the United States. Or perhaps it's something as simple as watching the sun set from Florida's southernmost point, Key West. Whatever the activity, the important thing is that it takes places outdoors, while everyone wears shorts and T-shirts, even in the dead of winter.

Understandably, the Keys are a very popular destination, but during the winter months they're not as crowded as you might think. The biggest migrations occur at Christmas and Easter, the period between drawing only a moderate flock of "snowbirds," as winter visitors are known.

The forty-two islands that make up the Keys curve 150 miles out into the Gulf of Mexico from the southern tip of Florida's peninsula. Arranged like carefully placed stepping stones dotting the water, they originally were a haven for pirates. Later, they became a major wrecking ground for Spanish treasure ships and, eventually, home to the British loyalists after the American Revolution. Today, the Keys are considered America's Caribbean Islands and one of the country's most popular winter playgrounds.

By far the best way to enjoy the romance and beauty of the Keys is to camp them. You can enjoy every sunset and hear the ocean breeze whistling through the trees. State-operated campgrounds are total just three, one each in the Upper, Middle, and Lower Keys. Private campgrounds quite plentiful throughout the

The best way to enjoy the romance and beauty of the Keys is to camp them.

entire chain, many of them miniresorts with a swimming pool and boat docks fronting the ocean or Gulf. Tents and RVs are both welcome at most campgrounds. A complete list of Keys camping facilities is presented in Appendix E.

Note that many of the campgrounds have a Mile Marker number posted with them. Mile Markers are how directions are given in the Keys, and the system couldn't be more precise. Mile Markers are easy to spot: small green signs with white numbers. Mile Marker 126 is the most northerly, located just south of Florida City. Mile Marker 0 is located in Key West at the corner of Fleming and Whitehead streets, though the sign is occasionally stolen by souvenir hunters.

Hauling an RV through the Keys was a nerve-wracking experience until all the narrow bridges linking the islands were replaced with more modern, wider thoroughfares. Not only do the bridges handle campers better, but also many of the major population centers have four-laned their main streets, so traffic no longer moves along at a snail's pace. However, there is one important exception: Sunday afternoon and evening, when lines of weekenders exodus home to Miami and other parts of South Florida.

If you've never visited the Keys before, you should be aware that America's version of the Caribbean has been so romanticized in films and song that you may have some misleading images about what you'll find. Perhaps the greatest misconception is that you'll find island after island of beautiful sandy beaches perfect for secluded picnics and swimming. Unfortunately, for the most part, that's just not so. Instead, the Keys are mostly hard coral rock bordered by thick ribbons of mangrove. But, there are some excellent beaches at the larger resorts—and most of the campgrounds.

Also, don't expect the islands to be lush, tree-covered oases. Shade in the Keys tends to be scarce—except at the campgrounds. More than anywhere else, the campgrounds contain all the natural features you expect but which can be so hard to find.

Throughout the Keys, you'll find some of the finest seascapes around: the blue waters of the Atlantic to the east and south and the green seas of the Gulf of Mexico on the northern side. As you drive along the Overseas Highway (US 1), a completely toll-free road with bridges as short as thirty-eight feet and as long as seven miles, you'll be surrounded on all sides by sea and sky.

In mapping out a trip to the Keys, keep in mind that they are usually divided into three distinct sections: Upper, Middle, and Lower Keys. It requires at least a week to take them all in. With so much to do in a relatively compact area, many visitors never leave the Upper Keys, spending their entire time there.

UPPER KEYS

The Upper Keys extend from Key Largo to Lower Matecumbe. After Key West, Key Largo is probably the most famous destination in the Keys, and not merely because of the Humphrey Bogart film, *Key Largo* (shot mostly in Hollywood). This is the most popular place for snorkeling and scuba diving in the entire United States: Key Largo is home to the John Pennekamp Coral Reef State Park, the first underwater park in the country. The twenty-one-mile-long, three-mile-wide park is the permanently protected home for 650 species of colorful reef fish (neon colored queen angels, grunts, snapper, and grouper) and more than 40 kinds of coral. Numerous dive shops line US 1 near Pennekamp, all of them reputable and most in business for many years. They have snorkel and dive trips that leave both morning and afternoon.

One of the most famous snorkeling spots is the "Christ of the Deep," a nine-foot-high bronze Christ statue standing in about fourteen feet of water. Surrounding it are large coral heads and numerous small tropical fish that make this an excellent introduction to the park.

Around Pennekamp, dive shops tend to be like convenience stores, located on almost every corner. A complete list of all the Pennekamp area dive shops as well as those located throughout the Keys is available in Appendix F.

Pennekamp Park is one of several camping places in Key Largo. It has forty-seven sites, all with tables and charcoal grills and some with electrical hookups and water. A swimming beach has a roped-off area not far from the campgrounds. Reservations should be made in advance. If Pennekamp is full, try the Key Largo Campground just to the south. It is a beautifully shaded camp resort, with a game room, laundry facilities, and a large swimming pool.

Serious anglers will want to camp a few miles farther south at Islamorada, the fishing capital of the Keys. This is where highly skilled guides stalk the wary bonefish, while the big sportfishing boats go forth to do battle with sailfish, kings, and dolphin at the edge of the Gulf Stream. Arrangements for guides and boat rentals can be made at the Caloosa Cove Marina and Bud 'n' Mary's Marina.

Bonefish: Bonefish provide the premier light tackle sport for all the Keys. Bonefish can be a powerful challenge, since you sight-cast to the notoriously spooky fishing using spinning tackle with a steady, smooth drag and 6-pound test monofilament. Bonefish, which typically weigh between three to six pounds, are amazingly powerful for their size.

In terms of looks, the bonefish is flashy: its elongated torpedo shape has bright silver scales that may also have hues of pearl and blue-green. Its small mouth, located under a piglike snout, is used for grubbing the bottom for crabs and other crustaceans. When feeding nose down in shallow flats, a bonefish's tail is often visible above the water. This behavior, known as tailing, is one of the first things a guide looks for when scanning the flats.

Although greatly sought, bonefish are only for sport, not eating. As their name implies, they are far too bony for most people's taste. If a fish is released as soon as it's caught, it should be none the worse for the struggle.

Everyone remembers their first bonefish. Mine raced away, out of control, with a pink jig firmly clamped in its mouth. I watched the line feed out at an unbelievable speed, a hundred feet of 6-pound test monofilament stripped off in the wink of an eye. It was as if I had hooked on to a passing powerboat going full throttle. Unable to stop the fish's progress, I was as helpless as a rider on horseback who's been bounced out of his stirrups. My ultra-light spinning rod danced and bent like a divining rod gone mad. The line was so tight from the fish's continual pull that it hummed dangerously in the wind, seemingly ready to part.

All good things, even a bonefish's incredible stamina, end eventually. Five minutes later I boated the fish, which was so exhausted it was swimming on its side. We resuscitated the fish by moving water through its gills before releasing it. Then my guide returned to the high platform of our shallow draft skiff and resumed poling over the clear-water flats.

It was wonderful. No wonder the bonefish's tenacious strength attracts dedicated anglers from around the country to try their luck. It's often been said that when you really want to test your angling ability, to see if you're as good as you think you are, the bonefish is the target to seek out.

Bonefish are literally everywhere throughout the Keys, although most anglers concentrate their search from Islamorada down to the region of Big Pine Key. However, you don't need a boat to catch bonefish. Almost all the oceanside flats from Key Biscayne to the tip of the Keys are prime bonefish territory. You can locate bonefish by quietly stalking from shore and simply wading the flats. Or you can hire a qualified guide to find them for you with his boat. It all depends on how much time, and money, you can invest in this quest.

Whether you're wading the flats or fishing from a skiff, bonefishing is unique in that your hook never touches the water until you first spot the fish you intend to throw a lure to. Your casts must be precisely aimed, placed just beyond and in front of the fish, so the lure can be slowly retrieved across the fish's path. If you put the lure too far beyond, the a bonefish will swim by without seeing it. Plop it on top of the fish and it will spook, disappearing instantly.

Such precision casting definitely requires some previous skill with a fly or spinning rod. It also helps to have strong nerves to bolster yourself each time the fish and lure make their close encounter. If the fish passes up the lure (as it usually does), it's try, try again.

On occasion, hooking a bonefish can be relatively easy if the fish are in the mood to eat and you tip your jig with a piece of shrimp as an added enticement. But most often bonefish are unbelievably wary and easily spooked. They seem to live in a constant state of alarm. I've known periods when all the fish were so wary they would vanish from sight once the lure was cast but before it hit the water.

Such is the challenging unpredictability of bonefishing.

Permit, Me! Here is yet another fish to truly rejoice over if it happens to take your lure. As hard-fighting as bonefish and tarpon, ounce for ounce, the permit has them both beat. Permit, which range between ten to forty pounds, may demand as much as three hours of hard fighting on light tackle. Permit never quit.

The Atlantic permit, sometimes called great pompano, are present throughout the Keys, but they are seldom seen. Bonefish are hook-hogs in comparison. The greatest concentration of permit appears to be from the Middle Keys, south. The Content Keys are especially noted for their large numbers of permit.

In the past, lucky anglers have been able to see as many as a hundred in a day. Even in such excellent circumstances, it seems you hook only one fish for every three-score you see. Permit are not as visible because they spend a great deal of time in holes and channels and, like bonefish, come up on the flats at flood tide.

However, because permit are so deep bodied, they require twice as much water as a bonefish before they make their flats entry. You can usually spot their tails and dorsal breaking the surface when the fish are feeding. Smaller permit usually travel in schools, while larger fish tend to be loners.

Live crabs are the permit's favorite bait on a 2/0-size hook and 12-pound test line with a 30-pound monofilament leader to withstand the abrasion as the permit scours the line all over the bottom. How close you cast a bait to a fish depends on what it is doing: cruising, feeding, or loafing.

If permit are out for a lazy swim over the flats and don't seem intent on feeding, plunk your bait at least ten to fifteen feet ahead of them to provide enough lead. As sight-feeders, permit tail just like bonefish, their head concentrating on a small patch of bottom. When a fish is feeding, you can afford to cast a lot closer, within several feet, without scaring it. Permit can be incredibly choosy, and you may cast a dozen times before they bother to acknowledge your offering. If spooky, they may be gone before you complete your cast.

Some anglers specifically seek out permit and wait at the edges of deep channels for the fish to present themselves. For most, permit are usually targets of opportunity, met by happenstance when you're out looking for bonefish. To be prepared for both, you need to keep two different outfits handy and ready: one for bones, the other for permit. Neither species will give you time to re-rig.

Landing a permit on a fly is a major accomplishment, one truly to be proud of. Check locally with one of the tackle shops about the pattern that seems to be working. Usually, it's a crab imitation that may be difficult to purchase anywhere outside the Keys.

Cuda! Cuda! Another feisty flats resident is the barracuda, often mistaken for a bonefish because its shadow looks much the same from a distance. Barracudas, regardless of size, are a fun fight. Their razor-sharp teeth demand that you reserve a special rig just for them: highly effective is a brightly-colored tube lure made of surgical tubing tied to a wire leader.

The tube lures can be trolled behind the boat when you are motoring from one flat to the next, or you can sight-cast to barracuda just as you would a permit or bonefish. Silver spoons work well, too.

Like bonefish and permit, cudas should be released unharmed to fight another day. They, too, are considered inedible because their flesh often contains a powerful toxin, which will either make you deathly ill or dead. Net rather than gaff a cuda so it can be released; when you're working the hook free, grasp the cuda's head firmly behind the gills—and don't let go until your task is finished and the fish dumped back over the side, no matter how much it squirms.

Fishing Offshore: At Islamorada, you'll also find a fleet of big charter boats that carry up to four persons for $400–$600 per trip. These thirty- and forty-foot sport-fishermen troll the edge of the Gulf Stream, just a few miles offshore, where sailfish and dolphin provide most of the action. Charter captains provide all the heavy tackle for trolling, but you are expected to bring your own lunch and drinks. Also, be sure to check at the time of booking who keeps the fish you catch—you or the boat. If the boat keeps the fish, they may offer a discount on the charter cost.

For offshore, you might want to bring along light spinning rigs in case you encounter a school of small dolphin. Once a single dolphin is hooked, the rest of the school normally stays around the boat as long as a single fish remains on the line. That can provide some frantic, fantastic fishing.

If you're lucky enough to catch a billfish and want to have it mounted to take back home, keep in mind that gamefish mounts are made mostly of fiberglass. Very little of the real fish you caught gets used. Therefore, since billfish are in short enough supply as it is, it's more sporting to release the fish unharmed after you measure its length and girth. A complete mount can be made using these dimensions, but you need to let your captain know in advance so the fish isn't gaffed and killed.

Other Interesting Sites: Near Mile Marker 78.5 is the Lignumvitae Key State Botanic Site, a 280-acre island located a mile offshore in the Gulf, reached by regular tour boats from Robbie's Marina. The botanic site contains the last virgin tropical hammock of typical West Indian trees, including the lignumvitae tree, an incredible durable hardwood said to live a thousand years. Just think: in 3001, some of the young saplings growing today will just be reaching old age.

The Keys claimed many Spanish galleons, and a mile south of Lignumvitae on the Atlantic side it's possible to view the remains of a wrecked galleon at the San Pedro Underwater Archeological Preserve. The site, in only eighteen feet of water, contains original ballast stones, anchors, bricks, and seven concrete cannon replicas. A hurricane sank the "San Pedro" in 1733.

MIDDLE KEYS

With so many popular activities in the Upper Keys, many people never drive beyond Islamorada. Consequently, the facilities farther south usually aren't as crowded. As in the Upper Keys, fishing and diving are the principal interests. Marathon, a city that ranks second only to Key West in size, is the headquarters for the party-boat fleet that specializes in full- and half-day bottom fishing trips for yellowtail, snapper, and grouper.

Rods are usually an extra charge and are adequate for hauling fish up from the bottom. If you're going to bottom fish regularly, it would be better to use your own rig, with 30 pound test line.

Party boats have a tendency to roll in the waves, and some people do get seasick. Seasickness is one of the worst non-fatal illnesses you can endure. However, seasick remedies are available in the drugstores throughout the Keys, particularly a product called Triptone, which everyone swears by. But you must take the medication at least an hour before leaving shore.

Bottom fishing may not be as challenging as bonefishing, but the results are a lot more edible. Through his bottom recorder, the captain identifies reefs and wrecks that have lots of fish hanging over them. Using mullet or other cut bait supplied without charge, you drop the line to the bottom, then crank the reel four to five turns to get the hook off the bottom and the bait more visible. Then, you wait.

The best place to fish on a party boat is at the stern, since the lines are less likely to get tangled there. However, tangled lines are a normal part of party-boat fishing. The mate can usually untangle them without cutting anyone's line, but in extreme cases such surgery may have to be performed.

The Marathon area has two interesting land-based places to explore. Pigeon Key, which is reached by walking over the ocean on the old Seven-Mile bridge, was a base camp for the construction of Henry Flagler's railroad that went to sea. In 1908, the Pigeon Cay camp included a dock, awarehouse, and several bunk houses that still exist today. There is a small admission fee and scheduled tours are available. Flagler's railroad, which reached Key West in 1912, was an enormous expense and an incredible engineering feat: it's been compared to having a single person sponsor and build the Alaska Pipeline. The railroad was destroyed by a monster hurricane in 1935, but the old railroad bed was turned into the foundation for US 1, the Overseas Highway. Until new overpasses were built in the 1980s, even Flagler's old railroad bridges were used by the highway.

In the middle of Marathon itself is one of the Key's most environmentally sensitive and important archeological sites, the 63.5-acre Crane Point Hammock. It contains North America's sole remaining virgin palm hammock and the remnants of an old Bahamian village. A museum at the site also displays evidence that this cay has been inhabited for the last 5,000 years. The walkway through the palm forest and to the old village offer one of the longest natural hikes anywhere in the Keys.

There is no state park in the Middle Keys itself for camping, but Long Key State Park north of Marathon, near the town of Layton, is an unbeatable camping spot. Located right on the ocean, all campsites face the beach and are canopied by tall, stately Australian pines. It is the finest public camping site anywhere in the Keys. Again, reservations are a must. You will never tire of the wind rustling the branches of the tall Australian pines, one of the most relaxing sounds you could possibly fall asleep to.

Diving in the Middle Keys doesn't receive a lot of publicity, but it can be quite good. The Arch at Sombrero Reef provides a remarkable photo op, a coral bridge that stands eight feet high. French grunts, yellowtails, and angelfish swarm through the shallows here, which vary from only a few feet to a maximum of thirty, ideal for both snorkelers and divers. Good snorkeling continues at nearby Delta Shoal, where a barge rests in the shallows. Unusual reef formations characterize Coffins Patch, loaded with rare pillar corals. Area dive shops are located in Appendix F.

LOWER KEYS

This area officially begins at the southern end of the famous Seven-Mile bridge. Except for Key West and parts of Big Pine Key, the Lower Keys are not nearly as developed. One of Florida's finest Atlantic beaches is located in Bahia Honda State Park, located at MM 38–37. Bahia Honda park is also the only public campground in the Lower Keys.

The best season to enjoy Bahia Honda's long and narrow beach is in fall and winter, when the prevailing winds come from the west. In summer, when the wind tends to come more from the east, the beach is often covered with seaweed. It is state park policy not to remove the stuff since seaweed is a normal part of nature. If the Atlantic beach is unappealing because of the weed clumps, try the much smaller beach on the Gulf side. In some ways, it is far more picturesque because of the old Overseas Highway bridge that can be viewed from there. Both beaches have sand bottoms, something quite normal elsewhere but rare in the Keys.

One of the nation's rarest animals is found in the National Key Deer Refuge located on Big Pine Key. Only about 300 of the deer exist, and it seems unlikely the population on Big Pine will grow much larger because of the heavy traffic going across Big Pine to Key West. Between fifty and seventy deer are killed by autos annually. These animals are wonderful photo subjects (see Chapter 3). Stop at the Blue Hole, which has the largest supply of freshwater in the Keys. Here you'll probably see a couple of alligators, something rare in the Keys where salt water dominates.

Big Pine Key is also the entrance to the Looe Key National Marine Sanctuary, home of the finest coral and fish concentration outside of Key Largo/Islamorada. The spur and groove formation of Looe Key, so classic throughout the Keys chain, is well illustrated at Looe Key. It is also the wreck site of the HMS Looe, a British frigate that sank on the reef in 1744. Ballast stone and the anchor still remain, but are now so overgrown they are difficult to distinguish from the reef itself. See Appendix F for local dive shops.

Big Pine Key is also a good place to join a kayaking tour through the Great White Heron National Wildlife Refuge located offshore. The great white heron, once thought to be a white phase of the magnificent great blue heron, is an uncommon bird found only in Florida and the Caribbean. A wading bird that stalks the shoreline for its food, the great white heron is distinguished from the similar-looking and similar-sized great white egret by its leg color. The great white heron has long yellow legs, while the great white egret has black stilts. The only way to explore the heron refuge is by boat, with the kayak providing the quietest, least disturbing passage through the mangrove islands (see Chapter 7).

Going south, you might want to keep an eye out for the famous bat tower on Sugarloaf Key. It's one of the most ingenious failures in Keys history. Many decades ago, a fish camp owner figured he could reduce the mosquito population and make his guests happier by attracting bats to dine on the ferocious insects. The bats never came, the fishing camp folded, and the tower still stands as part of the Keys zany history.

Key West: After driving through the sparsely populated keys that lead to it, Key West with all its glitz and glitter may come as a shock. Some people compare it to the French Quarter of New Orleans. Others refer to it as the T-shirt capital of the world. Both descriptions are appropriate.

Originally, the city was a combination of Southern, Bahamian, Cuban, and Yankee influences in a unique culture that can be seen in its architecture, tasted in its cuisine, and felt in its relaxed, individualistic atmosphere. Over the years, fishermen, artists, and writers were drawn to the tranquil slip of sand and sea. Ernest Hemingway was among its early devotees, but he would probably hate today's crowds.

Still, Key West has many interesting attractions including Hemingway's former house; the marker which pinpoints the southernmost point in the United States, which actually is not here but in the Dry Tortugas; the Lighthouse Museum with it mementos of the Spanish-American War; and Mel Fisher's Treasure Museum featuring gold, emeralds, and other priceless riches from the wreck of the *Atocha*, the richest Spanish galleon ever found.

Old-time Key Westers proudly refer to themselves as "conchs" (pronounced "konks"), the nickname given Loyalists who fled from the United States to the Bahamas during the Revolutionary War. Many of these people later moved to Key West. The conch was such a popular local symbol that when the British moved the Spanish out of Key West, the victors celebrated the occasion with a conch shell mounted at the end of a flagstaff.

The term "conch" derives from the pink, hard-shelled marine animal sold in huge piles in front of many stores and whose meat is served in delicious fritters, salads, and chowders. The entire Keys are known as the Conch Republic. However, conch are so scarce in the Keys that it is now illegal to harvest them. Much of the conch served here comes from the Bahamas or the Caribbean.

Key West deservedly is famous for its most spectacular sight: sunset. Just prior to the fiery display, sunset watchers are entertained by jugglers, amateur magicians, musicians, and politicians; virtually the entire town turns out to put on its own show. But it's the spectacular sunset everyone comes to see, and a good one often draws a standing ovation from the crowd.

Key West has a number of good dive sites around it, but the city also serves as the staging ground for exploring the remote Dry Tortugas, another sixty miles farther south. Using a live-aboard dive boat for their platform, divers can survey seldom-visited reefs and wrecks that are continually bathed by the warm, clear waters of the Gulf Stream, where visibility ranges an incredible 80 to 100 feet much of the year.

One of the most unusual day trips from Key West is by seaplane to Fort Jefferson in the Dry Tortugas, seventy miles south of Key West. It's even possible to camp there overnight. See Chapter 21, "Getting High Over Florida," for more details. The seaplane people have been dealing with campers for years, so they can offer good advice as well as transport.

Key West Tarpon: Key West is particularly noted for its tarpon fishing, which begins in mid-December and runs into late spring. Tarpon are caught in every way imaginable—trolling, flies, natural bait. Where the fish are at any particular time depends on the weather. When it's been calm and warm for several days in a row, the fish can be taken on the shallow flats. But if one of the all too common cold fronts stirs things up, the fish disappear into deeper water, which calls for a whole new approach.

It's an exciting prospect to sight-cast to an 80- or 100-pound silver king, watch them roll, and wait for one to take the bait. It's also a good idea to use a guide on your first tarpon trips before trying it on your own. Their busiest time is April through June.

Who

A centralized telephone number will send you complete information on any activity anywhere in the Keys. Try to be as specific as possible, so you aren't buried with only general information. Call toll free 800/FLA-KEYS. The Florida Keys and Key West web site is at http//www.fla-keys.com.

As in deep sea-fishing, the person most responsible for a successful bonefishing trip is the guide. Through his long years of experience, he is the one who knows on which flats the fish will be according to how high or low the tide. More importantly, he has the ability to spot fish that most anglers never see. The extreme glare that bounces off the water can be an impenetrable fog, even for those wearing the mandatory polarized sunglasses that help reduce it. The majority of anglers simply never see the dark torpedo shapes swimming over the sand until their guide points them out.

But a good bonefish guide can pick out a bonefish from among the eelgrass and other bottom cover from as much as thirty yards away. When bonefish are spooky, you must cast to them from extreme distances; precision casting becomes next to impossible when you can't see the fish.

A good guide is capable of talking an angler into making a winning cast with instructions like "Bonefish at two o'clock, ten yards out." Of course, the bonefish is apt to be unappreciative of all your efforts and pass up your lure.

What

A complete list of Keys campgrounds is located in Appendix E. Dive shop operators are detailed in Appendix F. The great majority of Keys fishing is done in the Islamorada area. The following marinas have a list of guides for both backcountry and offshore angling: Bud 'n' Mary's Marina at 305/664-2461 and Holiday Isle Marina at 305/664-2321

Small boats can be rented at Bud 'n' Mary's Marina; at Robbie's Marina, 305/664-9814, Islamorada; and CoConut Palmas, 305/743-0552, Grassy Key.

In Key West, the main charter docks are at Garrison Bight and on adjacent Stock Island. The boats usually return around 4 PM, a good time to show up and see who caught what. It's no guarantee the same boat will do as well (or as poorly) tomorrow, but by showing up you can get a feel for the different boat captains and their crews and which ones suit your temperament best.

The easiest and least expensive way to fish the Keys is from the bridges (see Chapter 8 for the proper way to land fish from bridges: it can be tricky). Presently, there are more than forty bridges that can be fished in the Keys. Otherwise, unless posted, you can consider all bridges to be angler friendly. Normally, however, you'll be fishing old US 1 instead of the new thoroughfare, which, from a pedestrians point of view, is far preferable than sharing the road with fast-moving vehicles.

The number of bridges available in the three different parts of the Keys varies dramatically. In the Upper Keys, which extends roughly down to Mile Marker 65, there are a grand total of only a dozen bridges. The Middle Keys, which extends roughly to Mile Marker 40 when the Seven-Mile Bridge is included, contains only three bridges. In the Lower Keys, from Little Duck Key southward, you'll find more than twenty bridges from which to fish. Many are quite short. Because of the intense sun, anglers use a variety of techniques to shelter themselves. Perhaps the most novel, and most thorough for overnight trips, is using a dome tent for a sleeping and sun shelter. Since most dome tents do not need to be anchored into the ground, they are ideal for setting up and sacking out in. Bring a ground cloth to help protect the flooring from abrasion.

During winter, the Florida Keys are the warmest place anywhere on the East Coast. However, the same cold fronts that dump snow and sleet in the Northeast may also impact the Keys with high winds and turbid water, conditions not favorable to either fishing or diving. At the same time, these are the best months for camping. High seas may last only for a few days at a time, so anyone on an extended visit should have no trouble getting offshore.

The surest months for calm conditions are generally from mid-April to November. The waters tend to be the flattest and clearest in the middle of summer, also the time of highest temperatures and regular afternoon showers. Summertime camping without air conditioning can be brutal, but with AC, the Keys are as comfortable as anywhere else.

Hurricanes and tropical storms typically occur between August and November. Since the highest land anywhere in the Keys is only a few feet above sea-level, evacuate to the mainland if there is a storm warning. And don't wait until the last minute, since there are only two two-lane roads that lead out of the Keys. Any evacuation doesn't have to be long or permanent. Within two or three days of the first warnings, the storm is past. Unless the Keys have suffered a direct hit, feel free to return and set up camp again.

Yes, weather in the subtropics may make things uncertain, but it's never boring!

24

Stalking
the Wily Lobster

Locating lobsters can be a lot like finding a needle in a haystack. In both instances you must rely on eyesight instead of feel, or the search could be painful. After all, if you go sticking your hands into coral crevices for lobsters you might come out with a moray eel instead, and chances are you don't want one.

The lobster is the undisputed delicacy of the sea. It is craved by jewfish, octopus, skates, and sheepshead and other predators, which, in addition to man, dine on the tasty crustacean whenever possible.

Realizing its appeal is more than shell deep, the lobster has adopted the policy of many movie stars and taken to a sheltered reclusive life. As a result, snorkelers and divers will usually find lobster fairly difficult to locate. Normally, all you see are the thin waving antennae protruding out from under ledges, crevices and holes, and reef caves.

Sometimes the antennae can be mistaken for soft octocorals moving with the current unless you know exactly what to look for. With patience and practice, it doesn't take long to turn into a competent lobster hunter.

Just as grits, cornpone, and good chili are peculiar to one part of the country, so it is with the southern lobster. *Panulirus argus*, as it is formally known, is quite distinctive in its lack of claws, a prominent feature much coveted on its northern counterpart. This has both its good and bad points: it means the southern lobster is easier to catch since you don't have to worry about your fingers getting crushed in a hearty handshake, but there's also less of the lobster to eat.

Unlike the cold-water namesake, the southern lobster comes in for a lot of bad names. Evidently, since it doesn't have claws, people feel they can call it about anything they want: crayfish, crawdad, bug. They believe if it doesn't have claws, it doesn't have class. The southern lobster is known most commonly as spiny lobster, receiving the name from the many sharp spines that protrude along its sides and its spiny-looking antennae.

The spiny lobster, found from Florida southward into the Caribbean, normally migrates in the fall following spawning and molting. These mass movements can involve thousands of the creatures in Florida and Mexico after the first winter storm. The lobsters seem compelled by some mysterious force to move to deeper water, forming long lines in the open as they travel—a movable feast for the diver lucky enough to find them.

Normally, however, you have to be content to take lobsters one at a time. During the day they are usually located around reefs, but don't confine your activities just to there. Lobsters also reside around jetties and artificial reefs made of old cars or tires. Since artificial reefs are visited mostly by line fishermen, these areas can be well worth regular weekday visits when angling activity is minimal.

In shallow water you can cover considerable lobster territory by dragging a snorkeler slowly behind a boat. Then, when a lobster is spotted, the snorkeler simply lets go and descends to capture his meal.

No one should tackle a spiny lobster bare-handed. It's not that it bites or anything, but the shell is sharp and can be unpleasant to grab. Heavy cotton or nylon gloves are almost essential.

The first time you spot a lobster, the natural urge is to grab the ends of the exposed antennae. That's fine if all you want is a matched set of antennae, which are too delicate to endure much manhandling and normally break off. However, sometimes a lobster has to be nabbed by the antennae because it's wedged in too tight to reach it any other way. Grab it at the antennae base. Any higher up and the antennae will break off.

Lobsters are fairly curious and not very bright, so if you haven't spooked one too badly you may be able to lure it out of its cave by cunning and guile. How? Simply beckon to it with your finger while the rest of you stays motionless. The lobster may become curious enough about the movement that it will move from its hiding place so you can grab it. Sound absurd? I agree.

I'll never forget the time I was diving at about sixty feet with a friend named Tony. We had our minds on things other than lobster, so we were surprised to see a large bug of about four pounds peering at us from under a ledge. Since Tony was the veteran lobster-catcher and I had my hands filled with camera gear, Tony had the honors.

Tony wasn't diving with gloves, and he wasn't thrilled with the idea of simply reaching in and grabbing the lobster by the carapace unless forced to. So he simply lay flat in front of the cave and motioned to the lobster to come out; the lobster did, part way.

When my strobe went off the lobster must have realized it was about to star in an epic it wanted no part of, for it retreated a little. Fortunately, it still was out far enough for Tony to grab it easily by the base of the antennae. The lobster was now destined to be the main course at Tony's anniversary banquet.

Once Tony had the lobster in a firm grip with both hands, he had no worry about keeping it. He handled it freely for me to take close-up pictures of its head, shell, and legs.

At one point the lobster almost exploded backwards out of Tony's right hand, but his grip was too firm. Even if it had escaped, chances were good it would only be temporary.

If a lobster gets free, swim after it as fast as you can. Although lobsters do move extremely fast when they snap backwards like a shrimp, an escaping lobster shouldn't be considered lost. While it may appear to be moving at jet speed, the burst often occurs only once and the flight path is normally in a straight line. Before too long, you'll probably see it resting on the bottom (undoubtedly thinking nasty thoughts) or crawling along slowly.

To try again, approach slowly and distract the lobster's attention with one hand while you catch it with the other. Sometimes a lobster will remember it has seen that trick somewhere before and keep up a fast, steady retreat. In this case, you might as well give up unless you feel like some futile swimming practice.

Suppose your lobster doesn't want to play games but wants to stay at home. How do you dislodge it from its hiding hole? The obvious answer is to reach in and grab it with your glove-covered hand.

The only problem is that many reef creatures, including lobsters, sometimes have roommates you wouldn't want to meet on a blind date: sea urchins, scorpionfish, moray eels.

On the other hand you may discover a lobster has a boyfriend or girlfriend and you find two where you had expected only one. The procedure, in any case, is to indelicately grab the lobster by the head and pull strongly, twisting at the same time, to dislodge it. Or, if there's room, spread your hands, reach in the opening, and grab.

Understandably, some people are squeamish about sticking an appendage in any place where it might be punctured or nibbled. For them (and I include myself in this group) there are several other methods equally effective.

If the lobster's hiding place has a sand or mud bottom, you can stir it up with your hand or an old broom handle. After you've done this, get back to the edge of the muddy water. A lobster evidently doesn't appreciate water pollution and will usually leave its cave: grab it.

Lacking a dirt floor, you can try "tickling" the lobster. This is really a misnomer, since it's doubtful a lobster feels anything funny through its shell. In tickling, you take a blunted broom handle or stick and reach into the hole and tap the lobster on the shell. You shouldn't need to jab or gouge to get it to come out.

If things that go bump in the night don't bother you, late evening or after sunset is perhaps the best time to dive for lobsters. At night, the spiny lobsters themselves venture forth in search of food. The creatures are actually scavengers, although if given a choice they will dine on other lobsters, sea urchins, crabs, and other smaller crustaceans.

You will sometimes find lobsters in the strangest places at night. I still vividly remember coming back to shore from a night dive and encountering a spiny lobster in less than three feet of water only a couple of yards from the beach. What made this so unusual was that a fairly large number of divers were continually going in and out of the water, yet this four-pound lobster walked casually over the sand bottom.

My light seemed to temporarily startle the bug, just as the sight of it surprised me, for it ran a rather confused pattern before making its way to deeper water.

Since lobsters often move onto shallow sandy flats at night, netting can some-

You have to be content to take lobsters one at a time.

times be more efficient than diving. To net, you need a bully net, which has a long handle and a hoop attached at a right angle.

With a bully net you pole or drift quietly across the flats until your light either picks up the lobster or its orange-red eyes. Then you keep the light on the lobster and continue to approach quietly. When you're close enough, scoop it into your net.

Because of heavy lobstering pressure each year, the size of the average legal lobster is only a pound. The law says a legal lobster is one with a carapace of more than three inches, measured from the depression behind the eye horns to the rear edge where it joins the tail. Unless you're eating on board, tail and carapace are not supposed to be separated until you return to shore. Once wrung, a legal tail is supposed to measure six inches from the top of the shell to the tip of the tail fin.

The spiny lobster is not only a delicacy, it is delicate and must be handled properly after capture to prevent spoilage. It should be kept cool in some way, either immediately put on ice in a wet burlap sack or, best yet, in a refrigerator. Lobsters, like crabs, can sometimes be kept alive for several days in a refrigerator or ice chest.

Once a lobster dies, it should be cooked immediately or the tail removed. This last point is crucial if the lobster is to be kept from spoiling. Once a lobster dies, the digestive juices of the intestines and stomach may seep into the tail, causing contamination. This is why they should be put on ice immediately after capture.

Many people make the mistake of eating only the lobster tail and discarding the rest of the animal. That's extremely wasteful, almost like throwing away the rest of the cow after taking out the tenderloin. It's even sillier when you realize the tastiest part of the lobster isn't even the tail. The tastiest meat is in the legs.

Assuming you cook a whole lobster by whatever method (we'll mention a couple of favorites shortly), this is how you make the most out of your catch.

Wearing a pair of your well-padded gloves, first twist the antennae off at the base. Then crack open the antennae for the appetizing chunks in the base. Next, remove the tail from the body by twisting the lobster halfway and pulling. If you're really hungry, you can attack the tail section immediately. This is done by cutting the underside of the taillengthwise with a pair of scissors or a sharp knife. Bending the tail backwards will split it open. After pulling out the tail meat, remove the intestinal vein.

To extract the meat in the body, first unhinge the back shell. Next, remove the stomach sac from behind the eyes. Everything else in there—the liver, the roe of the female, the white meat—is edible. Only the spongy gills are not. Don't forget also to crack open the lower part of the body. There's a lot of white meat in there, too.

On a large lobster, you've saved the best, the legs, for last. The legs are cracked open just like a crab's. You may find big chunks of succulent, very tender meat in the legs. Unfortunately, there's not enough to bother with on small, skinny-legged lobsters.

Lobsters can be cooked in any number of ways. The easiest method is boiling. You simply drop the live lobster into the boiling salted water head first, making sure you have enough water to cover the tail. Place a lid on and bring the water back to a boil. Cooking time depends on the size of the lobster. It takes 7 minutes for a one-pound lobster, 12 minutes for a two-pounder, 15 minutes for three to five pounds, and about 20 minutes for a big bug going six to ten pounds. Once cooked, the lobster should be placed under cold water for a few seconds, then served while still hot.

However, my favorite cooking method is grilled surf and turf on the beach at sunset served along with salad, garlic bread, and wine or beer. The combination of food, drink, and sunset on the water is unbeatable.

To prepare the lobster for the charcoal, simply wrap either tails or split lobster in aluminum foil and place them about three to four inches above the ready coals. A one-pound lobster should cook about fifteen minutes with the shell side down, then turned and cooked another ten minutes. The lobster needs to start cooking well before the steaks. If you want the lobster a little firmer and darker you can remove it from the foil and grill it another minute or two before serving.

Just before the steaks and lobster are ready, place the buttered garlic bread on the grill and toast both sides. Then take a sip of wine. After diving all day, you've earned it.

I know of no finer way to greet the night.

Who/Where

Spiny lobsters can be found from Palm Beach County southward through the Keys; they are also sometimes caught as far north as Daytona Beach. A complete list of Keys dive operators is found in Appendix F. A list of dive shops serving Miami and the Gold Coast is presented in Appendix G.

What

The taking of lobster is carefully regulated. To harvest them legally, you need a Florida Saltwater Fishing License with a current crawfish stamp. The following laws are subject to change at anytime, so always check locally at a dive shop before you reach for that first lobster, or contact the following authorities. For regulations covering state waters (three miles on the ocean side and out to nine miles in the Gulf), call the Florida Marine Patrol at 800/DIAL-FMP. Federal regulation begins where the state boundaries end. For the latest federal regulations, call the National

Marine Services Fisheries at 813/570-5305 or 305/743-2437.

Crawfish or lobster must remain whole while being transported on or below the waters of the state. You will be in violation of this provision if you remove the tail before you are back on land.

No egg-bearing females can be taken. Spears, grabs, and hooks are prohibited. Divers are required to have a carapace measuring device with them and take the necessary measurements when in the water. For a lobster to be legal, the carapace must be more than three inches long. Tails that have been separated from the body must measure greater than five-and-a-half inches; authorities sometimes do check ice chests.

You're limited to six lobster per person per day, and the diver's down flag must be posted. Boats are not supposed to come within a hundred yards of the diver's down flag. Lobstering at night is not permitted in the Keys, but is legal in other state-protected waters. Lobstering is also illegal in the waters of Everglades National Park, Biscayne Bay/Card Sound Spiny Lobster Sanctuary, Dry Tortugas National Park, and Pennekamp Park (during the sport season and in certain areas during the regular season).

Warning: One of the worst things to get caught doing is stealing lobsters from a commercial trap. If the law catches you, it's a minimum $250 fine. If the lobster-man catches you, it could be a bullet. That's no exaggeration. Since they've been shut out of Bahamian waters, commercial lobstermen are getting touchier than ever (not that they've ever taken kindly to sport lobstering). A number do carry guns to protect their traps.

When

Lobster season runs from the beginning of August through March. The last full weekend before August is a special period for recreational harvesting only. The waters are well patrolled then, and limits are strictly enforced.

25

Getting Wrecked
in Miami

At first, the outline of the big ship is hazy and indistinct. As we swim closer, it slowly becomes a massive, shadowy apparition. This tanker rests in ninety feet of water, so it is shrouded in perpetual twilight even on the brightest day. We glide down to stand on the deck. I look behind me and see the empty, windowless bridge, which looms over us like a burned-out skyscraper.

In the waters surrounding us are more than two dozen other ship wrecks that rest in less than 100 feet of water. These are not relics of some great World War II battleground—in fact, most are within eyesight of the Dade County shoreline.

Surprisingly, Dade County now has more diveable wrecks than almost anywhere in the world. And the wrecks are all relatively new ones, sunk since 1981, which means there's little danger of one crumbling down around us while we're swimming inside a corridor or cargo hold.

Why was the ocean floor off Miami deliberately "junked" with these ships? To create a whole new system of artificial reefs that would increase fish and other marine life. As on land, the sea is mostly devoid of animal life except in those rare places where shelter and food are readily available. In the ocean, these essential factors are supplied by a three-dimensional structure of some kind—a natural reef, a sunken ship, a downed airplane, whatever, as long as it enables some animals to build on the outside and others to hide on the inside.

The best diving is found on the five most accessible artificial reef sites, all of which contain multiple wrecks. They are Government Cut, Anchorage, Key Biscayne, R.J. Diving, and Haulover.

In Key Biscayne alone, you can dive the 105-foot-long tug, *Rio Miami*, sunk in seventy feet of water. Joining the *Rio Miami* is a three-ship package known as the

Belzona Triangle named after the corporation provided the funds that acquired the ships.

The marine growth on several of the older vessels is incredibly prolific and colorful. The ships are not merely bare metal hulks, which, when first seen from a distance, are only briefly dramatic. Instead, these ships are packed with far greater numbers of passengers than they ever held while afloat. A few are so encrusted they look like they have been down for decades.

The Department of Environmental Resource Management (DERM), is the agency in charge of finding and positioning these artificial reefs. DERM has placed over 500,000 cubic yards of reef material, including a couple of Tenneco Oil platforms. The oil platforms, located on the Dade/Broward County line, form the largest single artificial reef on the entire East Coast of the United States.

A good number of these new "shipreefs" came from the Miami River, once home to many abandoned vessels. Unfortunately, those have been used up, so now DERM is relying on donated ships or buying confiscated vessels from the U.S. Coast Guard. The key to creating a living shipreef is to sink a vessel shallow enough to permit sunlight penetration so the ships can provide the foundation for marine growth. Anything over 100 feet is too deep for this to occur.

Depth is not the only consideration in creating a successful artificial reef. It must also be placed on a barren sand bottom where it won't compete with or disrupt any part of the natural reef system.

The coral and sponge growth that attaches to the outside of a ship provides a food supply first for the juvenile fish that take up residence. After that, larger species move in to take advantage of the newly created food chain. In essence, the artificial reef program simply speeds up the natural process. It takes about twenty years for a wreck to fully duplicate a natural reef system.

Creating any artificial reef is a costly and time-consuming process, and it's especially so with ships. First, a vessel has to be cleaned of all fuel, fluids, freons, hydrocarbons, and anything else not compatible with sea life. Also removed are doors and anything else that might float off to become a hazard to surface craft.

Within hours of sinking, fish begin appearing at their new reef. They apparently begin schooling out of curiosity, then remain because the living conditions are ideal.

Algal growth, the first important element of the new reef system, appears within a few weeks, followed by the corals and sponges. Anywhere from six months to a year after sinking, divers will find a new community that didn't exist before. The site only gets better and better every year, as new residents move in and old ones expand.

Divers are able to approach quite closely the fish schooling over the wrecks, as long as they don't use quick jerky movements with their arms. To fish, such move-

Sunken ships act as artificial reefs. They enable some animals to build on the outside and others to hide on the inside.

ment looks menacing and threatening; the fish may mistake you for a predator and depart very quickly. Instead, glide or drift toward a wreck on an imaginary flight path like an airplane landing smoothly on the deck of an aircraft carrier. As long as you appear harmless, fish often assume you are.

The coral growth on some ships is incredibly profuse, and it should be treated with the same respect and consideration as a natural reef. That means no kicking, pulling, or souvenir collecting.

The 200-foot freighter *Almarante* was one of the first artificial reefs. It sits in 130 feet of water off Elliott Key. It is heavily coral encrusted and alive with fish, particularly French angels, grunts, and a roving patrol of barracuda. You'll also find lots of beautiful gorgonian fans, colorful encrusting sponges, hydroids, and ascidians. If you visit, carry a flashlight, even in daytime, to appreciate the incredible colors growing on the open decks as well as in the hidden nooks and crannies.

The *Ultra Freeze* was sent down in the summer of 1984. Bottoming out at 120 feet, she is one of the most popular deep dives. The top is as shallow as seventy feet. From the very beginning one of the wreck's main attractions has been a large school of horse-eye jacks.

The *Orion* was a tugboat that worked in the Panama Canal. Sunk in the early 1980s and still looking very much like a tugboat, it sits in ninety-five feet of water, listing slightly to starboard. You'll find a tremendous photo opportunity in the still intact wheelhouse. It's possible to swim through the entire ship, especially the holds usually filled with glassy sweepers. Like most Miami wrecks, it has several entrances and exits for divers and current to flow through.

One of the oldest wrecks is the *Biscayne* in about sixty feet of water. It's a forty-foot descent to the top of the deck, and the water here is normally clear and calm. The big schools of fish are diver friendly, including morays that eat out of your hand. Because of its age, the *Biscayne* has an amazingly thick coating of coral and sponges, on par with famous Caribbean wrecks.

Another deep Miami wreck is the *Blue Fire*, in 120 feet of water with 100 feet to the main deck. There is very little to see on the sand areas around this or any of the ships. The best coral formation is always on the top deck. Schools of snapper often hover around the superstructure, which has fallen off to the side.

The *Sarah Jane* is actually a group of wrecks assembled in the same area. A main showpiece is a metal barge, but others are made of wood, which decompose fairly rapidly. Wooden wrecks also have been found to attract a different type of fish and marine growth, plus they lose their high profile very quickly.

The *Belcher Barge*, donated by the Belcher Oil Co., consists of huge concrete pipes and debris that has one of the largest collections of barracuda in the Miami area. In the winter, hundreds of cudas will sometimes be stacked up from the sand all the way to the surface.

The *Shamrock* is north of Government Cut, one of South Florida's main cruise-ship channels. When the tide flushes water out of Biscayne Bay through Government Cut it goes north, so wrecks north of the Cut develop differently. The water north of the Cut is not as clear, but also the growth is faster and the fish life more concentrated. The concrete pipes around the *Shamrock* are one of the best spots for macro photography because of all the tiny marine life.

The *Police Barge* was a wreck that laid undiscovered for many years. Once found, concrete pipes large enough for a diver to swim through were added to take advantage of the rich coral and sponge growth. Lots of grouper and cobia on this wreck, and at night, sportfishing boats like to try for the mutton snapper and cobia.

Dive shops normally schedule their night dives on the wrecks on Saturday evenings, though the schedule may be expanded to weeknights in summer if there is enough interest. Boats leave the dock around 6 PM and anchor over their site just as the sun is setting. By the time you surface, the sun is well set. The dive boats then move shallower to another wreck or to a reef.

Best night dives are on the older, deeper wrecks containing the most coral growth, such as the *Orion* and *Blue Freeze*. After sunset, all the coral polyps on both ships make the wrecks appear like a garden in bloom.

Although sunken ships have worked quite well in providing new habitat for marine life, some future reefs may consist of specially prefabricated items since wrecks offer a limited habitat according to the size of their entrance and exit areas.

Designing certain size openings that fish are known to prefer will only enrich the habitat that much more.

Who/What/Where

For information on the newest artificial reefs or to make a donation to DERM's artificial reef program, call 305/375-DERM. For a complete, current listing of wrecks, make out a $5 check to DERM and mail it to: DERM, 33 SW 2nd Ave., Suite 300, Miami, FL 33130-1540.

In addition to Miami, you'll also find many more diveable wrecks along the Gold Coast, which includes Ft. Lauderdale and extends north through Palm Beach County. You could spend a two-week vacation wreck diving and never come anywhere near seeing them all. A complete list of all the dive shops serving these areas is available in Appendix G.

When

Florida boating and diving are strongly impacted by cold fronts that begin moving into the state in November and last until April. March is almost always a very windy month. Summer is the best period for calm seas and good visibility. Of course, anyone who decides to take a snow break in December or January will certainly find plenty to do on land if the wind shuts down diving. Unless the front is a serious one, conditions should improve after a few days so that the boats are able to go out again.

26

Diving
EPCOT's Living Seas

The giant view ports are packed three deep with people gazing into the interior of the 5.7 million-gallon aquarium. Called the "world's sixth largest ocean," EPCOT's Living Seas aquarium is packed with more varieties of fish than I've ever seen in the real ocean.

As hundreds of fascinated onlookers stare into one of the world's largest fish tanks, I look back at them. I'm inside the tank, swimming underwater with myriads of creatures, including turtles, rays, a sawfish, and many other remarkable animals.

This is not my first visit inside Disney's underwater preserve. When the Living Seas aquarium first opened, I visited with other writers and photographers to take a swim to help promote the new attraction. After a number of months, the Living Seas was closed to all but Disney divers. Ever since, I've regretted I didn't take better advantage of the opportunity to swim here.

As part of Disney's DiveQuest program, any certified diver can now enter the huge tank. Though open to the general public, it still is a privilege to get inside— the number of divers is limited to just sixteen a day. I'm back this time to shoot underwater pictures to accompany a story about DiveQuest that will appear in *Rodale's Scuba Diving* magazine.

This dive is a double treat for me. Not only am I back in the tank, but also I'm here again with a camera, which has required special permission. Underwater photography is not permitted as a normal part of the DiveQuest program because too many photographers chase and spook fish while trying to get their pictures. By mandate, the only things allowed to be spooked on Disney property are visitors in the Haunted Mansion.

I settle to the floor and rest my knees on the bottom of the twenty-seven-foot-deep tank. I am surrounded by a carousel of brightly colored fish. With about 200 species in the tank, it's possible to count more rare creatures in a single dive than most divers will ever see in a lifetime.

Swimming above me now is one such fish, a 500-pound jewfish, so tremendous it looks almost like a dirigible. A fish like this would rarely be sighted in the open ocean, due to fishing and spearing pressure in many parts of the world. I've seen a large jewfish only once before, off the coast of Mexico. It was probably about 300 pounds, not nearly as large as this behemoth. Disney divers have nicknamed this huge fish "Orson" after the late actor Orson Welles, a man of gargantuan size just before he died.

Just a few feet away from me is a sawfish, another incredible rarity for a diver to see closeup. The serrated knobs on the edges of its long, flat snout make it one of the tank's most dangerous-looking animals. Like a broom, the sawfish's nose sweeps back and forth over the bottom as it swims. Fearsome in appearance, this fish may be one of the friendliest fish in the tank according to Disney divers. I will have to take their word for it since visitors are not allowed to have any interaction with the fish. This is strictly a look, don't touch venture. Even so, it's a heck of a floor show.

Overhead, a small squadron of spotted eagle rays are circling, while just a few yards away several endangered green sea turtles rest on the bottom, entirely motionless, imitating rocks. I'd been warned the turtles are the most "dangerous" animals in the tank; they have poor eyesight and can't distinguish fingers from food.

The schools of fish surrounding me are mostly Florida and Caribbean species, many of them collected from the Keys. It's amazing how well they adapt to this manmade environment. The queen angels stay close to the reef, perhaps for protection, while the bolder gray angels follow us to one of the diving bells.

I take a few moments to inspect the detail that went into making this underwater terrain appear so genuine and lifelike. The coral heads are not real but painstaking manmade replicas outfitted with individual sponges and different varieties of corals. They were formed from molds of the real marine animals.

The shapes may be exactingly authentic, but to me it is obvious the colors have been exaggerated. They are glaring, almost neon-bright, to compensate for the low light level inside the tank. This improvement on nature is something quite obvious to me as a diver, but it is not so apparent to the hundreds of people looking through the six- and eight-inch-thick lexan view ports. Just as the Disney imagineers intended, everything to the audience outside appears real, almost magically so.

Most of all, I'm impressed at how well fed all the aquarium residents seem to be, since they show no inclination to dine on each other. Different fish have very different food preferences and different ways of feeding, so it had to be a logistical nightmare to figure out how to satisfy everyone.

For instance, it is in the very best interests of all to keep the sharks well fed. It turns out the sharks have a particular liking for mackerel, so Disney divers use tongs to feed chunks of mackerel to the circling sharks. The sharks seem to be content with this arrangement, and the divers get to retain all of their fingers.

Large reef fish, on the other hand, are fed shrimp, while their medium-sized cousins receive krill, a much smaller shrimp. The tiniest critters are fed very small brine shrimp and flaked food which is sprayed around the coral mounds with a large syringe. Some fish, however, need to graze on coral, algae, or plants. Parrotfish, for instance, are coral feeders who use their hard, beaklike mouths to break off hunks of living coral for their food. This is an inborn preference that must be satisfied in a way that keeps the fish from destroying the carefully arranged scenery.

The problem has been handled in an ingenious way. The aquarium's synthetic coral is made of dental plaster that has ground fish and other foods embedded in it. When the coral crunchers do what comes naturally, they literally eat up parts of the reef. Divers replace the chewed up sections with fresh clumps of food-saturated dental plaster. A perfect arrangement for everyone.

Plant- and algae-eating fish also need special consideration. Plants can't grow without sunlight, which is never present in the aquarium. Furthermore, the tank is kept at a cool 74 degrees Farenheit to suppress algae growth, which has a tendency to get out of hand and take over the best-maintained aquariums. Ironically, the needs of the vegetarians turned out to be especially easy to accommodate—by leaving heads of romaine lettuce out on the reef. Even the coral crunching parrotfish liked the lettuce, too, and they regularly line up to feed at the underwater salad bars.

In all, the aquarium residents consume about 500 pounds of food a day. Each day's feeding is stored in a freezer, then thawed and inspected before introduction into the tank. If approved, the food is prepared in a special stainless steel kitchen. Some items, such as the shrimp, are of such high quality that they could be served to guests in any of Disney's upscale restaurants.

The more I swim about the tank, noting how natural and normal everything looks, the more impressed I am. It was a tremendous feat of engineering to build and fill this 27-foot-high, 203-foot-diameter tank. The weight of the 5.7 million gallons of water filling the tank is tremendous, so well before construction of the aquarium began, the tank site was surcharged with soil that equaled 1.5 times the anticipated tank weight. That involved piling up the dirt and letting it sit. That way, any ground settling likely to occur would take place before building the aquarium ever started.

I swim slowly to one side and run my hand over the reinforced concrete walls. They measure three feet thick at the base and gradually taper to one foot near the top. Before the first fish was introduced, these walls were extensively checked for leaks. The tank was filled with fresh water, and over a space of about three weeks, divers marked about ninety minor cracks. Water pressure allowed many cracks to seal themselves, while others had to be injected with epoxy or have epoxy grout applied.

The people standing so nonchalantly next to the aquarium portholes probably have no idea of the tremendous pressure pushing against the sides of the tank and its acrylic windows. The spectators don't have much to worry about, since the windows are designed with a safety factor of twenty, according to a Disney spokesman. "Even if a 320-pound lemon shark hit a window at twenty-two knots, the shark would lose," he said. Just the kind of painstaking care that Disney is noted for.

Later, after the dive is over and I resurface, I'm surprised at how unsalty the water tastes. The fish and I are not swimming through real sea water but freshwater that's been treated to approximate the ocean. The sea is loaded with a lot more than salt, and so is this aquarium. This particular formula was made from twenty-seven truckloads of non-iodized salt, 400 tons of magnesium chloride, 300 tons of magnesium sulfate, plus large amounts of trace elements and other compounds.

If the aquarium's chemical balance ever got seriously out of balance, a lot of residents would start going belly up, not a sight tourists want to see. The tank's filtration system prevents this by working continually, so the water remains pure and the fish don't become stressed. Nothing that I see indicates how this is done, and there is no mechanical noise I can detect inside the tank except that made by our regulators. Yet the 5.7 million gallons are recirculated every two hours and forty minutes.

I look at my watch and realize the dive is two-thirds over. I swim over to a diving bell where compressed air is being pumped into and then trapped inside the bell's bubbletop. I enter the bell simply by popping up through the opening in the bottom. The air inside is quite breathable, the ideal place for two divers to meet and discuss the next stage of their dive.

Yet, of all the equipment used here, the only item I truly covet is the full-face mask equipped with a radio transmitter that enables a Disney diver to talk to his team members as well as the spectators outside the tank. Maybe someday we'll all get one of those. But then, what Jacques Cousteau called the "silent world," will never be the same again.

All too soon I notice the divemaster signaling it is time to surface. I look toward the ceiling, where multicolored lights shine on the water. I'm sorry the dive is over.

Then a new thought strikes me. There are sixty-one acrylic windows and several 8-by-24-foot observation panels in the aquarium, all packed with people. I've been so engrossed with the inside of the tank I hardly noticed the spectators who've been waving and are attempting to shoot flash pictures of me. I wave back, then look through my underwater camera's viewfinder and fire my strobe at one panel, even though I'm out of film. Waving arms and hands greet me as if I've just scored the winning touchdown at the Super Bowl.

I wave back and smile as I swim for the surface. It is just dawning on me that my dive is part of an elaborate, expensive show. And that now, just like Mickey and Donald, I've been a star in a Walt Disney production. It's taken so much time for me to realize this fact that I feel a little goofy.

Who

Divers must present a certification card. Reservations need to be made well in advance since space is limited to just sixteen divers a day. Call 407/WDW-TOUR.

What

This is an expensive sightseeing swim: $140 per diver, with a 20 percent discount for American Express card users. You don't have to pay the normal fee to get into EPCOT, a good thing since the dives don't begin until late afternoon. The first group gathers at the EPCOT entrance at 4:30 PM, the second at 5:30 PM. Divers see a short film describing the attraction, then are lead to a locker room. Divers need to bring their own swimsuit, but shorty wet suits and all other gear is provided in the admission price. Next, it's up to the top of the tank where the gear is ready at the edge of the pool. After a short briefing, it's into the tank in two groups of four for a thirty-minute dive. Afterwards, divers are shown a video of their experience. The tape costs another $35. Overall, the entire outing takes between two and two-and-a-half hours.

Although the huge aquarium is the focal point of the Living Seas, there is plenty to see outside of it, including numerous displays designed to promote a better understanding of our reliance on the sea, our past relationship with it, and the role the sea will play in our future.

It's interesting to note that a poll conducted at Disney World revealed that 37 percent felt ocean exploration was more important than exploring outer space; 48 percent said it was of the same importance; and 11 percent said it was less important. The remaining 4 percent, apparently brain dead, had no opinion.

The program is offered daily, year-round. No matter how hot, cold, or windy it is in the real world, the aquarium is always Disney-perfect, with never a current or rogue wave to worry about.

27

Swamp Buggies
and Airboats

You're lost in the Florida wilds and night is fast approaching. It's hot and the mosquitoes are going to be ferocious. On your right is a freshwater marsh with a picturesque pond and tall grass surrounding it. To your left is the edge of a cypress swamp where the water is knee-deep and the interior is already cast in gloomy shadow.

Unprotected by a tent, which is the better place to spend the night, out in the open or in the swamp?

If, like me, you instinctively say "Stay out under the stars!" I'll see you at the hospital in the morning. The mosquitoes will be far worse around the lake, where the quiet marshes provide a prime mosquito-breeding opportunity.

Water in a cypress swamp, on the other hand, is rarely stagnant. It does move, if slowly. Furthermore, the tannin-colored swamp water often houses the gambousia or mosquito fish, each of which can consume over a hundred mosquito larvae an hour.

I am relieved that I didn't learn this lesson in mosquito control firsthand, but that it happened while I was sitting high and dry in a monster machine called a swamp buggy. This survival knowledge is just one of the information nuggets swamp buggy driver Brenda Solveson imparts to her passengers as we roll from one watery habitat to the next. She reels off more valuable facts pertaining to the wetlands of South Florida than I've ever heard at one time. She talks nonchalantly while shifting gears, fording small creeks and plowing through deep swamps. Sometimes she drives through water that is above waist-high, and therefore impassible to most normal four-wheel-drive vehicles.

When making these crossings, our camouflage-painted swamp buggy must appear like the landing craft used in World War II at the beaches of Normandy on

D-Day. If you can recall what it was like to ride a school bus, you'll know exactly what this sensation is like, because this swamp buggy is an old school bus.

Yet I find it hard to imagine this particular vehicle ever transported children to school, not only because of its military-style paint job. For one, we are rolling around on huge, oversize rubber tires, the kind found on monster trucks. And the windshield, sliding windows, and metal roof all have been removed. We're completely open-air except for a canvas top that deflects the sun and rain.

Custom-made swamp buggies like this one are created not only from old buses but also bread trucks and delivery vans, anything with a wide base that will carry a lot of passengers. Swamp buggies are quite common in the wetlands of South Florida, much of which is actually part of the watery Everglades. In addition to the high water table here, swamp buggies sometimes become essential to move around parts of South Florida because of the frequent flooding caused by heavy, steady rains that bury even highways under water. As much as fourteen inches of rain can fall in a single day.

Due to all the standing water, travel in South Florida has always been a challenge. The Seminole Indians moved around the Everglades by poling their canoes over the grassy waters. In the early 20th century, regular outboard boat motors and their underwater propellers were paralyzed by the Everglades' thick saw grass. Swamp buggies helped open the region for greater exploration and recreation, as did another ingenious invention, the airboat.

Although swamp buggies and airboats can take you to many of the same places, what you see and hear along the way are vastly different.

An airboat, essentially a flat-bottom boat with an airplane engine affixed to the back, is the fast, sports-car-way of traveling across the grassflats. The airboat originally was developed to hunt alligators and gig frogs.

Airboats, however, have a few more drawbacks than swamp buggies. Their engine noise is tremendous. You can hear an airboat from miles away, and riding in one for hours without ear muffs is a good way to get a headache and ringing ears.

Furthermore, a small, speeding airboat needs to avoid running over gators or logs; otherwise, if the driver strikes the animal at just the right angle, the craft might flip and everyone could join the gator in the soup, an unhappy prospect. Flipping, however, is not a hazard on large, commercial airboats used to carry passengers.

Although swamp buggies and airboats can take you to many of the same places, what you see and hear along the way are vastly different. A swamp buggy tour is the Florida version of a leisurely African photo safari where a guide/driver narrates the sights and stops whenever there's something interesting. For instance, my buggy trip will cover about seven miles during a ninety-minute period, a relaxed pace that is like a slow stroll through the wetlands.

An airboat could cover this distance in a fraction of the time, but it would scare away the wading birds, the wild turkeys, and other animals I might photograph from the swamp buggy. In Disney theme park terms, a swamp buggy tour is like the Jungle Cruise but with real animals (and none of the corny jokes), while an airboat trip is more akin to Mr. Toad's Wild Ride. Both are fun and ought to be experienced; they're just very, very different.

My swamp buggy operates on the 90,000-acre Babcock Ranch, east of Punta Gorda and north of Fort Myers. This is a heck of a lot of land: enough room to build a city for two million people. Even with such huge land tracts available, swamp buggy and airboat tour operators avoid wandering all over the countryside and employ a regular route in order to minimize their vehicles' impact on the environment. A familiar routine also allows drivers to become more acquainted with the natural community of a specific region and even allows them to stage hands-on demonstrations with plants and animals now and then.

In addition to hosting swamp buggy tours, this particular ranch raises cattle, bison, and alligators. None of the livestock is caged. The bison and cattle are kept fenced in their respective sections (there are 300 miles of barbed wire fence criss-crossing this ranch), while the alligators roam freely wherever they want, along with white-tailed deer, wild hogs, and wild turkeys.

The bison, which have a small group of wild hogs feeding near them, are the first big animals the buggy takes us to. The herd is modest, only about thirty animals, but the creatures themselves are impressively large. The males weigh as much as 3,000 pounds, the females, 800 pounds. The bison grow virtually the same wooly winter coats here as they would in the sub-zero, snow-covered Great Plains. As a result, the animals spend a good deal of time trying to remove the thick covering by scratching against trees.

We're lucky to still see American bison anywhere, according to guide Brenda. It seems that when the Smithsonian Institution did its first study of the bison population in the third quarter of the 1800s, they found an estimated sixty to seventy-five million bison roaming the Great Plains, perhaps the most animals of a single species ever to exist anywhere on earth. Just ten years later, in 1886, bison in the United States numbered fewer than 600 animals, a fact I have difficulty believing. How could the slaughter of so many animals be so complete in such a brief period? Brenda says the animals were killed not just for meat and hides, but that many were butchered only for their tongues, considered a delicacy.

Leaving the buffalo, I begin counting the different bird species we see in the next five minutes: great white egrets, great blue herons, snowy egrets, and the very distinctive white ibis with their long curved orange beaks. These are all typical Everglades birds.

We arrive at a freshwater marsh and approach the first of many alligators. The best way to estimate the size of a gator, I learn, is to figure the distance between the animal's curved snout and its eyes. For every inch, the alligator is one foot in length. If it's twelve inches between the animal's snout and its eyes—the part which is almost all mouth—the gator should be twelve feet long. Regardless of size, all alligators come equipped with eighty razor-sharp teeth.

Alligators reared commercially meet their end when they attain six feet, an ideal size for harvesting the animals' tail meat and its soft, pliable belly skin for making boots and handbags. In the wild, a gator grows about a foot a year; in captivity, it can be accelerated to two feet annually by keeping an animal's temperature constant and feeding it a high-protein diet.

In addition to bison and cattle, the Babcock ranch is engaged in alligator ranching, which is different from alligator farming. Brenda explains the difference: "Alligator ranchers allow their animals to roam free over the countryside instead of keeping them in pens. As a result, the ranchers must search for the nests, an expensive and time-consuming process."

The nests, essentially nothing but a compost pile, contain between thirty and sixty eggs. In the wild, only about 10 percent of the eggs hatch, and the rest are lost to natural predators. When ranchers gather the eggs and incubate them, about 90 percent hatch. Every August, Brenda continues, the Babcock ranch employs a helicopter to locate its nesting gators, but only an estimated 10 to 30 percent of the nests are ever spotted. Once pin-pointed, the nests are examined by state wildlife authorities who determine how many eggs can be harvested that particular season. Although there are an estimated million alligators roaming around Florida, they are still considered a threatened species, so the state is closely involved in the raising and harvesting of the animals. In an extremely wet year, when many nests are flooded out, few if any eggs are collected.

Gathering gator eggs from the nest must be an exciting job, one I don't think I'll ever apply for. It requires two people: one person keeps the very protective mother away from her nest while the second worker—who's fervently praying his companion is doing his job properly—removes the eggs.

One of our best alligator-viewing sites on our swamp buggy tour is in the middle of a bridge that spans a wide creek. Although stained a light tea color by the tannin in the cypress trees that line the creek bank, the water is still quite clear. Normally, gators live in much darker water, which makes it difficult to view any of the body that's below the surface. But here, I can see the entire bodies of several gators and watch how their tails and legs move as they swim.

Leaving the creek, we keep looking for gator nests but fail to spot any. The nests are usually well exposed to the sunlight, which is important for a nest to produce both male and female gators. The amount of heat inside a nest determines whether the eggs will produce male or female alligators. The warmer eggs near the top produce males, the cooler eggs on the bottom become females, while eggs in the midrange also tend to become female.

In addition to bison, swamps, mosquitoes, and gators, Brenda fills us in on Florida's poisonous snake population, the early "cracker" cowboys, how to make swamp cabbage, the plight of the Florida panther, and perhaps a dozen other natural history topics. This swamp buggy tour is a better show-and-tell than any I had in school. And I leave with plenty of exposed film of lots of different critters to prove it.

Who/Where

Airboat rides are popular from the tip of the peninsula to Central Florida. Swamp buggy tours are more typical of South Florida, where shallow water covers so much of the landscape.

Always call ahead for reservations since swamp buggy and airboat rides are extremely popular.

Babcock Wilderness Adventures near Fort Myers offers an excellent ninety-minute swamp buggy tour; it's the one described above. The 10,000-acre Telegraph Swamp here is so picturesque and representative of the Everglades that the 1995 film *Just Cause* starring Sean Connery and Lawrence Fishburne was filmed here. One set piece, the old gator poacher's cabin, is now a museum displaying Florida fossils. Tours by reservation only. For information, call 813/338-6367. For reservations, 813/489-3911. Entrance to the Babcock ranch is 15 minutes from exit 26 on I-75. Follow the signs.

Old Tamiami Nature Tours and Swamp Buggy Rides in Bonita Springs takes buggy trips through three different wilderness environments. Water birds, gators, gopher tortoises, and raccoons are all commonly seen. Take exit 18 off I-75, go west to Old US 41, south one mile on the left; call 813/498-9050.

Wooten's, located south of Naples, is one of the oldest outfits offering Everglades excursions. Started in 1953, Wooten's has swamp buggies for touring the cypress swamps and airboats for traveling over the wet grassy plains. Snakes and gators are also featured in displays on the property. Located 35 miles south of Naples on U.S. 41 (Tamiami Trail) in Ochopee; call 800/282-2781. No reservations necessary.

Captain Doug House's Florida Boat Tours near Everglades City has six different airboats to search for gators, birds, raccoons, and manatees. No reservations necessary. Located on State Road 29, 1 mile past the bridge in Everglades City. Call 800/282-9194.

The Kissimmee Billie Swamp Safari, located on the Big Cypress Seminole Indian Reservation midway between Naples and Ft. Lauderdale, offers both airboat rides and swamp buggy tours. Also animal displays and the opportunity to spend the night in a modified "chickee," the elevated platforms that many Seminole still used for homes until the 1950s; call 800/949-6101. Also refer back to Chapter 19, Seminole Swamp Safari.

Miccosukee Indian Village and Airboat Rides, on the Tamiami Trail, is a combination cultural and nature tour. Traditional artisans in the village demonstrate doll making, wood carving, and bead making. The airboats visit an Indian camp in use for more than 100 years. Located at Mile Marker 70 on the Tamiami Trail (US 41) between Miami and Naples. Call 305/223-8380 or 223-8388.

Everglades Holiday Park Airboat Tours is near some very large Gold Coast cities, but it's a short ride from its headquarters to visit both the Everglades and the Seminole Indians. Located at 21940 Griffin Rd., Ft. Lauderdale; Call 800/226-2244.

Airboat Rides, located near the town of Christmas between Orlando and Titusville on US 50, offers ninety-minute tours of the St. Johns River. This section of the river is frequently filled with water birds; Call 407/568-4307.

Cypress Island near Kissimmee offers airboat rides as well as the chance to photograph exotic animals kept on a private island. From the intersection of the Florida Turnpike take Exit 244 and US 192 in Kissimmee, turn onto Shady Lane and follow the signs to the Cypress Island Country Store; Call 407/935-9202.

The best times to see animals regardless of vehicle are early and late in the day. Avoid mid-day during summer, when nothing moves except the wind pushed by the blades of an airboat. Showers will often make afternoon trips in summertime impossible. Airboat rides can be quite chilly on cool, overcast days, since the craft move as fast as 20 to 30 mph; have a jacket handy.

A

Appendix:
State-Owned Lands

THE NORTHWEST

Big Lagoon
State Recreation Area
12301 Gulf Beach Highway
Pensacola, FL 32507
904/492-1595

Blackwater River State Park
Route 1 Box 57-C
Holt, FL 32564
904/623-2363

Dead Lakes
State Recreation Area
P.O. Box 989
Wewahitchka, FL 32465
904/639-2702

Falling Waters
State Recreation Area
Route 5, Box 660
Chipley, FL 32428
904/638-6130

Grayton Beach
State Recreation Area,
Route 2, Box 6600
Santa Rosa Beach, FL 32459
904/231-4210

Henderson Beach
State Recreation Area
17000 Emerald Coast Parkway
Destin, FL 32541
904/837-7550

Perdido Key
State Recreation Area
c/o Big Lagoon State Recreation
Area
12301 Gulf Beach Highway
Pensacola, FL 32507
904/492-1595

**Ponce de Leon Springs
State Recreation Area**
c/o Falling Waters
State Recreation Area
Route 5, Box 660
Chipley, FL 32445
904/836-4281

**Rocky Bayou
State Recreation Area**
4281 Hwy. 20
Niceville, FL 32578
904/833-9144

**St. Andrews
State Recreation Area**
4415 Thomas Drive
Panama City, FL 32408
904/233-5140

St. Joe Peninsula State Park
Star Route I Box 200
Port St. Joe, FL 32456
904/227-1327

BIG BEND REGION

Econfina River State Park
Rt. 1, Box 255
Lamont, FL 32336
904/584-213

Florida Caverns State Park
3345 Caverns Road
Marianna, FL 32446
904/482-9598

John Gorrie State Museum
P.O. Box 267
Apalachicola, FL 32320
904/653-9347

**Lake Jackson Mounds
State Archaeological Site**
1022 Desoto Park Dr.
Tallahassee, FL 32301
904/922-6007

**Lake Talquin
State Recreation Area**
1022 Desoto Park Dr.
Tallahassee, FL 32301
904/922-6007

Ochlockonee River State Park
P.O. Box 5
Sopchoppy, FL 32358
904/962-2771

**Tallahassee-St. Marks
Historic Railroad State Trail**
1022 Desoto Park Drive
Tallahassee, FL 32301
904/922-6007

St. George Island State Park
HCR Box 62
Eastpoint, FL 32328
904/927-2111

**Three Rivers
State Recreation Area**
7908 Three Rivers Road
Sneads, FL 32460
904/482-9006

Torreya State Park
Route 2, Box 70
Bristol. FL 32321
904/643-2674

Wakulla Springs State Park
1 Spring Drive,
Wakulla Springs, FL 32305
904/922-3633

NORTH CENTRAL FLORIDA

Devil's Millhopper
State Geological Site
4732 Millhopper Road
Gainesville, FL 32606
904/336-2008

Gold Head Branch State Park
6239 SR 21
Keystone Heights, FL 32656
904/473-4701

Gainesville-Hawthorne
State Trail
Region 2 Administration
4801 SE. 17th Street
Gainesville, FL 32601
904/336-2135

Ichetucknee Springs State Park
Route 2, Box 108
Fort White, FL 32038
904/497-2511

Manatee Springs State Park
Route 2, Box 617
Chiefland, FL 32626
904/493-6072

O'Leno State Park
Route 2, Box 1010
High Springs, FL 32643
904/454-1853

Paynes Prairie State Preserve
Route 2, Box 41
Micanopy, FL 32667
904/466-3397

Peacock Springs
State Recreation Area
Route 4, Box 370
Live Oak, FL 32060
904/497-2511

Silver River State Park
c/o Lake Griffin
State Recreation Area
103 Highway 441/27
Fruitland Park, FL 34731
904/787-7402

Stephen Foster
State Folk Culture Center
Post Office Drawer G
White Springs, FL 32096
904/397-2733

Suwannee River State Park
Route 8, Box 297
Live Oak, FL 32060
904/362-2746

NORTHEAST FLORIDA

**Amelia Island
State Recreation Area**
c/o The Talbot Islands GEOpark
11435 Ft. George Road East
Ft. George, FL 32226
904/251-2320
904/261-4878 (Seahorse Stables)

Anastasia State Recreation Area
1340-A A1A South
St. Augustine, FL 32084
904/461-2033 or
904/461-2000

Big Talbot Island State Park
c/o The Talbot Islands GEOpark
11435 Ft. George Road East
Ft. George, FL 32226
904/251-2320

Bulow Creek State Park
3351 Old Dixie Highway
Ormond Beach, FL 32174
904/677-4645

**Bulow Plantation Ruins
State Historic Site**
P.O. Box 655
Bunnell, FL 32010
904/439-2219

Fort Clinch State Park
2601 Atlantic Avenue
Fernandina Beach, FL 32034
904/277-7274

Guana River State Park
2690 South Ponte Vedra Blvd.
Ponte Vedra Beach, FL 32082
904/825-5071

Little Talbot Island
c/o The Talbot Islands GEOpark
11435 Ft. George Road East
Ft. George, FL 32226
904/251-2320

Tomoka State Park
2099 North Beach Street
Ormond Beach, FL 32174
904/676-4050

WEST FLORIDA & THE GULF COAST

Anclote Key State Preserve
c/o Gulf Islands GEOpark
#1 Causeway Blvd.
Dunedin, FL 34698
813/469-5918

Caladesi Island State Park
#1 Causeway Blvd.
Dunedin, FL 34698
813/469-5918

**Crystal River
State Archaeological Site**
3400 N. Museum Point
Crystal River, FL 34428
904/795-3817

**The General James A. Van Fleet
State Trail**
Region 3 Administration
12549 State Park Dr.
Clermont, FL 34771
904/394-2280

Hillsborough River State Park
15402 US 301 North
Thonotosassa, FL 33592
813/987-6771

**Homosassa Springs
State Wildlife Park**
9225 West Fish Bowl Drive
Homosassa, FL 34448
904/628-2311

**Lake Griffin State Recreation
Area**
103 Highway 441/27
Fruitland Park, FL 34731
904/787-7402

Lake Louisa State Park
12549 State Park Drive
Clermont, FL 34711
904/394-3969

**Little Manatee River
State Recreation Area**
215 Lightfoot Road
Wimauma, FL 33598
813/671-5005

Rainbow Springs State Park
19158 SW. 81st Pl. Rd.
Dunnellon, FL 34432
904/489-8503 or
904/489-5201 (camping information)

Withlacoochee State Trail
Region 3 Administration
12549 State Park Drive
Clermont, FL 34711
904/394-2280

CENTRAL FLORIDA

Blue Spring State Park
2100 West French Avenue
Orange City, FL 32763
904/775-3663

**De Leon Springs
State Recreation Area**
P.O. Box 1338
De Leon Springs, FL 32130
904/985-4212

Highlands Hammock State Park
5931 Hammock Road
Sebring, FL 33872
941/385-0011

Hontoon Island State Park,
2309 River Ridge Road
Deland, FL 32720
904/736-5309

Lake Kissimmee State Park
14248 Camp Mack Road
Wales, FL 33853
941/696-1112

Lower Wekiva River
State Preserve
c/o Wekiwa Springs State Park
1800 Wekiwa Circle
Apopka, FL 32712
407/884-2009

Rock Springs Run State Reserve
c/o Wekiwa Springs State Park
1800 Wekiwa Circle
Apopka, FL 32712
407/884-2009

Tosohatchee State Reserve
3365 Taylor Creek Road
Christmas, FL 32708
407/568-5893

Wekiwa Springs State Park
1800 Wekiwa Circle
Apopka, FL 32712
407/884-2009

SOUTHEAST FLORIDA

Fort Pierce Inlet
State Recreation Area
905 Shorewinds Drive
Fort Pierce, FL 34949
407/468-3985

Hugh Taylor Birch
State Recreation Area
3109 East Sunrise Blvd.,
Ft. Lauderdale, FL 33304
305/564-4521

John D. MacArthur Beach
State Park
10900 SR 703 (A1A)
North Palm Beach, FL 33408
407/624-6950

John U. Lloyd Beach
State Recreation Area
6503 North Ocean Drive
Dania, FL 33004
305/923-2833

Sebastian Inlet
State Recreation Area
9700 South A1A
Melbourne Beach, FL 32951
407/984-4852

St. Lucie Inlet State Preserve
c/o Jonathan Dickinson State Park
16450 SE. Federal Highway
Hobe Sound, FL 33455
407/744-7603

Jonathan Dickinson State Park
16450 SE. Federal Hwy.
Hobe Sound, FL 33455
407/546-2771

SOUTHWEST FLORIDA

Cayo Costa State Park
c/o Barrier Islands GEOpark
P.O. Box 1150
Boca Grande, FL 33921
941/964-0375

Collier-Seminole State Park
20200 E. Tamiami Trail
Naples, FL 33961
941/394-3397

Don Pedro Island
State Recreation Area
c/o Barrier Islands GEOPark
P.O. Box 1150
Boca Grande, FL 33921
941/964-0375

Fakahatchee Strand
State Preserve
P.O. Box 548
Copeland, FL, 33926
941/695-4593

Gasparilla Island
State Recreation Area
c/o Barrier Islands GEOPark
P.O. Box 1150
Boca Grande, FL 33921
941/964-0375

Lake Manatee
State Recreation Area
20007 SR 64
Bradenton, FL 34202
941/741-3028

Myakka River State Park
13207 SR 72
Sarasota, FL 34241-9542
941/361-6511

Oscar Scherer State Park
1843 S. Tamiami Trail
Osprey, FL 34229
941/483-5956

SOUTH FLORIDA & THE KEYS

Bahia Honda State Park
Route 1, Box 782
Big Pine Key, FL 33043
305/872-2353

Bill Baggs Cape
Florida State Recreation Area
1200 S. Crandon Blvd.
Key Biscayne, FL 33149
305/361-5811

Indian Key State Historic Site
c/o Lignumvitae Key State Botanical
Site
P.O. Box 1052
Islamorada, FL 33036
305/664-4815

Long Key State Recreation Area
P.O. Box 776
Long Key, FL 33001
305/664-4815

John Pennekamp Coral Reef
State Park
P.O. Box 487
Key Largo, FL 33037
305/451-1202

San Pedro Underwater
Archaeological Preserve
Long Key State Recreation Area
P.O. Box 776
Long Key, FL 33001
305/664-4815

Park Activities

Coastal Camping Parks
Anastasia
Big Lagoon
Cayo Costa
Collier-Seminole
Econfina River
Fort Clinch
Grayton Beach
Jonathan Dickinson
Little Talbot Island
Oscar Scherer
St. Andrews
St. George Island
St. Joseph
Sebastian Inlet
Tomoka

Inland Camping
Blackwater River
Blue Spring
Dead Lakes
Falling Waters
Florida Caverns
Gold Head Branch
Highlands Hammock
Hontoon Island
Lake Griffin
Lake Kissimmee
Lake Manatee
Little Manatee River
Manatee Springs
Myakka River
Ochlockonee River
O'Leno
Paynes Prairie
Rocky Bayou
Suwannee River

Three Rivers
Torreya
Wekiwa Springs

Florida Keys Camping
Bahia Honda
John Pennekamp Coral Reef
Long Key

Parks with Cabins
Bahia Honda
Blue Spring
Cayo Costa (primitive)
Gold Head Branch
Hontoon Island (primitive)
Jonathan Dickinson
Myakka River
St. Joe Peninsula

Good Birding Areas
Anastasia
Bahia Honda
Big Lagoon
Big Talbot Island
Caladesi Island
Cayo Costa
Collier-Seminole
Fakahatchee Strand
Fort Clinch
Fort Pierce
Guana River
Hontoon Island
John D. MacArthur
Jonathan Dickinson
Lake Kissimmee
Little Talbot Island
Long Key

Myakka River
Ochlockonee River
Oscar Scherer
Paynes Prairie
Perdido Key
San Felasco Hammock
St. Andrews
St. George Island
St. Joseph Peninsula
Sebastian Inlet
Tosohatchee
Wakulla Springs
Wekiwa Springs

Boat Camping
Bahia Honda
Cape Florida
Caladesi Island
Hontoon Island
John Pennekamp

Snorkeling
Bahia Honda
Blue Spring
De Leon Springs
Ichetucknee Springs
John D. MacArthur
John Pennekamp
Manatee Springs
Peacock Spring
Rainbow Springs
San Pedro
St. Andrews
St. Joseph Peninsula
St. Lucie Inlet
Wekiwa Springs

Fishing
[sw: salt water]
[fr: fresh water]

Anastasia [sw]
Bahia Honda [sw]
Big Lagoon [sw]
Big Talbot Island [sw]
Blue Spring [fr]
Caladesi Island [sw]
Cayo Costa [sw]
Collier-Seminole [sw]
Dead Lakes [fr]
Econfina River [fr]
Fort Clinch [sw]
Fort Pierce Inlet [sw]
Grayton Beach [sw]
Guana River [both]
Hontoon Island [fr]
John Pennekamp [sw]
John U. Lloyd Beach [sw]
Lake Griffin [fr]
Lake Kissimmee [fr]
Lake Manatee [fr]
Lake Talquin [fr]
Little Manatee River [fr]
Little Talbot Island [sw]
Myakka River [fr]
O'Leno [fr]
Ochlockonee River [both]
Paynes Prairie [fr]
St. Andrews [sw]
St. George Island [sw]
St. Joseph Peninsula [sw]
Sebastian Inlet [sw]
Three Rivers [fr]
Waccasassa Bay [sw]

Parks with Bicycle Trails

[x: fat tire bikes needed]

Fort Pierce Inlet
General James A. Van Fleet Trail
Green Swamp Trail
Gainesville-Hawthorne Trail [x]
Tallahassee-St. Marks Trail
Tosohatchee [x]
Withlacoochee Trail [x]

Parks with Horse Trails
Econfina River
Florida Caverns
General James A. Van Fleet State Trail
Highlands Hammock
Jonathan Dickinson
Little Manatee River
Lower Wekiva River
Myakka River
O'Leno
Paynes Prairie
Rock Springs Run
Tallahassee-St. Marks Trail
Tosohatchee
Wekiwa Springs

Parks Offering Canoeing
[r: parks offering canoe rentals]

Anastasia
Big Lagoon
Blackwater River
Blue Spring [r]
Bulow Plantation Ruins
Collier-Seminole
Dead Lakes
De Leon Springs
Econfina River
Florida Caverns

Gold Head Branch
Guana River
Hontoon Island
Hillsborough River
Hugh Taylor Birch
Ichetucknee Springs
John Pennekamp Coral Reef [r]
John U. Lloyd Beach
Jonathan Dickinson
Lake Griffin
Lake Kissimmee [r]
Lake Louisa
Lake Manatee
Little Manatee River
Long Key
Lower Wekiva River
Manatee Springs
Myakka River [r]
Ochlockonee River
O'Leno [r]
Oscar Scherer
Paynes Prairie [r]
Rainbow Springs
Rock Springs Run
St. Joseph Peninsula
Stephen Foster
Silver River
Suwannee River
Three Rivers
Tomoka [r]
Waccasassa Bay
Wekiwa Springs

Hiking and Jogging
[bk: best backpacking]

Big Talbot Island
Blackwater River
Blue Spring
Bulow Creek

Cayo Costa

Collier-Seminole

Econfina River

Florida Caverns

Fort Pierce Inlet

Gold Head Branch

Guana River

Hillsborough River

Jonathan Dickinson [bk]

Lake Kissimmee [bk]

Little Manatee River

Little Talbot Island

Lower Wekiva River

Manatee Springs

Myakka River [bk]

O'Leno [bk]

Paynes Prairie [bk]

Rock Springs Run

Stephen Foster

St. George Island [bk]

St. Joseph Peninsula [bk]

Suwannee River

Tallahassee-St. Marks Trail

Torreya [bk]

Tosohatchee

Wekiwa Springs [bk]

Camping Reservations

Accepted in person or by telephone at many parks. Reservations accepted up to 60 days in advance of check-in date and must be made between 8 AM and 5 PM according to the time zone in which the park is located.

Reservations for cabins will be accepted no more than one year in advance, and a deposit equal to a two-night stay is required for a confirmed reservation. Call between 8 AM and 5 PM, Monday through Friday.

B

Appendix:
Florida's Canoe Trails

From the Panhandle to South Florida, you'll have plenty of places to paddle. Most navigable rivers and creeks are in the northern or central parts, since the great grass swamp known as the Everglades covers most of South Florida. Part of the Florida Recreational Trails System, these thirty-six canoe trails offer almost 950 miles of paddling.

Perdido River

The gently curving Perdido River forms the border between Florida and Alabama. It passes through woodlands of pine, cypress, and juniper. Several small ponds and sloughs provide additional canoeing opportunities along the way.

Length: 24 miles

Difficulty: Easy

Access: Three Runs; Old Water Ferry Landing (5 m); Barrineau Park Br, SR 184 (9 m); Muscogee Br, SR 184 (9 m).

Coldwater Creek

Crystal clear water and white sand bottoms are favorite features of this river. You'll find numerous sandbars perfect for camping or picnicking. Like other west Florida streams, the current of this creek can be faster than many rivers on peninsular Florida.

Length: 18 miles

Difficulty: Easy-Moderate

Access: SR 4 Br; Coldwater Recreation Area (4 m); Berrydale Br (5 m); Tomahawk Landing (4 m); Old Steel Br (2 m); SR 191 Br (3 m).

Sweetwater/Juniper Creeks

You'll encounter narrow winding curves and swift water in Sweetwater Creek. Once it joins Juniper Creek, the creek becomes wider and the curves are gentler. Clear spring runs trickle into the Juniper. Look for rapid water level fluctuations during heavy rains.

Length: 13 miles

Difficulty: Easy-Moderate

Access: SR 4 Br; Munson School Br (2 m); Red Rock Br (5 m); Indian Ford Br (6 m).

Blackwater River

The Blackwater's dark, tannin-stained waters contrast sharply with the pure white sandbars found along many bends. The trail is lined with cedar, maple, and cypress. The official trail segment of this fast flowing river ends at Blackwater River State Park.

Length: 31 miles

Difficulty: Easy

Access: Kennedy Br, SFR 24; Peadon Br, SFR 50 (6 m); Cotton Br, SR 4 (5 m); Blackwater River State Park (8 m);Bryant Br, SFR 21 (12 m).

Yellow River

The upper portion of the Yellow River drains Florida's highest elevation points, so the water is fairly fast. You'll pass hardwood forests and high sandy banks. Downstream, the river deepens and slows as you paddle through cypress and gum swamps. Part of the trail borders Eglin AFB. A base recreational permit is required.

Length: 56 miles

Difficulty: Moderate

Access: SR 2 Br; US 90 Br (17 m); Boat ramp off SR 189 (19 m); SR 87 Br (20 m).

Shoal River

A good trail for enjoying nature. The narrow river winds its way through wilderness where the surrounding forest is a mixture of maple, birch, oak, gum, and cypress. It's also bordered by high broad sand bars and sandy hills.

Length: 27 miles

Difficulty: Easy

Access: 285 Br; SR 393 Br (10 m); US 90 Br (8 m); SR 85 Br (9 m).

Holmes Creek

This trail is slower than some other west Florida waterways. The creek threads past high sandy banks and through lush swamplands. Watch for low hanging branches and sharp twisting bends.

Length: 16 miles

Difficulty: Easy

Access: Vernon Wayside Park, SR 79 Br; Brunson Landing (9 m); Hightower Springs Landing (1 m); Live Oak Landing off SR284 (6 m).

Econfina Creek

This fast flowing stream may be something of a technical challenge even for experienced canoeists. Virtually unspoiled, this clear, spring-fed stream moves through swamp, hammocks, and pine flatwoods. A very scenic treat.

Length: 22 miles

Difficulty: Moderate-Strenuous

Access: Scott's Br; Walsingham Br (10 m); Econfina Outfitters (5 m); SR 20 Br (1 m); SR 388 Br (6 m).

Chipola River

The trail begins at Florida Caverns State Park and goes for 50 miles through swamps and hardwood forests. Look for high limestone bluffs and caves, many of which are accessible from the river. Rapids (by Florida standards, anyway) include "Look and Tremble Falls." If the idea of rapids seems intimidating, begin at the SR 167 access.

Length: 52 miles
Difficulty: Easy-Moderate
Access: Florida Caverns State Park; SR 167 Br (1 m); SR 28G-A Br (10 m); SR 278 Br (10 m); SR 274 Br (8 m); SR 20 Br (10 m); SR 71 Br (13 m).

Ochlockonee River (Upper)

The narrow upper portion near the Georgia state line twists past cypress knees and blowdowns as it flows toward Lake Talquin. Low water will probably require portaging and pullovers.

Length: 25 miles
Difficulty: Easy-Moderate
Access: SR 12 Br; SR 157 Br (14 m); Tower Rd (6 m); US 90 Br (5 m).

Ochlockonee River (Lower)

You'll get a good look at the Apalachicola National Forest's high pine bluffs and dense hardwoods since over 50 miles of the trail wind through it. The trail ends at Ochlockonee River State Park, where the river widens and motor boats are more common. The water level varies according to the releases from Jackson Bluff Dam. You'll find plenty of campsites and fish camps.

Length: 67 miles
Difficulty: Moderate
Access: SR 20 Br; Pine Creek Landing (15 m); Ocklockonee River State Park (52 m).

Sopchoppy River

Also passing through the Apalachicola National Forest, this fast, dark-colored river twists and bends its way around cypress knees. Expect numerous pullovers and some wading during low water periods. Check with the U.S. Forest Service for water level information.

Length: 15 miles
Difficulty: Easy-Moderate
Access: Oak Park Cemetery Br, NFR 365; Mt. Beeser Church Br, NFR 343 (5 m); SR 375 Br (5 m); US 319 Br (5 m).

Wakulla River

This spectacular cypress–lined river's four-mile trail makes for a very pleasant half-day trip. The slow current makes for an easy round-trip; fencing at the state park prevents you from reaching a good deal of the run as well as the Wakulla Springs boil. Loads of wildlife.

Length: 4 miles
Difficulty: Easy
Access: SR 365 Br; US 98 Bridge (4 m).

Wacissa River

The narrow and swift Wacissa twists

and turns through the Aucilla Wildlife Management Area. Access to the lower section of the trail may be obscured by aquatic plants and overhanging willow trees. Look for it on the far right.

Length: 14 miles
Difficulty: Easy
Access: Wacissa Springs, SR 59; Goose Pasture Rec. Area (9 m); Nutall Rise Landing (5 m).

Aucilla River

Rapids and man-made dams make this a better trail for experienced canoeists. Conditions are at their worst during low water.

Length: 19 miles
Difficulty: Moderate-Strenuous
Access: US 27 Br; SR 257 Br (13 m); Logging Road (6 m).

Withlacoochee River (North)

You'll pass swamplands, sandy beaches and limestone outcrops. Anticipate several shoals areas. The trail ends at Suwannee River State Park.

Length: 32 miles
Difficulty: Easy
Access: SR 145 Br; SR 150 Br (4 m); SR 6 Br (16 m); Suwannee River St. Pk. (12 m).

Suwannee River (Upper)

The Suwannee River has what many consider to be Florida's only true rapids, known as "Big Shoals." You'll find numerous access points for exploring the pristine river swamp with wide sandy banks. The Stephen Foster State Folk Culture Center is accessible from the trail, which ends at Suwannee River State Park.

Length: 64 miles
Difficulty: Easy-Strenuous
Access: SR 6 Br; Cone Br Rd (10 m); US 41 Br (15 m); SR 136 Br (1 m); US 129 Br (17 m); SR 249 Br (13 m); Suwannee River State Park, US 90 (8 m).

Suwannee River (Lower)

Continuing from Suwannee River State Park, the lower section of the Suwannee River is very popular thanks to the scenery and abundant wildlife. It also contains numerous shoals which may require portage during low water.

Length: 62 miles
Difficulty: Easy
Access: Suwannee River State Park; US 90 Br (1 m); SR 250 Br (17 m); SR 51 Br (18 m); US 27 Br (26 m).

St. Marys River

Forming the state border, the St. Marys curves through the beautiful wilderness of Florida and Georgia. You'll find good camping on the numerous sandbars.

Length: 51 miles
Difficulty: Easy
Access: SR 121 Br; Stokes Br (9 m); SR 2 Br (12 m); Thompkin's Landing, SR 121 (17 m); Trader Hill, GA SR 121 (7 m); Boat ramp off of US 301 Br (6 m).

Santa Fe River

The lazy current begins just below

River Rise State Preserve where the Santa Fe returns to the surface after a three-mile-long underground journey. There are a few small shoals during low water, but they are generally passable. This is a good trail for beginners.

Length: 26 miles

Difficulty: Easy

Access: US 41-441 Br; US 27 Br (3 m); SR 47 Br (10 m); US 129 Br (13 m).

Pellicer Creek

You can easily make a half-day roundtrip on this short, four-mile trail.

Length: 4 miles

Difficulty: Easy

Access: US 1 Br; Faver-Dykes State Park (4 m).

Bulow Creek

The Bulow Creek Trail loops upstream from the Bulow Plantation Ruins State Historic Site. The creek returns to the trailhead before continuing on to the Intracoastal Waterway where it ends. It takes you through grassy coastal marshes typical of the Atlantic coast.

Length: 13 miles

Difficulty: Easy-Moderate

Access: Bulow Ruins St. Historic Site-loop upstream and return (7 m); Walter Boardman Lane Br, SR 201 Br (3 m); High Bridge Park (3 m).

Tomoka River

A 13-mile trail that loops upstream and narrows as it flows among cypress trees. downstream, the river widens through the open coastal marsh. It ends at Tomoka State Park.

Length: 13 miles

Difficulty: Easy-Moderate

Access: SR 40 Br-loop upstream and return (4 m); US 1 Br (4 m); Tomoka State Park Br (4m); Tomoka State Park Ramp (1 m).

Spruce Creek

You have a choice of two loops: a 5-mile round-trip upstream and a 9-mile round-trip downstream make up this trail. Both loops, which begin and end at Moody Bridge, pass through several habitats including dense hardwood forests and coastal saltwater marsh.

Length: 14 miles

Difficulty: Easy

Access: Moody Br-loop upstream and return (5 m); Loop downstream to horseshoe bend and return (9 m).

Rock Springs Run/Wekiva River

This is perhaps the prettiest trail in Central Florida; it is very popular on weekends. Rock Springs Run forms the border between Wekiwa Springs State Park and Rock Springs Run State Preserve. Rock Springs' clear water meets the Wekiva River at the park. The tannin-colored waters of the Wekiva River move through pine and hardwood uplands and dense swamplands and pass through the Lower Wekiva River, then flow into the St. Johns River.

Length: 25 miles

Difficulty: Easy

Access: Kings Landing; Wekiwa

Springs St. Pk. (7 m); Wekiva Marina (1 m); Wekiva Falls (10 m); Katie's Landing (1 m); Wekiva Haven (1 m); High Banks Rd. Landing (5 m).

Econlockhatchee River

The beginning of the "Econ," as it is known to locals, is narrow and shallow and twisting and calls for some canoeing skill for this to be something other than an ordeal. Downstream the river broadens and deepens and the curves are gentler.

Length: 19 miles

Difficulty: Easy-Moderate

Access: SR 419 Br; Snowhill Road Br, SR 13 (8 m); SR 46 Br (11 m).

Withlacoochee River (South)

The 83-mile-long Withlacoochee River trail begins in the foreboding sounding Green Swamp, actually a very important water recharge area. The river winds and twists through cypress swamps, hardwood and pine forests, and even a few residential areas. Good wildlife viewing along much of the trail. The river does not connect to the Withlacoochee River in the northern part of Florida.

Length: 83 miles

Difficulty: Easy-Moderate

Access: Coulter Hammock Recreation Area; SR 575 Br (2 m); US 301 Br (2 m); US 98 Br (2 m); SR 50 Br (6m); Silver Lake Recreation Area (7 m); SR 476 Br (9 m); SR 48 Br (9 m); Wysong Dam (11 m); SR 44 Br (4 m); SR 200 Br (16 m); US 41 Br (15 m).

Pithlachascotee River

This short trail on the Pithlachascotee has tight curves in the narrow upper segment which require good paddling skills. The river widens on the lower section to straighter stretches.

Length: 5 miles

Difficulty: Moderate

Access: Rowan Road Br; Francis Avenue City Park (5 m).

Alafia River

The Alafia bends and twists under a canopy of pine, cypress, and cedar trees. It flows swiftly over a limestone bed with shoals in low water.

Length: 13 miles

Difficulty: Easy-Strenuous

Access: Alderman's Ford Co. Park, SR 39; SR 640 Br (9 m); Lithia Springs Co. Park (1 m); Bell Shoals Road Br (3 m) Note: no parking at Bells Shoals Road Br.

Little Manatee River

A short trail that meanders through sand pine scrub, willow marsh and hardwood forests. The pristine trails ends at Little Manatee River State Recreation Area. This is a good half-day trip.

Length: 5 miles

Difficulty: Easy-Moderate

Access: US 301 Br; Little Manatee River State Recreation Area (5 m).

Upper Manatee River

This winding trail passes subtropical vegetation. An easy half-day trip, you can paddle both ways, making only one car necessary. Water levels and flow vary according to the amount of water released from Lake Manatee Dam.

Length: 5 miles

Difficulty: Easy

Access: Rye Road Br; Hagle Park Rd (2.5 m); Aquatel Lodge (2.5 m).

Peace River

The name says it all. This peaceful, very popular trail requires very little work as it meanders past sand bluffs, grassy areas, and dense forests. The Peace River, which originates in the Green Swamp, has many good opportunities for birding.

Length: 67 miles

Difficulty: Easy

Access: US 98 Br; SR 657 Br (3 m); SR 664 Br (7 m); SR 664-A Br (2 m); SR 664-A Br (4 m); SR 64-A Br (2 m); SR 652 Br (1 m); US 17 Br (4 m); Pioneer City Park, SR 64 Br (1 m); Gardner Boat Ramp (25 m); Brownsville Br (6 m); SR 70 Br (12 m).

Loxahatchee River

One of the few canoe trails in south Florida, this very special river is the only Florida waterway that's a designated National Wild and Scenic River. You get to enjoy 8 miles of it as it wanders through a lush cypress swamp with many ferns and orchids. Within the Jonathan Dickinson State Park, the Loxahatchee winds through mangrove swamps. A good variety of wildlife lives near the river.

Length: 8 miles

Difficulty: Moderate

Access: River Bend Co. Park, SR 706; Jonathan Dickinson State Park (8 m).

Hickey's Creek

The short Hickey Creek Canoe Trail meanders through subtropical hammocks. It ends at the locks on the Caloosahatchee River.

Length: 4 miles

Difficulty: Easy

Access: Bateman Rd SR 80 (2 m); Franklin Lock Ramp (2 m).

Estero River

A good one-day adventure that begins at the Koreshan State Historic Site which commemorates a religious sect that opposed sexual relations between men and women, even if they were married. Naturally, the sect died out, not leaving any followers. The trail twists among mangrove islands and coves, eventually opening into Estero Bay, which you are advised not to cross if there's more than a light chop. You return upstream.

Length: 7 miles

Difficulty: Moderate

Access: Koreshan State Historic Site; Carl Johnson County Park (7 miles).

Blackwater River/Royal Palm Hammock

A good trail for beginners, this 13-mile loop twists through the Collier–Seminole State Park. Tidal creeks and mangrove wilderness areas are still pristine. File a trip plan at the state park ranger station before setting out.

Length: 13 miles
Difficulty: Easy

Access: Collier-Seminole State Park-loop down Royal Palm Hammock Creek and return up to Blackwater River (13 m).

CANOEING REGULATIONS AND SAFETY TIPS

Safety Requirements:
- Flotation gear. (Florida law requires a Coast Guard approved personal flotation device for each occupant.)
- An extra paddle.
- First Aid kit; also insect repellent and sunscreen.
- Bow and stern lines.
- Flashlight and extra batteries.
- Drinking water.
- Place food and gear in water-tight containers and tie them securely to the canoe.
- Lock your car and take keys with you.
- Camp on sandbars to avoid trespassing on private land.
- A fishing license is required of everyone 16 years and older.

Allot the Right Amount of Time:
- Because of the mild river conditions, in Florida it generally requires an hour for every two miles of canoe trail.
- Remember, low water may expose logs, stumps or rocks, requiring many liftovers, or portages, which make the trip slower and more difficult.
- Rivers in north Florida are usually low in the fall and normal to high in spring and summer.
- Rivers in central and south Florida are usually low in spring and normal to high in summer and fall.
- Coastal rivers are most affected by tides: canoeing against the tidal flow can make a trip longer and more difficult.
- Winds can affect canoes, especially on wide or coastal rivers.

Maps:
Detailed, individual canoe trail maps are available from the Florida Deparrtment of Environmental Protection, Office of Greenways and Trails, Mail Station 795, 3900 Common wealth Blvd., Tallahassee, Florida 32399. 904/487-4784. No more than six maps may be required at one time.

C

Appendix:
Canoe Liveries & Outfitters

This list was current at presstime. To learn if any new operations have started up, contact:

Florida Department of Environmental Protection
Office of Greenways and Trails
Mail Station 795
3900 Commonwealth Boulevard
Tallahassee, Florida 32399-3000
904/487-4784

ALAFIA RIVER
  Alafia Canoe Rentals, Inc.
  4419 River Drive
  Valrico, FL 33594
  813/689-8645

ALAFIA RIVER
  See the following under Suwannee River: Suwannee River Canoe Outpost.

ALEXANDER SPRINGS CREEK
  Alexander Springs Concession
  49525 County Road 445
  Altoona, FL 32702
  904/669-3522

BLACKWATER RIVER (NORTH)
  Action on Blackwater
  Highway 4
  P.O. Box 283
  Baker, FL 32531
  904/537-2997

  Adventures Unlimited
  Tomahawk Landing
  Route 6, Box 238
  Milton, FL 32570
  904/623-6197
  1/800/239-6864

Andrew Jackson Canoe Rentals
4516 Water Street
P.O. Box 666
Bagdad, FL 32530
904/623-4884

Blackwater Canoe Rental
10274 Pond Road
Milton, FL 32583
904/623-0235
1/800/967-6789

Bob's Canoe Rentals
and Sales, Inc.
4569 Plowman Lane
Milton, FL 32585
904/623-5457

BLACKWATER RIVER (SOUTH)
Collier-Seminole State Park
20200 E. Tamiami Trail
Naples, FL 33961
941/394-3397

BLUE SPRING STATE PARK
Blue Spring Enterprises, Inc.
2100 West French Avenue
Orange City, FL 32763
904/775-6888

BULOW CREEK
Bulow Plantation Ruins State
Historical Site
P.O. Box 655
Bunnell, FL 32110
904/439-2219

CHASSAHOWITZKA RIVER
Chassahowitzka River
Campground
8600 West Miss Maggie Dr
Homosassa, FL 34448
904/382-2200

CHIPOLA RIVER
Bear Paw Canoe Trails
P.O. Box 621
Marianna, FL 32446
904/482-4948

COCKROACH AND
TERRA CEIA BAYS

COLDWATER CREEK
See the following under Blackwater River (North): Adventures Unlimited, Andrew Jackson Canoe Rentals, Blackwater Canoe Rental, Bob's Canoe Rentals and Sales, Inc.

CYPRESS SPRINGS
Cypress Springs Canoe
Trails, Inc.
P.O. Box 726
Vernon, FL 32462
904/535-2960

DE LEON SPRINGS STATE
RECREATION AREA
Post Office Box 1338
De Leon Springs, FL 32130
904/985-4212
(Spring Garden Run, Lake
Woodruff National Wildlife
Refuge)

ECONFINA CREEK
Econfina Creek Canoe Livery
Strickland Road
Route B, Box 1570
Youngstown, FL 32466
904/722-90

ECONLOCKHATCHEE RIVER
Hidden River Canoe Livery
15295 East Colonial Drive
Orlando, FL 32826
407/568-5346

ESTERO RIVER
Estero River Outfitters
20991 Tamiami Trail
Estero, FL 33928
941/992-4050

EVERGLADES REGION
Koreshan State Historic Site
Post Office Box 7
Estero, Florida 33928
941/992-0311

Everglades National Park
Boat Tours
Post Office Box 119
Everglades City, FL 33929
813/695-2591
1/800/445-7724 (in FL only)

Florida Bay Outfitters
Post Office Box 2513
Key Largo, Florida 33037
305/451-3018

**Flamingo Lodge Marina
and Outpost Resort**
No. I Flamingo Lodge Highway
Flamingo, FL 33034-6798
941/695-3101
305/253-2241

**Glades Haven R.V.
Park and Marina**
South State Road 29
Post Office Box 443
Everglades City, FL 33929-0443
941/695-2746
(November - April 10)

**North American
Canoe Tours, Inc.**
Everglades Outpost
and Ivy House
Post Office Box 503 8
Everglades City, FL 33929
941/695-4666

FLORIDA KEYS
Coral Reef Park Company
John Pennekamp Coral Reef
 State Park
Post Office Box 1560
Key Largo, FL 33037
305/451-1621

Long Key State Recreation Area
Post Office Box 776
Long Key, FL 33001
305/664-4815

Biscayne National Underwater Park, Inc.
8755 SW 328th Street
Post Office 1270
Homestead, Florida 33030
305/230-1100

Florida Bay Outfitters
(See Everglades listing)

HILLSBOROUGH RIVER
Hillsborough River State Park
15402 US 301 North
Thonotosassa, FL 33592
813/987-6771

Canoe Escape Inc.
9335 E Fowler Avenue
Thonotosassa, FL 33592
813/986-2067

HOLMES CREEK
See the following under Cypress Springs: Cypress Springs Canoe-Trails, Inc.

ICHETUCKNEE RIVER
See the following under Santa Fe River: Santa Fe Canoe Outpost.

JUNIPER SPRINGS RUN
Juniper Springs Canoe Rentals and Recreation Co.
24860 NE 147th Place
Fort McCoy, FL 32134
904/625-2808

LAKE GRIFFIN
Lake Griffin State Recreation Area
3089 Hwy. 441/27
Fruitland Park, FL 34731
904/787-7402

LAKE HOLATHLIKAHA
Fort Cooper State Park
3100 South Old Floral City Road
Inverness, FL 32650
904/726-0315

LAKE JOHNSON
Gold Head Branch State Park
6239 State Road 21
Keystone Heights, FL 32656
904/473-4701

LAKE KISSIMMEE
Lake Kissimmee State Park
14248 Camp Mack Road
Lake Wales, FL 33853
941/696-1112

LITTLE MANATEE RIVER
Wilderness Canoe Adventures on the Little Manatee River, Inc.
18001 U.S. 301 South
Wimauma, FL 33598
941/634-2228

LITTLE WEKIVA RIVER
See the following under Wekiva River: Katie's Wekiva River Landing.

LOXAHATCHEE RIVER
Canoe Outfitters of Florida, Inc.
16346 106th Terrace N.
Jupiter, FL 33478
407/746-7053

Jonathan Dickinson
State Park River Tours, Inc.
16450 S.E. Federal Hwy.
Hobe Sound, FL 33455
407/746-1466

MANATEE RIVER (UPPER)
Aquatel Resort
4315 Aquatel Road
Bradenton, FL 34202
941/746-6884

Ray's Canoe Hideaway
1247 Hagle Park Road
Bradenton, FL 34202
941/747-3909

MERRIT'S MILLPOND
Arrowhead Campgrounds
4820 Highway 90 E.
Marianna, FL 32446
904/482-5583

MYAKKA RIVER
Myakka River State Park Outpost
13207 State Road 72
Sarasota, FL 34241
813/923-1120

Snook Haven Restaurant
and Fish Camp
5000 East Venice Avenue
Venice, FL 34292
941/485-7221

OKLAWAHA RIVER
Oklawaha Outpost
15260 NE 152nd Place
Fort McCoy, FL 32134
904/236-4606

Canoe Excursions
4303 NW 26th Tr.
Gainesville, FL 32605
904/371-9600

OLETA CANALS
Oleta River State Rec. Area
3400 NE 163rd Street
North Miami, FL 33160
305/947-6357

PEACE RIVER
Canoe Outpost, Peace River
2816 NW CR 661
Arcadia, FL 33821
941/494-1215

Canoe Safari, Inc.
3020 NW CR 661
Arcadia, FL 33821
941/494-7865

PERDIDO RIVER
ST. MARY'S RIVER
SOUTH CREEK
Adventures Unlimited
Perdido River
160 River Annex Road
Cantonment, FL 32533
904/968-5529

PITHLACHASCOTEE RIVER

Cotee River Bait and Tackle
6241 Lincoln Street
Newport Richey, FL 34652
813/845-8330

RAINBOW RIVER

See the following under Withla-coochee River (South): Angler's Resort.

ROCK SPRINGS RUN

See the following under Wekiva River: Katie's Wekiva River Landing

ROYAL PALM HAMMOCK CREEK

See the following under Blackwater River (South): Collier-Seminole State Park.

ST. JOHNS RIVER

Blue Spring Enterprises, Inc.
2100 W. French Avenue
Orange City, FL 32763
904/775-6888

See the following under De Leon Springs: De Leon Springs State Recreation Area; Wekiva River: Katie's Wekiva River Landing, Wekiwa Marina, Inc.

Outdoor Adventures
6110-7 Powers Avenue
Jacksonville, FL 32217
904/739-1960

SALT RUN

Surf Station
1020 Anastasia Boulevard
St. Augustine, FL 32084
904/471-9463

SANTA FE RIVER

Ginnie Springs
7300 NE. Ginnie Springs Road
High Springs, FL 32643
904/454-2202
1/800/874-8571

Santa Fe Canoe Outpost
Post Office Box 592
High Springs, FL 32643
904/454-2050

Steamboat Canoe Outfitters, Inc.
Post Office Box 28
Branford, FL 32008
904/935-0512

SEBASTIAN RIVER

Bill Rogers Outdoor Adventures, Inc.
Post Office Box 1270
Homestead, FL 33030
305/230-1100

SILVER RIVER

See the following under Oklawaha River: Oklawaha Outpost.

Oscar Scherer State Park
1843 South Tamiami Trail
Osprey, FL 34229
941/483-5956

SPRING CREEK

See the following under Chipola River: Bear Paw Canoe Trails.

SUWANNEE RIVER

KOA Campground
Post Office Box 460
Old Town, FL 32680
904/542-7636

Manatee Springs State Park
Route 2, Box 617
Chiefland, FL 32626
904/493-9726, 493-9740,
or 493-1197

Otter Springs R.V. Resort
Route 1, Box 1400
Trenton, FL 32693
904/463-2696

River Run Campground, Inc.
Route 2, Box 811
Branford, FL 32008
904/935-1086

Suwannee Canoe Outpost
c/o Spirit of the
Suwannee Campground
Route 1, Box 98A
Live Oak, FL 32060
904/364-4991
800/428-4147

**Suwannee Outdoor
Adventure Center**
Post Office Drawer 247
White Springs, FL 32096
904/397-2347

SWEETWATER CREEK

See the following under Blackwater
River: Adventures Unlimited, Black-
water Canoe Rental and Sales, and Bob's
Canoe Rentals and Sales, Inc.

TOMOKA RIVER

Tomoka State Park
2099 North Beach Street
Ormond Beach, FL 32174
904/676-4050

WAKULLA RIVER

TNT Hideaway, Inc.
Highway 98
Route 2, Box 4200
Crawfordville, FL 32327
904/925-6412

WEKIVA RIVER

Katie's Wekiva River Landings
190 Katie's Cove
Sanford, FL 32771
407/628-1482

Wekiwa Marina, Inc.
1000 Miami Springs Road
Longwood, FL 32779
407/862-9640

WITHLACOOCHEE RIVER (NORTH)

See the following under Santa Fe
River: Steamboat Canoe Outfitters;

See the following under Suwannee
River: Suwannee River Canoe Outpost,
Suwannee Outdoor Adventure Center.

WITHLACOOCHEE RIVER (SOUTH)

Angler's Resort
12189 S. Williams Street
Dunnellon, FL 34432
904/489-2397

Big Bass Resort
Post Office Box 28
Istachatta, FL 34636
904/796-3784

Canoe Outpost, Withlacoochee
29135 Lake Lindsey Road
Post Office Box 188
Nobleton, FL 34661
904/796-4343

Florida Campland, Inc.
21710 Highway 98 North
Dade City, FL 33525
904/583-2091

Tumer's Camp
3033 Hooty Point
Inverness, FL 32650
904/726-2685

Baggett's Withlacoochee R.V. Park & Canoe Rental, Inc.
Post Office Box 114
Lacoochee, FL 33537
904/583-4778

NORTH FLORIDA AREA RIVERS

The Canoe Shop
11 15-B West Orange Avenue
Tallahassee, FL 32310
904/576-5335

Gulf Coast Excursions
Route 1, Box 3201
Panacea, FL 32346
904/984-5895

Pier 17 Marina, Inc.
4619 Roosevelt Boulevard
Jacksonville, FL 32210
904/387-4669

Outdoor Adventures
6110-7 Powers Avenue
Jacksonville, FL 32217
904/739-1960

CENTRAL FLORIDA AREA RIVERS

Florida Pack & Paddle
10705 SE 15 1st Street
Summerfield, FL 34491

Bill Rogers' Outdoor Adventures, Inc.
408 Ponoka Street
Sebastian, FL 32958
407/388-2331

SOUTH FLORIDA AREA RIVERS

Biscayne National Underwater Park
8755 South West 328th St.
Post Office Box 1270
Homestead, FL 33030
305/230-1100

Florida Adventures
1073 West Country Club Cir.
Plantation, FL 33317
305/584-7669

Outdoor Resorts of America
Post Office Box 429
Highway 29 South
Chokoloskee, FL 33925
941/695-2881

The Tree Gallery
8855-116 Terrace South
Boynton Beach, FL 33437
407/734-4416

D

Appendix:
Florida Canoe Clubs

Apalachee Canoe Club
P.O. Box 4027
Tallahassee, FL 32315
904/562-6087

Citrus Paddling Club
Route 1
Floral City, FL 32636

Coconut Kayakers
P.O. Box 3646
Tequesta, FL 33469

Florida Competition Paddler
4546 Huntington Street SE
St Petersburg, FL 33703

**Florida Sea Kayaking
Association**
3095 67th Avenue South
St. Petersburg, FL 33712

Florida Sport Paddling Club
11701 Spinnaker Way
Fort Myers, FL 33908
941/466-4678

Friends of the Sebastian River
P.O. Box 284
Roseland, FL 32957

King's Landing Canoe Club
5714 Baptist Camp Road
Apopka, FL 32712
407/886-0859

Mugwump Canoe Club
9025 Sunset Drive
Miami, FL 33173

Palm Beach Pack & Paddle
P.O. Box 16041
West Palm Beach, FL 33416
407/265-1018

Peninsula Paddling Club
8571 Shady Glen Drive
Orlando, FL 32819
407/352-1711

Seminole Canoe & Yacht Club
4619 Ortega Farms Circle
Jacksonville, FL 32210
904/388-2993

West Florida Canoe Club
P.O. Box 17203
Pensacola, FL 32522
904/557-2211

**Florida Canoeing &
Kayaking Assoc.**
P.O. Box 20892
West Palm Beach, FL 33416

Florida Audubon Society
1101 Audubon Way
Maitland, FL 32751
407/647-261 5

Florida Trail Association
P.O. Box 13708
Gainesville, FL 32604
904/378-8823
800/343-1882 (in FL only)

Florida Wildlife Federation
P.O. Box 6870
Tallahassee, FL 32314
904/656-7113

Izaak Walton League of America
c/o Manatee Community College
Dept. of Natural Sciences
Bradenton, FL 34207
941/755-1511 ext. 4561 (work)
941/792-8482 (home)

Florida Sierra Club
462 Fernwood Road
Key Biscayne, FL 33149

**Florida Association
of Canoe Liveries and Outfitters**
P.O. Box 1764
Arcadia, FL 33821
813/494-1215

E

Appendix:
Campgrounds of the Florida Keys

PRIVATE CAMPGROUNDS

America Outdoors
Rt.1, Box 38-A
Key Largo, FL 33037-9801
305/852-8054

U.S. Hwy 1 at mile marker 97.5, just 55 miles south of Miami.

700 feet of white sand beach, a 170-foot pier with slips and boat rentals. Breakfast and lunch dockside, complete store, laundry, A/C bath houses, heavily wooded sites, cable TV at every site.

Big Pine Key Fishing Lodge
P.O. Box 430513,
Big Pine Key, FL 33043-0513
305/872-2351

Mile marker 33 on the Atlantic Ocean, 28 mi. from Key West.

RV and tent camping, efficiencies, marina with good dockage. Convenience store. Direct access to Looe Key Marine Sanctuary, backwater flats, and deep water ocean fishing. Charter diving and fishing. Rental boats.

Bluewater Key RV Resort
PO Box 409,
305/745-2494
800/237-2266
Lower Sugarloaf Key, FL 33044-0409

Just off U.S. 1 at Mile Marker 14, Oceanside.

Close to Key West. RVs up to 45 ft., slideouts allowed. Children and pets ok. Self-contained RVs only.

Boyd's Key West Campground
6401 Maloney Avenue
Key West, FL 33040-6095
305/294-1465

On U.S. 1, mile marker 5, southernmost campground in the U.S.A.

Heated pool, boat ramp and docks, beach. Take city bus or rent a bicycle or moped and tour attractions.

Breezy Pines RV Estates
P.O. Box 43191
Big Pine Key, FL 33043-0191
305/872-9041
On U.S. 1, mile marker 30, Big Pine Key.
Shaded sites close to Key West, fishing, diving and snorkeling. Planned activities, potluck dinners, rec room, laundry, fresh water pool, shuffleboard, bike paths, cable TV.

Calusa Camp Resort
325 Calusa Road
Key Largo 33037-2699
305/451-0232
800/457-2267
On U.S. 1, 50 miles south of Miami at mile marker 101.5.
Pool, tennis, playground, boat ramp and docks. 50 miles south of Miami, 100 miles north of Key West. Tents to motorhomes on 3500 ft. of waterfront with access to Gulf and ocean.

Fiesta Key Resort KOA
P.O. Box 618
Fiesta Key 33001
305/664-4922
Go south from Miami on U.S. 1 to mile marker 70.
A 28-acre tropical island on the Gulf. Swim, dive and snorkel. Marina w/boat rentals, ramp and slips. Hot tubs, olympic-size heated pool, waterfront pub and restrained

w/patio, bike rentals. Motel units. 50 mi to Key West.

Florida Keys RV Resort
106003 Overseas Highway
Key Largo, FL 33037-8096
305/451-6090
800/252-6090
Go south from Miami on U.S. 1 to mile marker 106.
Shady, heated pool, volleyball, horseshoes, shuffleboard, and basketball. Laundry, hot showers and store.

Jabour's Trailer Court
223 Elizabeth Street
Key West, FL 33040-6671
305/294-5723
U.S. 1 south turn right onto Palm Ave. bridge to Eaton St., right on Elisabeth St.
Waterfront campground and lodging in downtown Key West. Guest room, cottage, trailer, mobile home rentals.

Jolly Roger Travel Park
275 Overseas Highway
Marathon, FL 33050-9756
305/289-0404
On U.S. 1 mile marker 59, 60 miles south of Homestead.
Shady grassy sites. Pets ok. Fishing, swimming, snorkeling, boat dockage and ramp. Coin laundry, AC motel rooms available. Free Cable TV.

Key Largo Kampground
101551 Overseas Highway
Key Largo, FL 33037
305/451-1431
800/KAMP-OUT

1 mile south of Penekamp State Park, Oceanside. Left on Samson Rd. Mile marker 101.5.

40 acres, shaded sites, 2 beaches, boat ramp, docks available, ocean access. Fresh water pool, playground, shuffleboard, volleyball. BBQ, picnic tables. Walk to shopping.

Key RV Park
6099 Overseas Highway
Marathon, FL 33050-2722
305/743-5164
800/288-5164

Between mile marker 50-51 on oceanside in the heart of Marathon.

Horseshoes, recreation hall with planned activities. Ocean access, close to shopping, public beach, walk to restaurants, 3 laundromat locations. Showers, phone, paved roads, boat ramp, boat dock, fishing. No pets.

Lazy Lakes Campground
PO Box 440154,
Sugarloaf Key, FL 33044-0154
305/745-1079
800/354-5524

U.S. 1 south to mile marker 19.8. Go left on Johnson Rd.

Fish from campsite. Swim and snorkel in lakes, paddle boats, kayaks, rec room, cable TV, heated pool, store, laundry. Cottage rentals. 16 miles from Key West.

Lion's Lair Travel Park
Rt. 1 Box 390
Marathon, FL 33050
305/289-0606

Take U.S. 1 south to mile marker 59. Lion's Lair on the left.

500 feet of ocean frontage. Sandy beach, boat ramp, fishing, rec hall, shady sites. No Pets. Efficiency rentals.

Pelican Motel & Trailer Park
Rt. 1 Box 528
Marathon, FL 33050
305/289-0011

On U.S. 1, 6 miles north of Marathon by mile marker 59.

Gulfside RV Park on Grassey Key. Motel and eff. apts. Docks, boat ramp, pool, showers and laundry room. Free cable TV. Pets welcome.

Sugarloaf Key Resort KOA
Rt. 2, Box 680
Summerland Key, FL 33042-0680
305/745-3549

Go south from Miami on U.S. 1 to mile marker 20.

Oceanfront beach near Key West. Snorkeling, fishing, marina, boat rental, canoes, fishing bridge, ramp and slips. Large pool, hot tub, restaurant.

Whispering Pines Trailer Park

Rt 2 Box 549,
Marathon, FL 33050-9764
305/289-1606

Go south on W.S. 1 from Florida City to mile marker 58.

Shady sites, marina slips on Gulf of Mexico. Adults only. No pets.

STATE PARKS

John Pennekamp State Park

P.O. Box 487,
Key Largo, FL 33037
305/451-1202

At the top of the keys an mile marker 102.5.

Tent and RV camping off the nation's only living coral reef. Glass bottom boat tours, snorkeling and scuba tours, canoeing, motor and sailboat rental.

Long Key State Recreation Area

P.O. Box 776,
Long Key, FL 33001
305/664-4815

Located north of Marathon at mile marker 67.5.

Beautifully shaded right on the Atlantic. Extremely popular. Swimming, fishing, hiking.

Bahia Honda State Park

Rt. 1, Box 782
Big Pine Key, FL 33043
305/872-2353

12 Miles south of Marathon.

Good beach, swimming, camping, boat ramps. This is Florida's southernmost state park.

F

Appendix:
Dive Shops of the Florida Keys

The following dive shops serve the Keys from Key Largo to Key West. Many of them plan their own lobster dives at the start of the season. They also can advise you of any changes in the law and provide the proper measuring instrument. All dive boats must pass Coast Guard inspection.

UPPER KEYS

Abyss Dive & Snorkel
MM 100, US Hwy. 1
P.O. Box 611,
Key Largo, FL 33037,
305/451-6030

Admiral Dive Center
MM 105 US Hwy. 1
1 Bowen Drive
Key Largo, FL 33037
Mailing Address:
P.O. Box 0113
Key Largo, FL 33037
800/346-3483, 305/451-1114
Fax: 305/451-2731

American Diving Headquarters
MM 105.5 US Hwy. 1
Key Largo, FL 33037
Mailing Address:
P.O. Box 1250
Key Largo, FL 33037
800/634-8464, 305/451-0037
Fax: 305/451-9291

Amy Slate's Amoray Dive Resort
104250 US Hwy. 1
Key Largo, FL 33037
800-4-A-MORAY, 305/451-3595
Fax: 305/453-9516

Aqua-Nuts
102970 US Hwy. 1
Key Largo, FL 33037
800/226-04151, 305/451-0414
Fax: 305/451-4892

Bud 'N' Mary's Dive Center
MM 79.8 US Hwy. 1
P.O. Box 1126
Islamorada, FL 33036
800/344-7352, 305/664-2211
Fax 305/664-5592

Capt. Chamber's Charters
PO Box 125
Key Largo, FL 33037
305/451-1805

**Capt. Corky's Divers World
of Key Largo Inc.**
10051 US Hwy. 1
Key Largo, FL 33037
Mailing Address:
PO Box 1663
Key Largo, FL 33037
305/451-3200

**Captain Slate's
Atlantis Dive Center**
51 Garden Cove Drive
Key Largo, FL 33037
305/451-3020, 305/451-l325
Fax 305/451-9240

Cheeca Lodge
81081 US Hwy. 1
Islamorada, FL 33036
800/934-8377, 305/664-2777
Fax 305/664-2893

Conch Republic Divers
90311 US Hwy. 1
Tavernier/Key Largo, FL 33070
800/274-DIVE, 305/852-1655
Fax 305/451-5273

Diver's Den
102965 US Hwy. 1
Key Largo, FL 33037
800/527-DIVE, 305/451-3481
Fax 305/451-0371

Florida Keys Dive Center
MM 90.5 US Hwy. 1
Plantation Key FL 33070
Mailing Address:
PO Box 91
Tavernier, FL 33070
800/433-8946, 305/852-4599
Fax 305/852-1293

Floridaze Dive Center
MM 90.8 US Hwy. 1
PO Box 1221
Tavernier, FL 33070
800/437-DIVE, 305/852-1432
Fax 305/852-1776

Hall's K-Hale Divers, Inc.
MM 99.9 US Hwy. 1
PO Box 1084
Bayside, Key Largo, FL 33037
800/859-3896, 305/451-6431

HMS Minnow Charters Inc.
MM 100 US Hwy. 1
Key Largo, FL 33037
Mailing Address:
PO Box 1687,
Key Largo, FL 33037
800/366-9301, 305/451-7834

Island Bay Resorts
PO Box 573,
Tavernier, FL 33070-0573;
800/654-KEYS, 305-852-4087;
Fax 305/852-2976

Island Ventures
103900C US Hwy. 1
Key Largo, FL 33037
305/451-4957, 305/852-4488

It's a Dive Watersports
Marriott Key Largo Bay Beach Resort,
103800 US Hwy. 1
Key Largo, FL 33037
800/809-9881, 305/453-9881
Fax 305/453-0093

Lady Cyana Divers
PO Box 1157
Islamorada, FL 33036
800/221 8717, 305/664-8717
Fax 305/664-4443

Ocean Divers
522 Caribbean Drive
Key Largo, FL 33037
305/451-1113
Fax 305/451-5765

Ocean Quest Dive Center
87000 US Hwy. 1
Islamorada, FL 33036
800/356-8798, 305/852-8770;
Fax 305-852-0013

Pennekamp State Park Dive Center
US Hwy. 1, MM 102.5,
Key Largo, FL 33037
Mailing Address:
5 Abaco Rd.,
Key Largo, FL 33037
305/451-6322;
Fax 305/451-9895

Quiescence Diving Services, Inc.
103680 US Hwy. 1
Key Largo, FL 33037
Mailing Address:
PO Box 1570
Key Largo FL 33037
305/451-2440, 305/451-4230
Fax 305/451-6440

Rainbow Reef Dive Center
85500 US Hwy. 1
Islamorada FL 33036
800/457-4354, 305/664-4600
Fax 305/664-2007

Stephen Frink Photographic Inc.
MM 102.5 U.S. Hwy. 1
PO Box 2720
Key Largo, FL 33037
305/451-3737
Fax 305/451-5147

Tavernier Dive Center
MM 90.5, US Hwy. 1
Tavernier, FL 33070
Mailing Address:
PO Box 465
Tavernier, FL 33070
3O5/852-4007
Fax 305/852-0869

The Reef Shop
84771 US Hwy. 1
Islamorada, FL 33036
800/741-4385, 305/664-4385

World Down Under
81586 US Hwy. 1
Islamorada, FL 33036
Mailing Address:
PO Box 1001
Islamorada, FL 33036-1001
305/664-9312
Fax 305/664-2260

MIDDLE KEYS

Abyss Pro Dive Center
Holiday Inn
13175 US Hwy. 1
Marathon, Fl 33050
800/457-0134, 305/743-2126
Fax 305/743-5460

Capt. Hook's Dive Center
11833 US Hwy. 1
Marathon, FL 33050
800/CPT-HOOK, 305/743-2444
Fax 3O5-289-1374

CJ'S Dive Center
2250 US Hwy. 1
Marathon, FL 33050
305/289-9433

Hall's Diving Center
1994 US Hwy. 1
Marathon, FL 33050,
800/331-4255, 3O5/743-5929;
Fax 3O5/743-8168

Marathon Divers
12221 US Hwy. 1
Marathon, FL 33050
305/289-1141

The Diving Site
12399 US Hwy. 1
Marathon, FL 33050
305/289-1021

Tilden's Pro Dive Shop
4650 US Hwy. 1
Marathon, FL 33050
800/223-4563, 305/743-5422
Fax 3O5/743-4739

LOWER KEYS

Admiral Busby's
Coral Reef Excursions, Inc.
508 South Street
Key West, FL 33041
3O5/294-0011, 305/745-5097
Fax 3O5/294-8272

Bonsai Diving
310 Duval Street
Key West, FL 33040
305/294-2921, 305/296-6301
Fax 305/296-6301

Captain's Corner Dive Center
0 Duval Street
Key West, FL 33040
305/296-8865, 305/296-8918
Fax 305/292-7685

**Cudjoe Gardens Marina
& Dive Center**
802 Drost Drive
Cudjoe Key, FL 33042
305/745-2357
Fax 305/745-2357

Fun Yet Charters
Rt. 4, PO Box 1119,
Summerland Key, FL 33042
305/872-3407

Genuine Draft Charters
Rt. 4, Box I 0.34-C
Little Torch Key, FL 33042
305/872-9722, 305-872-8120

Holiday Divers of Key West
3841 N. Roosevelt Boulevard
Key West, FL 33040
Mailing Address:
PO Box 2582
Key West, FL 33045
800/468-4242, 305/294-5934
Fax 305/296-5659

Innerspace Dive Shop
MM 29.5 US Hwy. 1
PO Box 430637
Big Pine Key, FL 33043
305/872-2319, 800/538-2896
Fax 305/872-3081

Key West Diver Inc.
MM 4.5 US Hwy. 1 Stock Island
Key West, FL 33040
800/87-DIVER
Fax 305/294-7612

Key West Pro Dive Shop
3128 N. Roosevelt Boulevard
Key West FL 33040
800/426-0707, 305/296-3823
Fax 305/296-0609

A Key West Reef
Safe Harbour Marina
6810 Front Street
Key West/Stock Island, FL 33040
Mailing Address:
PO Box 580
Key West, FL 33041-0580
305/292-1345, 305/292-4885

**Little Palm Island
Resort/Quarterdeck**
Rt. 4, Box 1036
Little Torch Key, FL 33042
800/343-8567, 305/872-2524
Fax 305/872-4843

**Looe Key Reef Resort
and Dive Center**
MM 27.5 US Hwy. 1
PO Box 509
Ramrod Key, FL 33042
800/942-5397, 305/872-2215
Fax 305/872-3786

Looker–Key West
PO Box 4035
Key West, FL 33040
800/245-2249, 305/294-2249
Fax 305/294-0421

Lost Reef Adventures
261 Margaret Street
Key West, FL 33040
800/952-2749, 305/296-9737

**Outcast Charters
& Vacation Rentals**
PO Box 1812
Big Pine Key, FL 33043
305/872-4680

Reef Runner Dive Shop
MM 25 US Hwy. 1
PO Box 11
Summerland Key, FL 33042
305/745-1549, 305/745-1575

Sea Clypse Divers
6000 Peninsula Avenue
Key West, FL 33040
Mailing Address:
PO Box 2122
Key West, FL 33040
800/626-6396, 305/296-1975
Fax 305/296-1975

Seahorse Scuba
PO Box 420811
Summerland Key, FL 33042
305/745-2315
Fax. 305/745-1659

Southpoint Divers
535 Duval Street
Key West, FL 33040
800/824-6811, 305/292-9778
Fax 305/296-6888

Strike Zone Charters, Inc.
MM 29.5 US Hwy. 1
PO Box 89A,
Big Pine Key, FL 33043
800/654-9560, 305/872-9863

Underseas Inc.
MM 30.5 US Hwy. 1
PO Box 319,
Big Pine Key, FL 33043
800/446-5663, 305/872-2700;
Fax: 305/872-0080

Viewfinder Dive Center
2728 N Roosevelt Boulevard
Key West, FL 33040
800/860-3483, 305/292-5000;
Fax 305/292-9557

G

Appendix:
Dive Shops of the Gold Coast/Miami

Both wreck diving and lobstering are popular off the Palm Beaches, Ft. Lauderdale, and the greater Miami area. These are the dive shops which serve this region. Keys dive operators are listed in Appendix F.

Dixie Divers Coral Springs
PADI 5 Star
2060 University Drive
Coral Springs, FL 33071
305/755-9858
Fax 305/755-3448

Dixie Divers Deerfield Beach
PADI 5 Star
1645 SE 3rd Court
Deerfield Beach, FL 33441
305/420-0009
Fax 305/420-0380

Aqua Specialty Dive Center
13710 W SR 84
Ft. Lauderdale, FL 33325
305/423-8340
Full Service Dive Shop - NAUI

Austin's Diving Center, Inc.
10525 South Dixie Highway
Miami, FL 33156
305/665-0636

Dixie Divers West Palm Beach
PADI 5 Star
1401 S Military Trail
West Palm Beach, FL 33415
800/456-3188
Fax 407/969-6722

B & B Aquatic Adventures, Inc.
1327 South Federal Highway
Dania, Florida 33004
305/920-3322

Boca Underwater Services, Inc.
P.O. Box 1402
Boca Raton, FL 33429
305/421-2601
Fax 305/425-0020

Florida Frogman Inc.
2852 NW 72 Avenue (Milam Dairy Rd)
Miami, FL 33122
305/599-9900
NAUI/PADI Referrals

H20 Scuba
160 Sunny Isles Boulevard
North Miami Beach, FL 33160
305/956-DIVE
Fax 305/956-9405

Adventure Scuba Inc.
150 N US Hwy. 1
Tequesta, FL 33478
407/746-1555
Fax 407/746-1555

Ameridive Scuba Center
9819-1 S Military Trail
Boynton Beach, FL 33436
407/732-0833, 407/732-0883

Anchor Scuba
1530 SE Cordova Road
Fort Lauderdale, FL 33316
305/763-DIVE;
Fax 305/792-3985

The Aqua Shop (B)
505 Northlake Blvd.,
North Palm Beach, FL 33408
800-331-3772,407-848-9042;
Fax 407/848-9232

Aqua Benture Dive Center
409 Lake Avenue
Lake Worth, FL 33460
407/582-0877, 407-582-0666

Biscayne Park Underwater Tours
PO Box 1270
Homestead, FL 33030
305/247-2400, 305/247-2402
Fax 305/242-9601

Coral Reef Scuba
9830 W Sample Road
Coral Springs, FL 33065
305/344-6333
Fax 305/345-9371
• 4984 N University Drive
Lauderhill, FL 33351
305/748-5105
Fax 305/748-6208

Deep Six Dive & Watersports
521 N US Hwy. 1
Fort Pierce, Fl 34950
800/732-9685, 407/465-4114
• 3289 NW Federal Hwy
Jensen Beach, FL 33457
800/732-9685, 407/692-2747

Destination Atlantis Inc.
3301 Rickenbacker Causeway,
Miami, FL 33149
305/541-5260
Fax 305/447-1609

Dive Shop II
700 Casa Loma Boulevard
Boynton Beach, FL 33436
407/278-9111, 407/734-5566

Divers Unlimited Inc.
6023 Hollywood Boulevard
Hollywood, FL 33024
305/981-0156
Fax 305/963-5255

The Diving Locher
223 Sunny Isles Boulevard
North Miami Beach, FL 33160
800/756-DIVE, 305/947-6025
Fax 305/947-2236

**Diver's World/Dream
Quest Adventure Charters**
3102 Reo Lane
Lake Worth, FL 33461
407/439-DIVE

Florida Frogman Inc.
2852 NW 72nd Avenue
Miami, FL 33122-1310
305/599-9900
Fax 305/591-2774

Force-E
877 E Palmetto Park Road
Boca Raton, FL 33432
407/368-0555
• 7166 Beracasa Way
Boca Raton, FL 33433
407/395-4407
• 1395 N Military Trail
West Palm Beach, FL 33409
407/471-2676
• 660 Linton Boulevard
Delray Beach, FL 33444
407/276-0666
• 2160 W Oakland Park Boulevard
Fort Lauderdale, FL 33301
305/735-6227

• 11911 US Hwy. 1
North Palm Beach, FL 33408
407/624-7136
• 2700 E Atlantic Boulevard
Pompano Beach, FL 33062
305/943-3483
• 155 E Blue Heron Boulevard
Riviera Beach, FL 33404
407/845-2333
• 8410 W Flagler Street
Miami, FL 33144
305/225-3483

Frank's Dive Shop
301 E Blue Heron Boulevard
Riviera Beach, FL 33404
407/848-7632

Hollywood Yacht Charters Inc.
1052 Ocean Dr. #5
Miami Beach, FL 33139
305/673-0832, 305/673-3755
Fax 305/966-7125

Lighthouse Dive Center
2507 N Ocean Boulevard
Pompano Beach, FL 33062
305/782-1100
Fax 305/781-4862

Ocean Diving Inc.
750 E Sample
Pompano Beach, FL 33064
305/943-3337
Fax 305/785-3483

Omega Blu, Inc.
P.O. BOX 10834
Pompano Beach, FL 33061
800/755-3111, 305/783-3111

Orbit Marine Sports, Inc.
101 N Riverside Drive, Suite 206
Pompano Beach, FL 33062
800/226-7303, 305/942-7333
Fax 305/785-9102

Palm Beach diving Headquarters
180 E 13th Street,
Riviera Beach, FL 33404
800/622-0555

Pier 66 Aquatic Center
2301 SE 17th Street
Fort Lauderdale, FL 33316
305/768-9500

Pro Dive
801 Seabreeze Boulevard
Fort Lauderdale, FL 33316
305/761-3413, 305/761-3414
Fax 305/761-8915

Rampage Dive Charters
P.O. Box 14808
North Palm Beach, FL 33408
800/525-0876, 407/626-1003
Fax 407/775-0283

The Scuba Club, Inc.
4709 N Dixie Hwy. 1
West Palm Beach, FL 33407
800/835-2466, 407/844-2466
Fax 407/844-8256

Reef Dive Shop
304 E Ocean Avenue
Lantana, FL 33462-3257
407/585-1425

Seascape Charters, Inc.
130 First Way
West Palm Beach, FL 33407
407/683-9177

Splashdown Divers
700 Casa Loma Boulevard
Boynton Beach, FL 33435
407/736-0712
Fax 407/364-4111

Team Divers South Beach
300 Alton Road
Miami Beach, FL 33139
800/543-7887, 305/673-0101
Fax 305-538-4894

Underwater Unlimited
4633 S Lejeune Road
Coral Gables, FL 33146
305/445-7837
Fax 305/445-7839

US1 SCUBA INC.
15 N Federal Highway
Fort Lauderdale, FL 33062
305/946-6055
Fax 305/784-8600

Whitecaps Scuba Shop
The Breakers Hotel
One S County Road
Palm Beach, FL 33480
407/659-8497;
Fax 407/659-8403

H

Appendix:
More Biking Trails

Listed below are state parks with on/off road trails for bicycles. In addition to designated trails for cycling, many state parks have scenic paved or dirt roads suitable for bicycling. Bicycles are allowed on any roads normally open to motor vehicles. Check with the park office for any scenic roads which may be available for use. See Appendix A for addresses.

PATHE/ROADS THREE MILES OR LESS:

Fort Pierce Inlet
State Recreation Area
(1 mile)
Ft. Pierce, FL
407/468-4007

Oleta River
State Recreation Area
(2.5 miles)
North Miami, FL
305/947-6357

Bill Baggs Cape Florida
State Recreation Area
Key Biscayne, Fl
305/361-5811

Jonathan Dickinson State Park
(2 miles)
Hobe Sound, FL
407/744-9814

Ravine State Gardens
(1.8 miles)
Palatka, FL
904/329-3721

OVER THREE MILES:

Highlands Hammock State Park
(1.5 miles)
Sebring, Florida
813/385-0011

Myakka River State Park
(25 miles)
Sarasota, FL
813/361-6511

**Tallahassee - St. Marks
Historic Railroad**
(15.8 miles)
State Trail
Tallahassee, FL
904/922-6007

Talbot Islands GEOpark
Fort George, FL
904/251-2323

Wekiva Springs State Park
Apopka, FL
407/884-2009

Withlacoochee State Trail
(5 miles)
Clermont, FL
904/394-2280

OFF ROAD BICYCLING:

Blackwater River State Park
Holt, FL
904/623-2363

Cayo Costa State Park
(5.5 miles)
Boca Grande, FL
813/964-0375

Cedar Key Scrub State Reserve
Cedar Key, FL
904/543-5567

Wakulla Springs State Park
Wakulla Springs, FL
904/922-3632

Guana River State Park
(9.5 miles)
Ponte Vedra Beach, FL
904/825-5071

**Gainesville-Hawthorne
Rail-to-Trail**
(16 miles)
Micanopy, FL
904/466-3397

Highlands Hammock State Park
Sebring, FL
813/385-0011

**Lower Wekiwa River
State Reserve**
Sanford, FL
407/330-6725

OFF ROAD BICYCLING (CONTINUED):

Manatee Springs State Park
(8.5 miles)
Chiefland, FL
904/493-6072

Myakka River State Park
Sarasota, FL
813/361-6511

O'Leno State Park
High Springs, FL
904/454-1853

Talbot Islands GeoPark
Fort George, FL
904/251-2323

Teneroc State Recreation Area
Lakeland, FL
813/499-2421

Tosohatchee State Reserve
Christmas, FL
407/568-5893

Withlacoochee State Trail
(42 miles)
Clermont, FL
904/394-2280

I

Appendix:
Maps & Charts

FLORIDA ATLAS
DeLorme Publishing Company
P.O. Box 298
Freeport, ME 04032
207/865-4171,800/227-1656
PUB. 1987. 127 pages.

FLORIDA COUNTY MAPS
Florida Dept. of Transportation
Map and Publication Sales
Mail Station 12
605 Suwannee Street
Tallahassee, FL 32399-0450
904/488-9220
   County maps showing highways, secondary and dirt roads, water bodies, and structures.

FLORIDA OFFICIAL ROAD MAP
Florida Dept. of Commerce
Division of Tourism
126 West Van Buren Street
Tallahassee, FL 32399-2000
904/487-1462

or:
Florida Dept. of Transportation
Map and Publication Sales
See Florida County Maps. Free.

NAUTICAL CHARTS
U.S. Dept. of Commerce
National Oceanic &
Atmospheric Administration
National Ocean Service
Distribution Division
Riverdale, MD 20737
301/436-6990
   Charts showing depths and contours of coastal waters and bays, major rivers and lakes. Often available at local marinas & map stores.

NAUTICAL CHARTS FOR THE
WILDERNESS WATERWAY
National Recreational Trail
   (Everglades City to Flamingo):
#11433(598 SC), #11430(642 SC).

SOUTH FLORIDA WATERWAYS

South Florida Water Mgt. District
P.O. Box 24680
West Palm Beach, FL 33416-4680
407/686-8800 Free.

District maps of Kissimmee Waterways and the Everglades, a Water Conservation Area Guide and Lake Okeechobee Recreation Guide.

SUWANNEE RIVER MAP

Suwannee River Water Mgt. District
Route 3, Box 64
Live Oak, FL 32060
904/362-1001, 800/342-1002

Pub. 1984. Free.

An 18' x 24' map showing river mileage, access points along the river and directions for reaching them.

TOPOGRAPHIC MAPS

United States Geological Survey,
Map Distribution Section
Federal Center
Post Office Box 25286,
Denver, CO 80225.
303/2367477.

Maps showing land contours, size and location of water areas, transportation routes, political boundaries, man-made features and land survey systems. Often available from map/book stores and engineering firms.

FLORIDA CANOE TRAILS

The canoe trail maps issued by the Department of Environmental Protection indicate which maps to order, or refer to the "Index to Topographic Maps of Florida" chart for names of applicable topographic maps.

J

Appendix:
Environmental Organizations

These organizations are at the forefront of protecting Florida's natural places:

Florida Audubon Society
460 SR 436
Suite 200
Casselberry, FL 32707
407/260-8300

The Nature Conservancy
Florida Chapter
222 S. Westmont Drive, Suite 300
Altamonte Springs, FL 32714
407/682-3664

Florida Conservation Association
1890 Semoran Boulevard
Winter Park, FL 32792
407/672-2058

Florida Trail Association
P.O. Box 13708
Gainesville, FL 32604
904/378-8823
800/343-1882 (in FL only)

Florida Wildlife Federation
P.O. Box 6870
Tallahassee, FL 32314
904/656-7113

Florida Sierra Club
462 Fernwood Road
Key Biscayne, FL 33
305/361-1292

K

Appendix:
Regional Mean Temperatures and Rainfall

Mean temperatures in degrees Fahrenheit.
Average monthly rainfall in inches.

CENTRAL FLORIDA

	Jan	Feb	Mar	Apr	May	Jun	Jul	Aug	Sep	Oct	Nov	Dec
High	71	73	78	83	88	91	92	92	90	84	78	73
Low	49	51	56	60	66	71	73	74	72	66	57	51
Rain	2.2	2.8	3.4	2.4	3.3	7.0	7.9	6.7	6.8	3.3	1.9	2.0

NORTH FLORIDA

	Jan	Feb	Mar	Apr	May	Jun	Jul	Aug	Sep	Oct	Nov	Dec
High	64	66	73	79	86	90	90	90	87	80	71	65
Low	42	44	49	55	63	69	72	72	69	58	48	43
Rain	4.1	4.8	5.2	3.9	4.1	6.6	8.0	7.0	5.4	2.8	2.9	4.3

SOUTH FLORIDA

	Jan	Feb	Mar	Apr	May	Jun	Jul	Aug	Sep	Oct	Nov	Dec
High	76	77	80	83	85	88	89	90	88	85	80	77
Low	59	60	63	67	71	74	76	76	75	71	66	61
Rain	2.0	1.9	2.3	3.6	6.2	8.6	6.7	7.4	8.3	6.7	2.8	1.8

About the Author

M. Timothy O'Keefe is also the author of *Caribbean Afoot! A Walking and Hiking Guide to Twenty Nine of the Caribbean's Best Islands*, also published by Menasha Ridge Press. With a Ph.D. from the University of North Carolina at Chapel Hill, Tim is a professor in the School of Communication at the University of Central Florida where he founded the journalism program. He has been a resident of the Sunshine State for almost three decades and was a field editor for *Florida Sportsman* magazine for 23 years. He is also the author of *The Hiker's Guide to Florida, Fish and Dive Florida & The Keys* (with Larry Larsen), *Manatees Our Vanishing Mermaids,* and *Seasonal Guide to the Natural Year: Florida with the Alabama and Georgia Coasts.* His personal, lively writing style and photographs have won more than 40 regional and national awards.